PRAISE FOR *JUNKYARD GIRL*

"*Junkyard Girl* is an astonishing tale, told by a gifted storyteller. Beautifully written, emotionally engaging and unrestrained in its intimacy, it is an honest account of a life unravelling. But as it is doing so, we do indeed begin to feel 'the divine hand at play.' This book is evidence; as heartbreaking as it is heartfelt. In the end, it is a celebration of the deepest mysteries of life, asking who we really are and where we really come from. A delightful read."

—Jay Rabinowitz, ACE, award-winning motion picture editor of
Requiem for a Dream

"Too many memoirs simply narrate a life story. Montes De Oca invites readers to live in her world and memories alongside her, capturing the passionate overlay of the past with an attention to detail that is the hallmark of excellence...*Junkyard Girl* is a cut above the ordinary. It is very highly recommended for memoir readers and libraries that seek not just an exploration of past links to present-day choices, but a vivid inspection of life that constantly presents solid reflections and captivating scenarios of change."

— D. Donovan, Senior Reviewer, *Midwest Book Review*

"What happens when you discover you are not who you thought you were? Buried secrets. Lies. A DNA test. These are the details that make *Junkyard Girl* a spell-binding, gut-wrenching page turner. Carlyn is a late discovery adoptee. This knowledge shatters her sense of identity and belonging, forcing her to look at family in an all-new way. The writing in *Junkyard Girl* is lyrical, exquisite. The story is unpredictable and true—the perfect recipe for a memorable read."

—Julie Ryan McGue, award-winning author of *Twice a Daughter:*
A Search for Identity, Family, and Belonging

"With brazen vulnerability, warmth, humor and emotional courage, Carlyn Montes De Oca takes us on a journey rife with laughter, tears, her junkyard childhood and a surprising secret enormous enough to eclipse everything she knew about herself as a fully-formed adult. Carlyn's prose and descriptions are like music that seduces and lights up our senses. She pours us into an irresistible and unimaginable tale that makes *Junkyard Girl* a most unexpected delight!"

—**Gary W. Goldstein, Producer of**
Pretty Woman* and *Under Siege

"I was spellbound by this author's life. Family secrets can sometimes knock us off the course we were on and return us to an entirely different world. And the thing about secrets is we never know when the truth will be revealed nor how it will affect our lives. Riveting, poignant, and unexpected, Montes De Oca's story reminds me why I love the memoir genre!"

—**Suzanne Simonetti, *USA Today* bestselling author**
of *The Sound of Wings*

"*Junkyard Girl* is utterly engaging from start to finish, an astonishing story of a secret adoption and a beautifully rendered tale of complicated family dynamics, the secrets we keep and the gifts we give to each other. I found myself utterly lost in the rich, compelling details of Carlyn's childhood growing up in a big, Mexican-America family. Montes De Oca has beautifully, and honestly, detailed her inner life, conflicts, and emotional journey of discovery and resolution—all with a healthy dose of humor. Reading this book has given me a clearer understanding of what my own adopted daughter may be feeling, or what she might go through in the future."

—**Maria Jacquemetton, Emmy award-winning**
television writer and producer

"A skilled and entertaining writer, Montes De Oca engages us throughout with her prose, but it's the unique and fascinating story of her adoptive mother that keeps us flipping pages. That and the two…big…secrets. One you'll discover early on. The other? You'll have to wait until the (satisfying) conclusion!"

—**David Aretha, award-winning author**

Junkyard Girl captures the surprising and emotional journey of a decades-old secret adoption. Told with honesty and humor, Carlyn Montes De Oca's remarkable memoir takes the reader through a story infused with emotion and depth. With vivid details and a longing for the truth, *Junkyard Girl* grapples with the meaning of familia, and the discovery of self."

—**James Wong, writer-producer and two-time Golden Globe winner of *The X-Files***

"In *Junkyard Girl*, Carlyn Montes De Oca tells two interwoven stories with sensitivity and courage. One is about a young girl raised in a junkyard, and the other about discovering the queen of all family secrets—how, at age 57, she discovered through a DNA test that she was adopted. She succeeds commendably with both."

—**Robert Basler, former reporter and senior editor for *Reuters* in Asia and America**

"*Junkyard Girl* is a poignant story of one woman's struggle to claim her true self. Written in eloquent prose, Montes De Oca invites us into her life, which ultimately inspires readers to better understand their own. Her characters are closely observed, well-drawn, and relatable. This book is a gentle reminder that our essence has little to do with where we come from, what we look like, what we do, or who we know. Human beings are never 'junk.' Our worth is inherent."

—**Bella Mahaya Carter, award-winning author of *Raw: My Journey from Anxiety to Joy***

"An intimate memoir written by a Late Discovery Adoptee as she grapples with the initial shock of finding out, at age 57, that she was adopted. In *Junkyard Girl*, Carlyn Montes De Oca takes us along her journey toward healing as she revisits her life experiences through this new adoptee lens and uncovers her full origins story. This is ultimately a narrative of acceptance, forgiveness, and the complex bonds of family—those we share blood with and those we've spilled blood with. The author's attentiveness to the synchronicities of adoption and lifelong companionship with animals will appeal to the soulful places of many, as they touched mine."

—Sara Easterly, Author of *Searching for Mom* and Founder of Adoptee Voices

"Trusting that the life we are living is built upon a foundation of truth, *Junkyard Girl* successfully shares with us what happens when a family secret is accidentally discovered that upends that notion. Beautifully written, Montes De Oca's memoir is an honest and poignant reflection on her journey after facing a new reality that had her call into question her origin story and identity. In the end, we fully understand how her amazing love for and connection with animals remain the grace that pulls her through a dark night into the light. An uplifting and inspirational must read."

—Meg Nocero, award-winning author of *The Magical Guide to Bliss, Sparkle & Shine* and *Butterfly Awakens*

"A strikingly emotional real-life narrative. With passion and courage, Carlyn Montes De Oca discloses how she unearths a flaw in her origin story. Drawing on the depth of her loyalty to her immigrant family and the love of her dogs, Carlyn conveys with determination and optimism what it's like to search for the truth of one's identity later in life. The result: *Junkyard Girl*—a treasure to behold."

—Valerie Taylor, author of the award-winning novels *What's Not Said* and *What's Not True*

"Most children, at some point, wish they belonged to another family somewhere somehow. For most, it's just a childhood fantasy; for Carlyn it was the truth. In a very personal and intimate narrative, Carlyn takes us on her personal journey as she uncovers her identity accompanied by the reliable and constant love of a dog. *Junkyard Girl* is a can't-put-down read from start to finish!"

—**Maria Milito, National radio personality and animal advocate**

"*Junkyard Girl* is an engrossing book that instantly connects you to a Latinx story of family, secrets, and identity. I immediately wanted to know more."

—**V. Alexandra de F. Szoenyi, writer at BoldLatina and LatinaMedia.co, co-founder, Latina Writers Community**

"Part drama, part comedy, part detective story, *Junkyard Girl* is compelling. Montes De Oca learns that her entire family had for more than 50 years kept secret that she was adopted. From that shocking news, she brings us along on a journey of discovery of who she is, who she was and who she will be moving forward. Taking us back in time with warm and wonderful, engaging and sometimes enraging stories, Montes De Oca captivatingly weaves the narrative of her life, teaching about acceptance and forgiveness, connecting with people and with animals, and doing it all with incredible honesty. From the very first sentence, we pull up to a spot right next to the determined, spunky and grace-full Montes De Oca—and stay with her every step of the way. And what an inspirational, inspiring trip it is."

—**Karen Pearlman, journalist, San Diego, CA**

Junkyard Girl

Junkyard Girl

A Memoir of
Ancestry,
Family Secrets,
and Second
Chances

CARLYN MONTES DE OCA

GOOSE HILL PRESS

Published by Goose Hill Press

For more information please contact: publisher@goosehillpress.com.

Edited by Krissa Lagos and David Aretha
Book design by Christy Day, ConstellationBookServices.com
Author photo credit: Michael Friel

ISBN (paperback): 978-0-9997812-2-7
ISBN (ebook): 978-0-9997812-3-4

Library of Congress Control Number: 2022917752

Printed in the United States of America

For Mary and Vincent, my mom and dad, who gave me this story.

Contents

"The blood of the covenant is thicker than the water of the womb."
—Anonymous

An Unexplainable Knowing

IT IS SATURDAY AFTERNOON and my imagination runs ablaze.

The rough surface of a weather-worn doghouse supports my weight as I rest on my back, watching an infantry of clouds sculpted by a teasing wind mutate into fantastical shapes above me. Leading the pack is a hunchback weighed down by a bulbous nose. Behind him, a baby elephant flouts a bouncy dress. A dragon's eye brings up the rear.

A passenger plane—an entity made not of vapors and wishes but of polymer and steel—flies past, piercing the dragon's eye and leaving a chalk-white wake in its path. Like ice water, the aircraft jars me from my reverie, reminding me that the only way I can get a ticket on board that flight, or any vehicle that might take me away from here, is to grow up. Something that, at eleven years old, feels as unattainable as the plane above, already disappearing into the horizon.

I am not alone as I daydream. My two-year-old black Labrador retriever, Orange—named by my brother Art after King William of Orange—is nestled up beside me. He watches me with half-open eyes, his slits revealing a soft, chocolate brown gaze. The sun penetrates his fur, creating a lustrous onyx sheen. Orange is my internal and external heating pad. He radiates warmth, offers comfort, and exudes love.

My other dog, a black and tan Basenji we call Bandit, spies a nearby fig tree where a trio of crows bides its time. The birds caw in unison, sharing secret plans with each other, calculating the ideal moment they will swoop down and steal the plump Mission fig dangling from an overhead branch. Bandit answers their chatter by scratching his flank before his head plops between his front paws and he recedes into an alert half-sleep.

On this day, the sun peeks through the fig tree's palm-shaped leaves, forming a brilliant afternoon star. As if speaking a silent language that only I understand, the star reveals her message, and a *knowing beyond reason or logic* permeates my being. I sense that the family I have grown up with since infancy is not my actual family. My true parents come from the stars, perhaps from another planet, or a foreign moon. Eleven years ago, for reasons unknown, they abandoned me here, in this tiny beach town alongside the Pacific Ocean, but . . .

"Someday they will come and take me away," I tell my dogs, as if saying it aloud confirms my suspicions.

Orange's mouth stretches into a high-pitched yawn, revealing brown-tinged canines with a string of spit stretched between them. His breath reeks of the Spam sandwich I refused to eat for lunch and that he found hidden in my napkin earlier today.

"This can't be my life," I say with certainty, as though speaking it will bend destiny to my will. "These can't be my parents." I stare into the clouds, trying to make contact with any deities who will listen beyond the chubby angel now being thinned by the breeze.

An errant cloud crosses the sun and the afternoon star fades. I leave the magical world above me and focus on my earthly surroundings—the true reason I gaze at the heavens and hunger for a different life.

While other kids my age tan at the local beach or entertain friends on playdates or race their bikes up and down our street, I'm inside a ten-by-twenty-foot dog kennel, sprawled across a structure whose peeling paint makes my legs itch and speckles my hands with green flakes. Yet inside this cage and among my dogs is where I find solace from what lives outside the enclosure.

Through the small rectangles of galvanized wire fence, my eyes settle onto a curious world: our backyard, a strange empire of junk that spans half a city block. Discarded patio furniture, buckets streaked with gray paint, and a mélange of flat tires rest against the outside of the kennel fence. Beyond those, between the dog's shelter and the house I live in with my parents, my sister, and two brothers, lie abandoned engine blocks, industrial drainage pipes, sheets of corrugated tin, piles of wooden planks, a line of crippled cars, and forty forgotten toilets. Together, these cast-offs wait day after day, season upon season, for the possibility of a second chance at purpose. But this chance rarely comes. The junk accumulates, propagates, and quarrels with any open space. Here, in my world, the junk always wins.

Our property is unlike any other in town. Rummage not only litters the yard but also the inside of our home where clutter is just another family member. The odds and ends my parents accumulate are not for profit but for survival. They don't see the relics they gather from swap meets, garage sales, and thrift shops as worthless; they perceive them as life. If the day ever comes when the entire planet goes to pot, by God, they will have the indispensable tool, mendable broken appliance, or invaluable spare part needed for their family to survive.

I don't see the world as my parents do. I feel nothing but suffocated by these poor man's riches. I long to be rid of all this *stuff*—to be free, to be normal.

"These are not my parents," I repeat like a witch casting a spell over a cauldron. "I know my real parents will come for me one day. This can't be my life.…

Though I wouldn't know it until many years later, this conversation with the heavens went beyond childish whim. That day, I stumbled into the mystifying world of *Unexplainable Knowing*—a place where hidden truths reside and where secrets patiently bide their time, waiting for their chance at revelation.

In my *Unexplainable Knowing* lived a secret fiercely guarded by my nuclear and extended family and enforced by my parents' silent dictate. This secret spread beyond the town I grew up in, beyond the confines of my state, and even beyond the country of my birth. Scores of people were privy to the truth but kept it buried, shoveling more earth over it whenever its memory surfaced.

This truth held the secret of my identity—a secret born not of spaceships, or parents from a distant moon, or fanciful clouds in the sky but of one woman's despair and another woman's unfathomable love. One day, the secret would surface and a reckoning would come. But this was a truth I would not suspect, entertain, or discover for more than five decades.

PART ONE

"Fear is the cheapest room in the house.
I would like to see you living in better conditions."
—Hafiz

CHAPTER ONE

DNA MIA

IT WAS A CHILLY DECEMBER dawn in Eldorado, a sleepy community on the outskirts of Santa Fe, New Mexico. Numb with grief, I didn't feel the cold.

I sat cross-legged on a yoga chair, huddled in my tiny home office. My fingertips tapped across my computer keyboard in a futile attempt to conjure the next line of my book. Try as I might to focus on the task at hand, my stare kept drifting to Rudy, my fourteen-year-old chocolate brown pit-lab.

Rudy was stretched across a dog bed near my toes, his once splendid, muscular frame thin and unmoving. His muzzle shone as white as the blanket of snow outside my window. As I watched him, checking on his uneven breathing every few minutes, he also observed me with dark fawn-colored eyes, heavy from age.

Just a few weeks before, our sixteen-year-old black chow-chow, Dakota, had passed away. That same day, our vet had gently informed us that Rudy was close behind her—words that reached through my chest, wrenched my heart, and refused to let go.

A notification popped up on my computer screen, interrupting my thoughts.

"Dang it!" I made a mental note to ask my husband, Ken, how to turn off these irritating messages even as I clicked on the notification to read it.

The message was from Ancestry.com, a genealogy website famous for helping people find blood relatives they don't know exist. I had friends who'd unearthed cousins, found siblings, and even discovered their biological father through this site—but I didn't expect this to be my experience. My mother and father, now long deceased, had been married for over six decades. And though the Montes De Oca–Curiel clan was considerable—over a dozen aunts and uncles, sixty-three first cousins, countless second cousins, a scad of nieces and nephews, plus all of our spouses—I figured that by this point in my life, I had a pretty good handle on everyone I was related to.

By the time we reach our fifties, most of us know our family members. We love and hate them. Seek and flee from them. And often, can't live without them.

I was no exception. I was clear who my clan was. My purpose for getting a DNA test was not to dredge up more relations but to look deeper into my geographical roots. When I was in college, I'd studied abroad in Spain and even visited the town of Montes De Oca, located in the Basque country. When I returned home, I'd brought back two things: a Spanish lisp and a fascination with our family tree. My sole interest in genealogy was to find out how much Spanish, Portuguese, and Jewish blood I contained in my lineage.

Eager to know my results, I still dawdled once the DNA test kit I'd ordered arrived, leaving it on my living room table for a month.

After Thanksgiving dinner, my stepdaughter, Gina, spotted the kit in exactly the same spot where she'd seen it the last time she visited.

"What are you waiting for?" she asked, annoyed by my procrastination. "Just go into the bathroom and spit into the tube."

"All right," I answered, irritated by my own laissez-faire attitude. Groggy after our hearty Thanksgiving vegan dinner, I slid slowly off my favorite wicker chair and grabbed the white box before heading for the bathroom.

Once inside, I set the contents on the counter, read the instructions on the pamphlet, and spit into the clear plastic tube, as directed. As I sealed the carton, I wondered how much Jewish ancestry would appear in my results. *Am I related to someone famous? Maybe I'm part Viking.*

Or perhaps I'd discover only that I'd just spent fifty-nine dollars for no reason.

The following morning, I slipped the boxed kit into our mailbox and did not give my DNA another thought . . .

Until today.

As I perused my DNA results on my computer screen, I discovered I was barely Jewish at all, was not related to anyone famous, and feasting in Valhalla with Vikings named Freya and Ragner was not in my future. The ancestry report showed I was 51 percent Indigenous American–Mexican, 36 percent Spanish, and 6 percent Other. In the *Other* category it informed me I was 3 percent Jewish. *Only 3 percent? How is that possible?*

Previously, a genealogist had traced the Curiel line on my mother's side of the family and discovered that two Jewish brothers, surname also Curiel, had fled to Portugal from Spain during the Spanish Inquisition. But the border between Spain and Portugal was not a boundary recognized by the Holy inquisitors. To avoid torture and death, the brothers had fled farther—to South America and then on to Mexico, the country my parents eventually emigrated from in their early twenties. The Montes De Ocas, in contrast, had been among the original conquistadors: conquering new lands for the monarchy, enslaving the native populations in the New World, and converting non-believers to Christianity.

It turned out that the towns of Curiel and Montes De Oca in Spain were only ninety-eight miles apart.

"Looks like your dad's family didn't have to go far to chase your mom's family out of town," Ken liked to tease.

I'd often wonder if he was right.

When I was just seven, I sat on my mother's bed, watching her get ready for work. Clad in a white polyester dress, matching shoes, and tan pantyhose—mom assessed the outfit in her antique vanity mirror with the poise of a general, though she worked as a beautician. A coat of rose red lipstick came next, before she kissed the back of her arm to remove the excess. In my starry eyes, *Mami* resembled a terracotta goddess.

Near the top of her head, she secured a fake brown hair bun with a generous mist of hairspray that tickled my nose with its strong chemical scent.

"Achoo!" I sneezed.

"God bless you," she said.

"Achooooo!" I sneezed longer and louder.

"Bless you," she repeated.

"Achoo, achooo, achoooo!!!" In quick succession I sputtered brief bursts, anointing the room with a different kind of spray.

"God bless you now and for the rest of the day!" Mami said with a conclusive tone as she hung a pearl tear drop earring through an ear lobe. Like magic, her proclamation put an end to my sneezing and replaced it with a giggle.

On my father's bed lay that morning's newspaper. Mami grabbed it and held up the front page for me to see. A black-and-white photograph of a young boy standing directly in front of an armored tank during the Six-Day War in Israel filled the top quarter of the page. The caption underneath identified the child as David Curiel. *Curiel*—Mami's maiden name.

"See?" she said in Spanish, the language she always spoke to her children. "We *are* Jewish."

This was the moment my mother's pride became my own. From that day on, I became enamored by Bible stories from the Old Testament—not because of their religious messages but because the Jews in those stories had kick-ass adventures. Joseph had a prophetic dream that averted a famine; the orphan Moses became a Prince of Egypt; and David's sling brought down a giant. In first grade, the nuns at St. Joseph's Catholic School told our class that the Jews were God's chosen people. Now, according to Mami, I was one of them.

My mother's voice faded as I skimmed my DNA results for any explanation of why I was not more Jewish. Why I was not one of the chosen people like my cousin Rob, whose test told him he was 40 percent Jewish.

"Three percent? Is that all?" I said out loud. Rudy raised his head, sensing something was amiss. I reached down and stroked the underside of his plush muzzle, assuring him all was well. He sighed and fell back to sleep, where he spent most of his time these days.

I continued analyzing my head-scratching DNA findings. *Maybe Ancestry made a mistake. Maybe I'm not reading the results correctly. Maybe it's all BS.*

Maybes consumed my thoughts and kept me from noticing a detail that should have set off an alarm in my psyche. On the top of the page, the name MARTHA BAPTISTA was written in plain sight and in capital letters. This name, Ancestry claimed, was a close relative.

If I had noticed this and investigated even further, I might have noted that beside this woman's name were the words *122 centimorgans (cMs)*. Of course, at the time I didn't know a centimorgan from a centipede—but if I had bothered to learn the difference, I would have discovered that a centimorgan measures genetic distance: how closely your DNA matches another human. Martha Baptista and I shared 1,575 cMs, which put her in the "very close family" range.

But I didn't recognize her name, and I was confident that I was on a first-name basis with all of my family members. Besides, I was busy: I had a fast-approaching book deadline and an upcoming talk to give. And, of course, there was Rudy, who was growing weaker by the day, teetering on the precipice between this life and the next.

I slid off my purple yoga ball chair and lay down beside my dog, cradling his fifty-pound body just as I had when he was a puppy. His breath warmed my cheek in shallow bursts. How many more times would his soulful brown gaze meet mine? Whatever it was, it would never be enough.

With this thought pressing against me, I put Ancestry, and the name Martha Baptista, out of my mind.

The following day, I received this email:

Hi my name is Martha Baptista. I've been checking on the ancestry site for years and never have come close to a DNA match. I am curious as to how we are related. If you want to contact me, we can compare our family line. If not, I will understand, I am very particular about my personal life. Thanks for reading my email. –Martha

I read Martha's words more than once, studying its content for peculiarities. How often did I received scam emails from people asking for money or even the numbers to my savings account? But her inquiry seemed to be neither. *Sure, why not?*

I sent Martha a brief response, accepting her invitation. I did not hear back from her.

Two weeks later, I'd forgotten all about Ancestry, about being only 3 percent Jewish, and about Martha Baptista. My mind was consumed with grief for Rudy, who had passed away as I held him just a few days earlier. The blow from losing both him and Dakota in such a short time had left my heart bruised and hollow.

I sat in front of my computer staring at a blank screen, fending off waves of sadness, when I received an alert notifying me I had a private message on Facebook.

"Crap!" I said, once again annoyed at my inability to turn off these interruptions.

The message came from a fellow named Adam who'd friended me on Facebook the week before. I'd accepted his friendship request because, judging by his posts, we shared a mutual love for dogs. I clicked on the notification and read the message:

"You look an awful lot like my wife."

Uh-huh, okay, that's nice, I thought. Adam was clearly flirting with me. Uninterested, I left his thought unanswered and returned to my monitor.

Adam answered my silence by sending me a picture of his wife.

"Don't you think you look like her?" he persisted. "Maybe you're related. A cousin or maybe even a sister?"

The brunette smiling back looked a few years older than me, her fine straight hair was set in a shoulder-length bob, similar to mine. Her brown eyes twinkled behind rectangular frames just like the glasses I fiddled with on the bridge of my nose. Other than this, I didn't see a resemblance.

"Do you think I look like this lady?" I asked Ken when he strolled into my office.

His tall, lean frame bent just enough to look over my shoulder.

"No," he answered with a smirk that informed me he thought I looked like this woman about as much as I resembled Angelina Jolie.

"Well, what do you think?" Adam asked in his next message. This guy refused to give up.

"I think your wife and I shop for glasses at the same store," I typed back.

"Well, Ancestry says different," he responded.

These words signaled the first of many instances to come where my world would suddenly grind to a halt. As I read the message a second time, I stopped believing that Adam was flirting and concluded instead that he was a stalker. *But how does he know about Ancestry?*

"What do you mean?" I demanded. "Who's your wife?"

"Martha Baptista," he replied.

I sat back in my yoga chair—and nearly fell off of it. His wife was the woman whose name was on my DNA results as a possible close relation? The same woman who'd emailed me?

Adam pressed on. "My wife has no relatives to speak of. Wouldn't it be nice if she and you are related somehow?

Just like before, I doubted that Martha was any relation to me. But what if someone in my extended family had had an affair? Perhaps she was the result of a secret liaison—someone's love child.

My writer's mind spends a fair amount of time immersed in imagination, and this story was piquing mine. I gave Adam my email address and told him that if Martha wanted to, she could contact me directly.

Twenty-four hours later, Martha did exactly that.

Hi, Carlyn. We don't know each other, but Ancestry says we are highly connected. My name is Martha and my maiden name is Gallegos, which was my mother's last name. She was born in Illinois. In 1954, she and my father fell in love. He was an established figure in his community and already married with children.

I grew up in Chicago, without many family ties, met my husband, married, and have four beautiful daughters. I see that you have a great love for animals, and I do as well.

Maybe you have insight into how we might be related. Or maybe you have a relative that might know. I see my grandkids' faces and I wonder who they resemble. I know that in families there is always a buried secret somewhere. At this stage of my life, I am just curious and would like to know some of my history.

Sincerely, Martha

In families there is always a buried secret somewhere.

I reread that line several times.

When it came to secrets, my family had its share. Not long before my father died, he told my husband that he had been in the Marines. When Ken shared the news with me, I was positive he had misheard.

"My dad was never in the Marines," I informed him as I poured my morning smoothie into a glass. "Besides, how do you even understand what he's saying to you? He's speaking Spanish and you don't even know the language."

"I understand him," Ken said, unruffled by my skepticism. "We understand each other."

"Uh-huh," I replied, unconvinced.

"He *was* in the Marines," my older sister, Lilly, said from the kitchen, where she was heating a corn tortilla on the stove, her radiant smile flanked by two exquisite dimples. "It was a terrible experience, so he never wanted to talk about it again."

I wasn't sure what was worse: the fact that my father had never shared this integral piece of information about his history with me or that he'd confided in Ken, who couldn't even order a pretzel from a pretzel vendor in Spanish and now was nodding his head as though vindicated.

A jagged scar lived on the back of my dad's neck. Although I'd noticed it over the years, I'd never asked him where he'd gotten it. If I had, perhaps he would have shared that during World War II, a torpedo had struck the ship he was assigned to and the resulting explosion had sent flying shrapnel into his nape.

But my father serving in the Marines wasn't the only Montes De Oca–Curiel secret.

Lilly also shared around that time that Abuelita, my mother's mom, didn't think highly of my father because his family was poor. Dad dismissed my grandmother for being a snob, and Mom ended up caught between them. Shortly after my parents married, Abuelita hired two men to kidnap Mami and bring her back home. For weeks, my parents hid in a relative's basement, a room flooded by the torrential summer rains. Friends brought them food, clean clothes, and other necessities. Weeks later, unable to locate their whereabouts, Abuelita abandoned her plan. Ultimately, my mother got her way.

My grandmother may have been bull-headed, but my mother was the *entire* bull.

I suspected there were other secrets belonging to the Montes

De Oca–Curiel tribe. What I didn't realize, and would soon discover, was that *I* was one of them.

I responded to Martha Baptista's email explaining that I didn't recognize any of the names on her list but could call my siblings, who were older than I, and might be aware of details regarding family history, clan politics, and hidden secrets that I was not.

I was the youngest in our family. Lilly, the next in line after me, was nine years older. Even though I was now in my fifties, the family dynamic was still to treat me like the baby.

When I was younger, this worked in my favor. I relied on my parents or siblings to figure out the complicated things in life, like the directions to my favorite board game (Monopoly), inflating the tires on my bike, or the art of heating up a tortilla over a burner on the stove. My family took care of business and made choices in my stead. When I left the nest, I tried breaking out of this long-held pattern countless times, but more often than not, when we interacted as family, we slipped back into our default roles. As the oldest, Ray, with his keen intellect was in charge when my parents were not. Art, born less than a year after him, was quick with a joke and the life of any party. Lilly was the nurturer we all turned to for comfort and wisdom. One thing all three of my siblings had in common was their unflinching devotion to and protectiveness of their little sister—*me*.

I informed Martha that if I discovered any worthwhile information, I'd let her know. I was sure that once I spoke with my sister and brothers, I'd come up empty-handed—but I would still ask. Her story pulled at my heartstrings. Martha was searching for family, and even in the impersonal vastness of cyberspace, I sensed her deep longing to connect. But how could I help her? I didn't know anything more than I'd already told her.

I was sure there was nothing I could offer Martha.

I was wrong.

CHAPTER TWO

The Visit

A WEEK LATER, I CALLED LILLY, filling her in about my ancestry test, the peculiar results, and Martha's email inquiry.

Lilly is not only my big sister; she is my lifeline. When she wraps her arms around me, I'm in the womb again, floating in a sea of calm, peace, and safety. If anything were to happen to me or if I needed her, I know she would drop everything and take the next flight out, whether I was in Santa Fe, New Mexico, or Wagga Wagga, Australia.

My raven-haired sister stands taller than me, but unlike my customary leggings and oversized shirts, Lilly has a flair for style. She is also very generous. Whenever I compliment her on her creative fashion choices, more often than not, she removes that piece of clothing and hands it to me. I've ended up with lots of cool earrings, elegant scarves, and colorful headbands after saying, "Wow, that looks so beautiful on you."

"Who knows?" I joked with Lilly on the phone that day. "Maybe Martha is someone's secret love child. We *do* have a big family."

My sister and I find most things in life funny. Our humor is sarcastic—sometimes hailing from the gallows—and frequently silly. Often, we are the only ones who think what we're joking about is drop-dead hysterical. But today, Lilly wasn't laughing at all. In fact, she barely said a word. I visualized her milky complexion and the sprinkling of tan freckles across the bridge of her nose and imagined a ripple of agitation crossing her face though I could not understand why my query would bother her in the least.

"Her husband, Adam, thinks we look alike," I persisted.

"Can you text me her picture?"

I did, and a moment later I heard Lilly's cell ding.

"What's her last name?" she asked, her voice unusually subdued.

"Gallegos," I said.

I waited for her response but got none.

"So, do you recognize any of the names Martha mentioned?"

"No." Lilly's voice sounded unusually curt. "I've never heard of them. I don't know anything."

My sister's words said one thing; her tone hinted at something different.

When I look back at moments like these now, I see there were several clues that should have alerted me that things were not as they seemed. More importantly, I *sensed* something was not right. Every year I promise myself I am going to heed my intuition more—that I will finally listen to that sixth sense I always thought I inherited from my mother. But in this moment, I trusted the words of others rather than listening to my inner guidance.

Then again, why *should* I question anything told to me by a sister whose hug felt like life itself?

As we spoke further, I analyzed Lilly's reluctance. *Had she quarreled with her husband, David? Perhaps she was just tired. Was she mad at me about something I wasn't aware of?*

I shifted the subject away from Martha and toward the latest in the political climate, family gossip, and John Snow sleeping with his aunt in *Game of Thrones*. Eventually, Lilly's voice relaxed, and it stayed that way until it was time to end our call.

"I love you, Looscious," I said.

"I love more, Carboonish," she answered.

We laughed, as always, at our silly nicknames for one another, as if it were the first time we had heard them, and then hung up.

As I stood there with the phone in my hand, however, something nagged at me like an irksome rock in my sock.

So, I dialed my brother Ray, told him about my DNA findings, and read him Martha's email.

Ray is a man of few words, but today he responded with none. "Do you know any of these people Martha's talking about?" I asked, breaking the uncomfortable quiet.

"No."

"Do you remember Mom or Dad mentioning someone named Baptista or Gallegos?"

"No."

I had no reason to doubt my big brother, yet I felt an unease under his silence, just as I had with Lilly.

"Maybe you know something about—"

"I don't know anything," Ray cut me off, echoing four familiar words—the same words Lilly had given me as her response.

"I got to go. Lilly is calling me on the other line," he said, sounding unusually rushed. I wanted to ask why my sister's call—she only lived two minutes away from him—was more important than mine. I opted for something different.

"Ok…well, talk to you later then?"

"Yeah, later." He hung up before I could say another word.

I spent the next couple of weeks preparing for an upcoming talk at a local animal shelter. Although I'd previously worked as a film editor for twenty years, then as an acupuncturist for fifteen, my true calling has always been helping animals by writing books and speaking out on their behalf. In Santa Fe, where Ken and I had just moved to nine months earlier, I'd found an appreciative community of animal lovers who welcomed my message of living a more compassionate and "pawsitive" life alongside our animal friends. For the first time in my life, like a bullet train speeding down an unimpeded track, I felt fully aligned with my purpose. Writing and presenting were also helpful distractions from my recent and ever-present grief over losing Rudy and Dakota.

Often, I fell asleep and dreamed about my dogs—standing outside in the deep snow and looking at me through the glass door, as if waiting for me to let them inside. I could never reach them in time before their faces faded away, and I'd wake up in a tangle of blankets in the middle of the night, the hole in my heart throbbing.

After waking from one of these dreams one night, as my vision grew accustomed to the darkness, I stared at the empty dog beds and inhaled Rudy and Dakota's scent, still lingering in the room. I wondered if my dogs felt me as I still felt them across space and time. My eyes scanned the wall and landed on a framed photograph of my mother; her familiar gaze all-knowing. I don't believe in regrets, but if there were anyone I wished I could talk with to make the past right, it would be her.

I decided to call Lilly again in the morning.

"I should really let Martha know if we know anyone she might be related to," I told my sister when she answered the phone. "Have you given it any more thought? Do any of those names she mentioned sound familiar? Do you think one of our uncles had an affair?"

"No," Lilly answered without elaborating. Lilly's reluctance to talk about Martha reminded me of my mother and father's mistrust of strangers. They may have smiled at newcomers; my dad may have taken a visitor's arm and acted like they were old friends; but in my family trust was hard-earned and not easily given to outsiders. The only exception I ever witnessed to this rule was with my husband, Ken. My parents liked his good-humor and dependable disposition from the get-go, which was one of many reasons I was certain he was special.

My mom had passed away sixteen years earlier and my father had been dead for a decade at this point, but their presence, power, and legacy still held each of their children captive in different ways. I concluded Lilly didn't trust Martha because she didn't know her, and as my big sister she was wary about this outsider's motives and wanted to protect me.

"Look, I think I know what's happening here," I said to Lilly. "It's that thing our parents had about not trusting strangers, right?"

She didn't answer me, so I kept talking.

"Martha isn't asking anything from us. She doesn't want money. She's just asking for information."

I waited for Lilly's response but got none. I pressed on.

"Martha doesn't have any family. I can't imagine what that must feel like. I've always had you guys. If that were me, I'd want to know where I came from, and I'd hope someone would help me."

Weeks later, Lilly confided to me that this was the moment she knew she would break the promise she'd made to our mother nearly six decades earlier. But in that moment, she simply echoed the same four words she'd said before: "*I don't know anything.*"

A week later, my cell phone rang and Lilly's name popped up on the screen.

"Hey," I answered.

"What are you doing?" she asked.

"Just tell me," I said, bracing for impact.

"Tell you what?" she asked.

"If you're calling me, something bad has happened. So just tell me what it is!"

As close as we are, Lilly rarely calls me. When I do get a call from her, I can usually count on it being unhappy news. But today she wasn't calling to say that someone in our family was terminally ill, missing, or dead. Her news was not bad at all—in fact, it wasn't even news. It was a question.

"Can I come visit you?"

I glanced through the French doors at the thick layer of white covering our front garden. A bitter wind howled outside, forcing a shower of snowflakes to defy gravity and fly horizontally as though gliding over a flat surface. The temperature that morning was in the low twenties.

"Now? It's the middle of winter," I answered, somewhat bewildered. Like me, Lilly is a California girl and accustomed to So-Cal's temperate Mediterranean climate. She did not consider the cold to be her friend.

"Are you sure you don't want to wait until the springtime before coming out? It'll be a lot nicer then and we can do more outdoorsy things."

"No," she answered firmly. "I need to come and get a hug from my sister."

At that, my Spidey sense went into full swing. Just like the other times we'd spoken in recent days, I sensed something was amiss but couldn't figure out what it was.

"Of course, whatever you want to do is fine," I said, unwilling to press the point any further.

If I was a different person, I would have forced a confession. I would have listened to my heart and not to her words. But insisting on explanations and urging answers from the reluctant is not something Montes De Oca women were raised to do. We were taught to accept what we were told by older family members and not create friction. It took decades for me to learn how to voice my needs, and by this time in my life I was fairly good at doing it in many of my relationships. But this family habit was a well-worn groove in a skipping record that was hard to break. I would wait until Lilly was ready to talk.

CHAPTER THREE

Shock & Awe

"SOMETHING BIG HAS HAPPENED in our family and I have to talk to you about it," Lilly said, as we stood in my kitchen in Santa Fe, a week later, watching the electric tea kettle boil.

"Is someone sick? Who died? Is Ray getting divorced? Is Art okay?"

I spewed out every conceivable disaster that came to mind. Lilly shook her head slowly, her complexion a tad more pale than normal. I realized if any of these catastrophes had actually happened, my sister would have simply picked up the phone. *What could be so important that she felt compelled to hop on a plane and fly three hours in the heart of winter to tell me in person?*

"Let's just get our tea and sit down, okay?" The tone of her words were missing their typical lilt.

Ever the caregiver, Lilly plopped tea bags into four colorful mugs. As she covered them with steaming water, I stepped behind her so she couldn't see me silently mouthing more potential calamities to my brother-in-law.

I must have looked ridiculous, because he half-heartedly chuckled—a sound that didn't match the worry in his gaze. His calloused hands gripped the counter behind him, as if steadying his brawny physique. He glanced at Ken, who offered no help whatsoever being in the dark as much as I was. David, a retired firefighter, always on the ready, was accustomed to facing all manner of emergencies. Today, he looked ready to battle a blaze.

The sixty seconds it took the four of us to walk from the kitchen into our living room and settle into our respective seats felt endless. *Something big has happened in our family*—Lilly's words echoed in my mind. I am not a patient human being. I seek efficiency; I like finding the quickest, smartest way from A to B. This brief minute of waiting was taking an abundance of self-control.

It'll be over soon, I told myself. *Be patient. In a few minutes you'll know what this is all about.*

Lilly sat beside David on our cat-scratched couch. Ken and I faced them on our wicker chairs. I crossed my legs tightly, holding the large arms of the seat for support, wondering if anyone else could hear the pounding of my heart. My sister said something unintelligible—then her eyes met mine, and she burst into tears.

"I'm sorry," she apologized through choked sobs. She turned to her handbag, rustled through it, then pulled out two sheets of paper and a pair of stylish reading glasses. "I thought this might happen, so I wrote it all down—about a dozen times—on the plane." She dabbed her cheeks with a Kleenex, slipped on her glasses, then held the pages out in front of her. Her actions gave her a few seconds to compose herself. She sat up straight—something my mother always nagged her to do—and, hands trembling, began to read.

Carlyn, about three weeks ago, you forwarded an e-mail from Martha Baptista. She wanted to get in touch with you and see if you knew how you might be related. At that point, I knew we needed to break a promise to my parents that we made as children.

When we were young, you mentioned to me how differently you felt about the world and from everybody else in the family. Then, as a young adult, how eagerly you looked forward to getting away and making your own life. Secretly, I envied your attitude. You began exploring different places and experiences with a passionate energy! You grew and developed into an extraordinary human being.

Today, I have a story to share with you, which began even before you were born. This story is the best I can remember, though not perfect . . . Carlyn, you were adopted.

And with these last four words, I was unmade.

As Lilly paused to take a sip of her tea, my world also paused long enough to spin off its axis as if the fibers that bound me to this planet were sheered of their power. I floated in the air for a moment, severed from all I knew to be true, watching my planet and life disappear beneath me. In the next breath, gravity lassoed me downward and smacked me hard against the ground, shattering my identity into a thousand tiny fragments.

My hearing diminished after Lilly said the word *adopted*. It was as if cotton balls had collected inside of my ears, muffling her voice into faraway echoes coming from the other side of an immense canyon. Like a lip reader, I stared at her mouth, hoping it would help me hear what she was saying.

Your birth mother's name was Maria Gallegos. She had two small children already (Martha and Robert) when she became pregnant with you. She wasn't married to your birth father. I don't know who he was.

The following information is what I remember of a story told to me in brief, guarded, and cautious conversations when I was a child and as a young teenager that our mother, Mary, had with me about how you became my sister.

Maria Gallegos was a distant relative of a woman named Molly. In 1952, Molly was Mary's roommate when they were both in the hospital delivering their respective daughters. They remained friends and our mother would visit Molly at her home in Montecito several times a year.

On one of those visits, Mary parked in Molly's yard and heard a woman crying inconsolably. When Molly came out, Mary asked her if she knew the woman. Molly responded yes, that it was her cousin. She said that this woman was unmarried, had two small children already, and a third one on the way. She wanted an abortion. Molly told her she wouldn't help her get an abortion, no matter how much she cried.

The cotton balls plugging my ears after Lilly said *adoption* multiplied exponentially when I heard the word *abortion*. My chest tightened around my lungs midbreath upon realizing how close I had come to never being born. *This can't be happening. It must be a mistake. Is this a joke?* My mind filled with denial.

I contemplated the alternatives. Humor, teasing, and laughter were Montes De Oca badges of honor. My brothers loved to taunt me. When I was a kid they tried for years to convince me I was born on April Fools' Day, not March 30, my actual birthday. They told me my parents felt bad that I was an April Fool, so they'd invented a new birthdate for me. They'd carried out this tease well into my adulthood by phoning me on April 1 to wish me a happy birthday. But this was not the secret Mom and Dad had actually protected me from.

I glanced up; Lilly's lips were still moving.

Our mother didn't believe abortion was an option. She and Dad had discussions, and they subsequently offered Maria a way to get out of her situation. They offered to adopt the unborn baby she was carrying.

Before you were born, Maria came to live with us with Robert (about age 3) and Martha (about 7). They lived as part of our family, sleeping at our house, eating at the same table, until Maria went to the hospital and gave birth to you.

My parents told us never to tell anyone that they had adopted you. They told us that if we shared this information, it would only be used to hurt you. It was the 1960s; they had been raised in a small, remote pueblo in Mexico in the early 1900s. They'd lived through revolutions and uprisings and the stigma, prejudice, and shaming of children left without fathers that led to them never being accepted as "real" members of a family. They felt it was the most compassionate, loving and protective decision they could make. They were firm about this, and we never broke our promise.

These are the facts as I remember them. We always meant well, but the process is difficult and unclear. This is shattering information. I hope you will eventually be able to put yourself in Mary, Vincent and Maria's place, to begin grieving your loss and understand that these decisions were made with a 100% loving intent. I have a sister that slept in my room, whom I played with, carried in my arms and in my heart, to love forever.

I don't know when Lilly stopped speaking. I'm not sure how long I remained quiet. I was not a fan of Humpty Dumpty; the image of an egg-shaped fellow tumbling off a wall never appealed to me. But now there was no one I could relate to more. Like Humpty, I'd fallen and been cracked open, and wasn't sure how or when I could be put back together again. *Adoption, abortion, secrets*—the words circled me like leaves caught in a spiraling gust of wind.

The silence in the living room demanded attention. I looked up from my lap, where for several minutes I had been studying a wisp of brown fur—Rudy's—that adorned my black leggings.

Everyone's attention was focused on me. Waiting. Wondering. Worrying. David's anxious eyes were wide, deer-like, and moist. Lilly's fair cheeks were flushed a rosy red, a look I'd envied when we were young; probably because my own tanned skin would not allow the bloom.

How must I look? I wondered. Was I wearing my typical half-grin? The one that lives on my face whether I'm having dinner with a good friend or my car has just been rear-ended with me in it?

Lilly told me later that my skin had lost all its color and that no grin, half or otherwise, was in sight. Somewhere during her revelation,

Ken rose from his chair and kneeled beside mine, his face ashen. He clenched my hand in his own. Now, our eyes met. Bulging saucers like I had never seen before had hijacked his soft brown pools, and his head was trembling ever so slightly. I felt as shattered as he looked.

Lilly's fingertips slid a black-and-white snapshot across the wooden table in front of me. In the photo, my brother Ray, fourteen and lanky, cradled me, in his arms, as a newborn. Next to him, Lilly scrunched her face up at the camera. Beside her, Art's hands rested on a three-year-old boy's shoulders. The boy's eyes refused to meet the camera lens, staring at his shoes instead, the noon-day sun too bright for him to attempt a smile. A little girl stood beside him, wearing a striped shirt and knee-length shorts. Her forefinger rested on her lips. She squinted at the camera, looking unsure.

"That's Martha, and that's Robert," Lilly said, her voice quivering as she pointed to the two younger kids. "Your sister and brother."

What??? My mind echoed. I had seen this photograph in a musty family album many times over the years. "Who are these kids?" I'd asked my mother and my sister repeatedly. An offhand response usually followed: *some neighbor kids; distant cousins; the children of a compadre of my father.* To be a compadre—a godfather—to someone's child was an honor my dad had been given by many. I'd accepted the answer I was told because there had been no reason for me to doubt it was true.

Paralyzed on my cushion, I stared at the glossy photo, refusing to touch it, as if handling the celluloid memory might actually make it real. I looked up at the faces of my sister and brother-in-law, who anxiously awaited my reaction. Perhaps they expected an explosion of anger—accusations. But there was no fight in me. Bewilderment consumed me. What does one say when they are told they are not who they thought they were? How are you supposed to react when you discover that the parents who raised you are not your actual parents?

My thoughts drifted to my extended family.

"Lilly, we have sixty-three first cousins. How many people know about this?"

Lilly shrugged. "I have no idea."

Sleep did not come easily that night. When it finally did, I dreamed I was a little girl standing on an immense plateau covered in fresh snow and surrounded by mountains. The myriad of puzzle pieces once forming my identity fell like snowflakes from the sky. Like a film strip moving at half speed, these fragments floated onto the white earth, settling beyond my vision. Frantically, I gathered them, trying to force them back together, but nothing fit as it did before. The lid on the puzzle box lay near my feet. With some effort, I yanked it from the ice and studied the picture.

A family get-together. My brothers, sister, and parents stand around me as I blow out a candle with the number six on it. Food, teasing, laughter.

As the sun rose, the picture faded.

I woke up in my bed laying beside Ken, reassured by his presence and the life we had made together until the tension in my chest reminded me something was amiss and I remembered.

Carlyn, you were adopted.

I lay awake watching baby blue and pink pastels cover the horizon outside our bedroom window, replaying the previous night's dream in my mind. My family history, origin story, the identity I once took for granted . . . it had all vanished overnight. To recover my identity, I would need to find where the new puzzle edges now interlocked. The picture it would paint would not be the image I'd once known. That life was gone forever.

A few hours later, Ken and I met Lilly and David at our favorite Mexican restaurant for breakfast. The aroma of freshly steamed tortillas and my sister's cheery face was a welcome break from an uneasy night.

When Lilly revealed the story of my beginnings, shock impeded my hearing. Later, I read, reread, and triple-read her two pages as if committing the details to memory. But no matter how many times

I pored over her words I couldn't help but interpret the subtext as: *You have a new family now. You should go be with them.* I felt stranded, abandoned, and cast off by the people I loved the most. I pictured spending Thanksgiving and Christmas Eve with strangers named Gallegos instead of Montes De Oca—imagined trying to fit in where I did not belong. The knot tightened in my chest and quickly spread to my belly as I picked at the inside of my breakfast burrito.

No one brought up the adoption. We spoke about the hotel Lilly and David were staying at, what they'd eaten for dinner the night before, and how bone cold the air felt outside. The elephant in the room sat silently in his place.

My parents taught us never to complain about the challenges we faced. We spent our formative years enrolled in the Buck It Up School of Life. But today, my inner turmoil, a storm threatening to burst and take no survivors, overcame my conditioning.

While Ken and David discussed the differences between Mexican and New Mexican cuisine, I leaned in and, as softly as I could, whispered to my sister, "I don't want to make a big deal out of this. But I think I was in shock yesterday, and I'm not really sure I heard everything you said. I need you to go over some things again so I can be clear."

Lilly met me halfway across the table. Her soft hands, infused with loving intent, covered mine.

"This *is* a big deal, and I am here to talk as often as you want and to answer any questions you have for as long as you have them," she said. I squeezed her hands.

David and Ken, overhearing our talk, apparently could have cared less about the differences between Mexican and New Mexican food; they were just waiting for me to make the first overture. With the elephant now free, and snacking on a chimichanga in the back of the room, everyone talked at once.

"My heart sank when I heard the name Martha Baptista," my sister admitted. "I was so scared she was going to tell you before I could."

"The other night I walked downstairs and saw Lilly and Ray sitting at the dinner table—they were crying, worried about how to tell you," David said.

My adoption news had been hard to hear, but picturing my brother and sister this upset made me realize how difficult the unveiling of the secret they'd kept quiet for so many years had been on them. Ray in particular was a man who kept his emotions under lock and key; for him to be this distraught made me feel that regardless of our genealogical severing, I was as important to siblings as they would always be to me—at least for now.

After breakfast the four of us strolled around the Plaza, the historic, Spanish-style square in the heart of Santa Fe where tourists and locals gather to hear music, shop in quaint adobe-style stores, and, on arid summer nights, dance. As our husbands chatted ahead of us, Lilly and I walked together, arm in arm, glued to each other like Siamese twins. I craved closeness to my sister, both physically and spiritually. I imagined myself as the puzzle pieces scattered in the snow—a leg here, an eye there, a crow pecking at the remains of a forgotten memory. The last thing I wanted was to join another family. Lilly was my family. Her arms were my haven, my sanctuary, my home.

"I like your scarf," I said, admiring the charcoal gray and lime green muffler. In typical *Lilly fashion*, she promptly pulled it off and slid it over my head and onto my neck, fiddling with it until she knew it was protecting me from the cold.

"Mom would have loved visiting here," Lilly said, taking my arm again as we walked through the narrow sidewalks of *The City Different* and past the displays of turquoise jewelry, resplendent, colorful tapestries, and lifelike animal sculptures.

"Why didn't you tell me, Lilly?" I blurted out, louder than I meant to. "You're my sister. I tell you everything."

We stopped in front of a large window display and feigned interest in some life-sized paintings. A couple passed us and, seeing our strain, looked away.

I lowered my voice. "I just can't imagine not telling you something like this."

Lilly's face flushed pale pink. "I was afraid. I thought you'd be so angry and that you would reject me, reject our family. Mom is dead, and so is Dad . . . I couldn't bear the thought of losing you too." Lilly tightened her arm around mine as she spoke.

I rested my head on her shoulder, reassured. The fear trailing behind us like a persistent pest, nipping in my ear, insisting I was being shipped off to a new family—it was wrong. The only thought in Lilly's mind was, *Please, don't push us away.* The only thought in mine was, *Please, don't let me go.*

CHAPTER FOUR

The Fallout

ONCE LILLY LEFT SANTA FE, the waterworks burst. And no plumber on earth could fix the flood.

It's just information—facts, I scolded myself every time I broke out crying and couldn't stop. *Nothing has really changed. I'm still me.*

To confirm this, I'd look in the mirror several times a day, searching for any changes to my face or the quality of my olive skin and peering deep into my dark brown eyes, as if learning that I was adopted might have altered my physical appearance in some way.

When I was young and the junkyard still held its mystique, I foraged its grounds with my dogs, searching for enchanted relics spellbound by a witch's curse that only I had the power to free. A rotted tabletop transformed into a shield, a pegleg from a discarded stool was reborn as a sword, and a go-kart shrouded in rust became my chariot. Dashing through the yard, I might trip over a protruding object that had not been there the day before. If my father was nearby, and heard me crying, he would temporarily abandon the engine part he was repairing and come find me.

"Don't cry, Chiqui," he'd say, inspecting my cut. His soothing words carried a little half-laugh, as if my injury was nothing at all.

Sympathy was not something I could expect if my mother found me sobbing, however. *"No llores,"* she'd insist, her honed voice like a samurai's katana slicing through the air, scaring away my hurt and rendering me silent. As a result, when I grew older and experienced sadness or grief, I didn't sustain tears for very long. I dealt with life's pain by either driving my feelings deep inside me or lashing out with anger. It would be years before I understood that this path only led to needless suffering.

Even with this knowledge, as an adult, crying had still never come readily to me—*until now.*

I washed my dinner dishes over the kitchen sink, my tears rinsing the plates. In the middle of Zumba class, Ricky Martin's "Living La Vida Loca" sent me weeping into a toilet stall. As I lay in bed beside Ken watching *The Walking Dead*, I grabbed a tissue and dabbed at my eyes.

"I've never seen you cry this much." Ken eyed me with concern, knowing zombies weren't to blame for my frequent outbursts.

"I don't even know what I'm crying about." I tossed the Kleenex skyward in a fit of frustration and then watched it slowly parachute down onto our duvet.

After several hours of sitting in front of my open laptop and not typing a single word, I gave myself permission to take a couple of days off from writing. On my journey to rebuild the cracked foundation of my identity, I could have, as a newborn, sought peace by plopping onto a cushion and meditating; or enjoying a soothing massage; or even soaking in a hot tub to relieve my tension. Instead, I found consolation elsewhere. I spent the next forty-eight hours lounging in bed, eating vegan chocolate chip cookies, drinking root beer, and binging on reruns.

Author and psychiatrist Elizabeth Kubler Ross says there are five stages of grief. Denial is the first. In the early days after my discovery, denial was my constant companion. At night I lay in bed, exhausted but wide awake, counting the stars above the falling snow outside the glass door, hoping for sleep to liberate me. But my spiraling thoughts would not allow it. I entertained the idea that my adoption might be a mistake. But then I systematically ran all the facts through my mind: Lilly had admitted it was true; Art and Ray had corroborated the story; and—who could deny the most obvious evidence of all?—the evidence had been staring at me from my reflection in every mirror I had ever come across.

Physically, I didn't resemble anyone else in my family. In a land of giants, I was a munchkin. Ray towered at six feet four inches; Art trailed behind him by only an inch. Lilly came in at five foot six. I was a mere five foot two and three-quarters. Except for his green eyes, Lilly and Art were carbon copies of my father: light-skinned, dimpled grins, aquiline noses. I had a permanent tan, could muster up a one-sided dimple only by tightly squeezing my cheek, and had a much smaller, rounder nose than my siblings. Cavities filled my siblings' mouths; up until now I'd never had a single one. I could say I favored Mom, whose complexion was darker and who stood three-quarters of an inch shorter than me, or that Ray with his darker skin did not resemble my parents either, but then there was the DNA test—hard science. It was impossible to argue with those facts.

And then, of course, there was Martha, my half-sister—living proof that despite my denial, this revelation was completely, undeniably, absolutely true.

What will my cousins think when I break the news to them? For days, I pictured my sixty-three first cousins, their surprise, disbelief, and astonished expressions when I told them I was adopted.

But after phoning them, the only one gobsmacked was me.

"Yeah, I knew you were adopted—didn't you?" Rob asked.

"Oh, what a relief that you finally know," Val said.

"I knew that ever since I could walk," Angie confessed. "That information was like a rite of passage for us kids."

Except for a few relatives, virtually everyone in my family knew I was adopted, including nieces and nephews who were born after me.

"How is this even possible?" I asked Ken before breaking into tears for the third time one morning. "How did so many people keep such a big secret?"

I thought of my six cousins whom I was close to—in age and in friendship—growing up. The highlight of my year had been visiting them in San Diego on our three-day drive to Mexico each summer. Late into the night, long after our parents put us to bed, we'd force ourselves to stay awake, whispering under the bedcovers, confessing our crushes on cute boys and sharing our hidden truths. Yet somehow the most powerful secret between us had never come up. Even when I solemnly placed a seaweed clump on my cousin Giselle's head at the beach and crowned her "Queenie: Queen of the Dorks!"—sending all the kids laughing and chanting, "Queenie! Queenie! Queenie!!!"— Giselle never retaliated against my insensitivity by saying, "*Well, I may be a dork but at least I'm not adopted!*"

When my cousins admitted knowing the truth and keeping silent about it, I responded with a snarky, "I am so going to kick your ass!" Word about my threat got around to the rest of the family and in short order I received an envelope in the mail from my cousin Lori containing several photographs from our childhood. Her note read, *Before I say anything else, I want to say yes, I knew you were adopted, so please don't kick my ass.*

When my cousin Jesse came to Santa Fe for a visit and shared what he remembered, I repeated my threat for comic effect.

Jesse, a bear of a man with a friendly nature was sitting in the same wicker chair I'd been in when Lilly broke the news, simply responded, "Well, if it was between you kicking my ass or my aunt doing it, I'd rather have had you do it."

"Just how many people knew about this?" I asked Lilly again, as if being told an exact number would diminish my distress. Being the last one to know information everyone else is aware of has been a lifelong pet peeve of mine. Once more, with the news of my adoption, I was the last invited to the party.

Lilly answered my question with a story.

In her mid-thirties, Lilly and her four-year-old daughter, Tracy, visited Mascota, the small town in central-western Mexico where my parents were born and raised, and that we visited every summer during my childhood.

Extinct volcanoes and pine-covered mountains surrounded the popular tourist mecca, known as the Emerald of the Sierra. Fourteen thousand people lived in Mascota, many of whom were acquainted with my parents. Some were relatives with the name Montes De Oca; others shared my mother's maiden name, Curiel.

As Lilly and Tracy strolled toward the family house where my father grew up, Lilly told me she heard the sharp click of high heels striking the cobblestone sidewalk behind her. She turned to find a middle-aged woman she had never met before running up to her.

"It's wonderful to see you here," the woman said, catching her breath when she caught up to them. "We never see your family anymore."

"I'm just here with my daughter, showing her where my parents grew up," Lilly told her.

The woman ignored Tracy and asked, "So, whatever happened to *that kid* your family picked up?"

Lilly looked at me, a flash of anger in her usually calm eyes.

"Carlyn, she said it like she was talking about a bag of trash someone found on the side of the road," Lilly said. "Then I realized she was talking about—*you.*"

I shook my head, realizing how far the secret of my beginnings had traveled and how wide the net of silence had been cast.

"Lilly, if a total stranger on the streets of Mascota knew about me, then everyone in that town did. You know how they like to gossip."

Lilly nodded sympathetically.

"So, what happened next?" I asked.

"Well," Lilly said in a dismissive tone as her fists landed on her hips, "I said to that woman, 'I simply don't know what you're talking about.' Then I took Tracy's hand and we crossed the street and never looked back."

I chuckled as I imagined Lilly marching off indignantly with Tracy in tow. The heart of an angel may beat inside my sister's chest, but when it came to me, it was crystal clear she would do whatever it took to keep me safe.

When I was only a few days old, my mother placed my crib in Lilly's room. As she and my brothers looked down at me, Mami told them, "This is your new sister. You will always treat her like a sister. And you will never tell her we adopted her."

My siblings did what we always did when my parents set down the law: they nodded, obeyed, and kept silent.

I'd been a pain in Lilly's ass and the love of her life ever since—a fact that never failed to warm my heart.

CHAPTER FIVE

Sister Stranger

ONE WEEK AFTER THE BIG REVEAL, I concluded that the only effect self-medicating with root beer and vegan chocolate-chip cookies was having was to increase the circumference of my waistline. I was beyond-the-moon appreciative that my adoptive parents had taken me in, given me a family, and ultimately saved my life—but the revelation was an earthquake, magnitude ten-plus. It had struck my core, and its aftershocks were unrelenting.

Two words kept repeating in my mind like a skipping record on a turntable: *adoption* and *abortion*. It was hard enough after fifty-seven years to discover that I was adopted and my entire family had kept it a secret from me. But hearing that my birth mother had wanted to end her pregnancy also made me realize how close I had come to never existing. Had my mom not visited her friend Molly at that precise moment; had she not felt compassion for the woman sobbing in her yard; had the stars not aligned in my favor; my life would not just be different, it might not *be* at all.

I believe wholeheartedly in a woman's right to choose. If having an abortion is your decision, that is up to you. But an unborn fetus is one thing; it is quite another to have been born and lived a full life, and then look back and realize you might never have experienced a single breath of it.

And, of course, beyond all these realizations, there was also Martha Baptista.

I procrastinated calling Martha for a week. In retrospect, I should have waited longer, much longer, to balance the emotional wrecking ball I was experiencing daily, before picking up the phone. But Martha had been waiting a lifetime to find out the information I had just discovered. In good conscience, I couldn't make her wait a minute longer.

So, on Valentine's Day 2019, after pacing my bedroom in the hopes that doing so would settle my nerves (it didn't), I picked up my cell and entered the numbers that connected me to an unfamiliar voice in Missouri.

"Martha? This is Carlyn Montes De Oca." I began the conversation in a professional tone, enunciating my last name clearly, as though it was a beloved toy I would not give up.

I didn't know what to expect when I heard her speak. Perhaps I anticipated a recognition, like a forgotten memory or déjà vu. That did not happen. Instead, I became a robot, recounting the details of the most impactful event of my life to a complete stranger. I shared how Maria had brought Martha and Robert to California as she sought an abortion; how my mom and Maria had met; and how my parents had taken her family to live with them until I was born. I didn't mention the unabating upheaval that had possessed me, an emotional roller coaster I couldn't find my way off of.

My words triggered a geyser of forgotten memories from Martha.

"I remember living in California! I remember your sister! And I remember your mother—*Mary Montes*—I remember that name!" Martha's voice quickly escalated from tentative to animated as she recalled how Lilly caught lizards in a glass jar near the creek behind our house, then set them free, and going to the drive-in theater to see *Cinderella* in a packed station wagon filled with kids, and how afraid she was of our yapping, nipping Chihuahuas.

With each recollection, her tone was more elated. *Does she really remember these details, or is it wishful thinking?* I wondered. Her next memory made it abundantly clear.

"I remember the house that moved!" she said.

I slumped onto my bed, unable to support my weight, my legs as weak as the foundation of the house that fifty-seven years ago was sinking into a marsh and had to be moved.

When I was born, our family's home was on a property of an exclusive prep school where my father worked. My mother wanted to own a home, but the expense concerned Dad. After all, we were lower-middle class, and now, with a newborn in the picture, there would be six mouths to feed. Regardless, Mami took their savings and purchased a 974-square-foot, three-bedroom house in Sandyland Cove, a posh beachside enclave in Carpinteria. The house was in danger of sinking, so my parents had it transported to a lot they bought on the other side of town. Six months later, *the house that moved* would become our home. A home that would preserve our future memories and hold as much junk as my mom and dad could fill it with.

"I have a sister—I have a sister!" Martha said like an enthused child unwrapping a long-awaited Christmas gift. "I knew something was missing—I just didn't know what it was. It was *you*."

As I listened to Martha's memories, it sank in that as difficult as this was for me, as much as I wished to rewind the tape and go back to my life before this new normal, this was not a fabrication, a mistake, or a dream I would just snap out of. My adoption was real; as concrete as the cell phone I gripped in my hand and the voice of the woman on the other end of it.

As Martha continued talking, I glanced over at Rudy and Dakota's empty beds, which after a month I couldn't yet bear to put into storage. Through every major life event, dogs, cats, or both had been at my side. Like Lilly's embrace and Ken stroking my head when I cannot fall asleep, animals had always comforted my heart and nurtured my spirit when I needed it most. But now, as my inner fabric searched for ways to mend, my dogs were not here to make me laugh by racing in circles around the yard, or to provide comfort with their tender nuzzles. This tsunami I would face on my own.

After an hour, Martha and I said our goodbyes. Like a wrung-out towel, I curled into the fetal position inside Rudy's donut-shaped bed and drifted off, warmed by the afternoon sun and consoled by the familiar potpourri of sweet and pungent canine scents.

During the following week, I exchanged several emails with Martha. She shared pictures of her daughters and various grandchildren, and also of my half-brother, Robert, whom she had not seen in over twenty years. She said I looked like him—a resemblance I could not see. Perhaps I didn't want to. In return, I emailed her pictures of Ken and my stepchildren, Greg and Gina. Then I rifled through old family photographs, wondering which ones to send her. *My family.* I was not sure what to call anyone anymore—my adopted family, my birth family, my sister, my adopted sister, my parents, my birth mother? These ping-pong semantics made my head ache.

Martha's excitement to connect with a new sister was understandable. She had been searching for something she was missing all of her life, and now she'd finally found it.

The opposite was true for me. I had not been searching for family, only information about my historical lineage. I already had parents, siblings, and sixty-three first cousins. Still, my curiosity to unearth every detail of my adoption proved stronger than my instinct for self-preservation. Like an undertow, my desire for the truth swept me out to sea, pulling me where I was not emotionally ready to go. As uncomfortable as my correspondences with Martha were, as much as her elation triggered my distress, I did not pace myself as I traversed this gauntlet.

My parents often bragged that as a toddler, I never took an actual "first step"—that I ran before I ever walked. I've been running ever since. Whatever I am curious or enthused about, I pursue with a passion. My adoption story was no different.

I emailed Martha photographs of the family I grew up with. The first was a black-and-white snapshot of my father standing in front of our house. In it, he wears a panama hat and holds a baby—me—in his arms, his dimples emphasizing his winning smile. In the second photograph, I am a child of three, my thick arms flung around Lilly's neck, my unconditional joy announcing to the world how much I adore my big sister.

I thought our photo exchange was over for the evening and was about to shut down my laptop when another email arrived with a photograph attached.

When I opened it, a woman's face popped onto the screen. Her gaze sent a chilled finger down my spine.

For fifty-seven years I grew up believing that a woman named Mary Montes De Oca, a force as unyielding as iron and as naturally beautiful as fresh cinnamon, was my mom. Until the day she died, Mami's skin was soft and wonderfully unwrinkled, the result of a lifetime of avoiding the sun's rays and morning and evening applications of Oil of Olay. This new mother, staring at me from my computer screen, was petite. Her lips were pressed tight into an uncompromising smile; a puffy blond wig was secure on her head. Maria's piercing black eyes sent goosebumps across every inch of me. I wanted to erase the email, delete the photograph forever, and plead to the gods for a do-over.

I am not a fearful person. In my twenties, I hitchhiked solo through northern Spain. As my stepson Greg's officiant, I skydived with the wedding party the week before his nuptials. On a dare, I even spent the night alone on the doorstep of an abandoned castle in Scotland. But now, instead of feeling a connection to the woman who gave birth to me, a surge of dread made me want to run from her.

During the fifteen years I practiced Chinese medicine as an acupuncturist, I learned that a person's face reveals clues about their well-being. A scan of my birth mother's features staring back at me on my computer screen filled me with a suspicion that Maria suffered from a Shen disturbance—or, as it's known in Western terms, *mental illness*.

Martha confirmed my hunch. On a subsequent phone call, she told me she believed my biological mother suffered from bipolar disorder.

Martha shared that Maria was often depressed and came to believe that a curse was the culprit for her dark moods. After she and her two children left Carpinteria, they lived in Chicago. There, Maria visited a *curandero*—a shaman—whom she believed could remedy her spiritual affliction. She dragged her children along with her to these encounters. While the curandero performed rituals and recited incantations over their mother, Martha and Robert cowered in a corner, terrorized as they witnessed the strange goings-on.

Bipolar disorder and shaman healings were not the only factors making life with Maria a bitter pill. Despite being born in Chicago, Maria had never learned to speak English. She couldn't hold down a job, so the family's clothes, food, and other essentials all came from an organization run by a group of nuns. Martha, meanwhile, didn't learn Spanish until she was older, and so had difficulty communicating with her own mother.

During high school, Martha began her day at 4:00 a.m. in order to attend school and work two part-time jobs.

"Christmas was the worst time of the year for my brother and me," she said. "We never celebrated it or any other holiday, and we never got presents. The only time we came close to having a normal Christmas was the year my Aunt Lena came over, bringing us gifts and dragging a Christmas tree behind her. I don't remember my mother ever hugging us or ever saying she loved us."

There but for the grace of God go I . . . I dwelled on these words I'd once heard in a priest's sermon. These might have been my Christmases had Mary Montes De Oca not felt swayed by Maria's tears.

Life with my birth mother was difficult for Martha and Robert, and it only got worse.

"Sometimes my mother would punish us by hitting us with a chain that she carried around with her," Martha told me. "My brother and I did nothing to warrant that type of abuse."

"No child ever warrants that," I told her, wishing life had been better for her and Robert. I asked, "Was there anything good that you remember about growing up?"

"I loved movies, and kids," she said. "On weekends I'd take the neighborhood children to a Saturday matinee."

As Martha spoke, I pictured the many times I went to movies on Saturday afternoon with Lilly at the local movie theater—how we laughed, the popcorn we ate, and the fun we had.

Did Maria love her children? That wasn't clear to me. But what was obvious was that Maria had considered them a burden. A third child might have become the tipping point that destabilized an already perilous balance.

At twenty, Martha met Adam, a self-assured security guard. They married and started the family she'd always longed for. But during this time, unbeknownst to her, the authorities evicted her mother and brother from their home.

"When I got there, they had thrown everything out," Martha said. "My mom kept an old suitcase filled with pictures and letters that I snooped through when I was little. I saw your mom's picture in there once. She looked so glamorous, holding a white purse in her hands. My mother carried that suitcase with her from place to place each time we moved. But it's all gone now."

Over the years, Maria's mental state shifted from depressed to bizarre. After Robert left home, she refused to tell Martha where he went. Regardless, Martha invited her mother to live with her. Maria moved in, but didn't stay long. Soon after, she began talking to herself and making disturbing comments. One day, she left—without a word, a note, or a goodbye. When Martha finally tracked her down, she was living in a run-down hotel in downtown Chicago. Maria refused to open the door or even speak to her. That was the last time Martha saw her mother.

"Do you think she's dead?" I asked bluntly.

"I think so," Martha said. "We lost touch twenty years ago. I can't imagine she's still alive. She'd be in her nineties if she was."

I decided Martha was probably right. How likely was it that someone with a severe mental illness—a nomad without family or financial means—could survive to that age?

Since Adoption D-day, I'd been calling and texting Lilly frequently, sometimes several times a day. I needed my connection with my big sister to remain strong to keep me from crumbling. After I finished up this latest conversation with Martha, my trembling fingers entered Lilly's phone number for the second time that day.

"I knew she was mentally ill," Lilly said after I told her the details of Martha's life with Maria.

"You were nine years old, Lilly. You told me you didn't even know Maria was pregnant when she was living with you—you said you thought she was getting fat. So why would you think she was mentally ill?"

"Because she had to be crazy not to want you," my sister said, as if stating a universal truth.

With those words, my sister's arms reached across two states and wrapped me tight in a wonderful cocoon of love and protection. I sighed, releasing the trapped breath in my chest, reassured that the tether between us held.

I filed Maria's picture into a folder and shut the lid on my laptop with a snap, convinced that my birth mother was now a concept relegated to a digital file that I would never see again. I forgot that saying the word *never* is an open invitation to the universe to pile on a second helping of what you least want, when you least expect it.

CHAPTER SIX

And the Hits Just Kept Coming

IT WAS LOVE AT FIRST SIGHT.

The intimate, pueblo-style house that Ken and I moved into just a few months before I received the news about my adoption delivered delicious views of the surrounding Sangre de Cristo and Oritiz mountain ranges. The neighboring stucco structures, colored in varying earthen hues, lay sprinkled across the landscape. Like a space colony on a semi-arid planet, the houses melded peacefully into the high desert's sandy hills and immense blue skies. Ken loved the brick floors and the impressive wooden vigas stretching across the ceilings. But all I saw were the large French doors, abundant windows, and four skylights. This home satisfied my number one desire in any place I live—*sunlight*. Lots of it.

With my head resting on a pillow and eyes closed, I was sitting in my wicker chair, relishing a sunshine bath, when my cell phone rang.

Martha Baptista. My jaw tightened—something that was occurring more and more whenever her name popped up on my device.

"Hello," I said politely as I put the phone up to my ear.

"I don't know what is going on in the universe," Martha blurted out. "But I just got a call from an attorney who told me our brother died from a heart attack a year ago."

Our brother. Although I had two marvelous older brothers, I'd once wished for a brother closer to me in age. When I was a child, I pretended I had a twin. For months, I spoke to my imaginary sibling as if he were a real boy made of flesh and bone. Now, a pang of disappointment shot through my belly. I'd never meet Robert, my half-sibling, the waif who refused to peek up at the camera and smile in the snapshot Lilly had given me three weeks earlier.

Well, I reasoned, taking in the news Martha was sharing, *look how thrown I was when I discovered I had a half-sister.* My nervous system might have short-circuited if I'd met a new brother who was not Ray or Art.

"The attorney said something else . . ." I heard Martha inhale loudly through the phone line.

Out with it, I thought with my typical impatience. I tamped the feeling down and instead chose my words carefully. "What's that?"

"Our mother is alive and in a state hospital in Chicago. She's in hospice."

Mother, alive, hospice—each of these words rattled my body like a jackhammer on pavement.

"Hospice? Do you . . . do you think you might go see her?" I asked, remembering the last time she'd seen Maria Gallegos was two decades before in a shoddy Chicago hotel.

"I was thinking about it . . . do you want to go?"

YES! my mind shouted, but I responded calmly, "Let me think about it, okay?"

Who was I kidding? The flames of a fire can tempt even when it burns. As upsetting, overwhelming, and all-consuming as my adoption discovery felt, I also was in the midst of an unbelievable adventure. My excitement and fear were magnetic forces both attracting and repelling each other in a never-ending dance. I was at the center of a story that unraveled daily—and however painful the truth might be, I needed to follow this cliffhanger to its end.

Ten minutes later, I called Martha back.

"I'm in," I said.

Online, I found an outrageously overpriced ticket to Chicago departing in three days. In just seventy-two hours I'd stand face to face with a half-sister I never imagined existed a month before, and my biological mother, whom I had only seen in a photograph. A cold tingle made its way down my spine as I pictured her face. What would I feel when I actually met my birth mother in person?

"Do you think my doing this would upset our parents?" I asked Lilly over the speakerphone while packing my clothes into my purple suitcase. "I kind of feel guilty. Like I'm betraying them by doing this somehow."

"You're not betraying them," Lilly said. "They never told you because they were afraid. "They lived through a time when people had a stigma against kids born out of wedlock. They didn't want you to carry that around your entire life."

But there were other reasons too.

"Did you ever see our father cry?" Art asked me when I rang him. Like my mother, Dad reminded me of a mighty Saguaro, the resilient cactus of the Sonoran Desert, who endured fierce heat and devastating storms yet remained standing. As a little girl, I'd clung to his bulging bicep and laughed with delight as he lifted me up and down as though he were a weightlifter and I was his dumbbell. I never saw Dad bend to weakness or give in to fear, no matter the hardships that came our way.

I did in fact see him cry, however—*twice*.

The first time was at my Abuelita's funeral. The proud matriarch who'd judged my father unworthy of her daughter, the determined mother who'd hired men to kidnap Mami after my parents married, the stubborn matron who'd said barely a handful of words to Dad through-out her life—this woman's death brought tears from my father's eyes, until he wiped them away forever with a swipe of his wrist.

The second time I saw Dad cry was a couple of years later, when I was in my mid-twenties and telling him the details of an upcoming solo trip. I explained how two weeks before, I'd stood in the local library, eyes closed, and spun a globe on a stand—and when I'd stopped the earth from spiraling, my fingertip had landed on Egypt. I'd then added Israel to my travel itinerary for good measure and booked a ticket to both.

When I picked up my pack and swung it onto my back, I saw Dad's face contort. The moisture misting his cheeks betrayed his concern. When he caught me watching, he turned away and pretended to inspect a doorknob, as if it might need repair.

"It's just because I'm so happy for you," he said, waving his hand as he walked out of the room. I didn't believe his excuse. But I also wasn't sure what to make of this man, larger than life, afraid of nothing, and now awkwardly looking away so I couldn't see his tears.

"No, I never saw him cry," I lied to Art.

"Well, he cried one day at The Studio," Art said, referring to his photography business based in Los Angeles. "We were in my darkroom and he says—'What if Carlyn finds out she's adopted? What if she goes looking for that woman?' I told him you were old enough to know the truth, that you could handle it, and they should tell you. But it was as if he couldn't hear me. 'What if she rejects us? What if she rejects your mother?' He just kept saying that over and over."

I couldn't imagine my father this distraught. My parents were the patriarch and matriarch of our huge extended family that spanned throughout California and Western Mexico. They were hardworking, self-sacrificing, and as tough as nails, and they'd taught us to be the same—or at least to pretend to be. But fear wears many masks—dons different manifestations. I thought Mom and Dad were omnipotent, and as a child I was powerless by comparison. But listening to my brother recount my father's despair made me conscious that besides my family, fear had also lived in the *house that moved*. It had shared a room with my buried secret. Until now, I had not realized how much real estate this pair had occupied.

I longed to talk to my parents—to hear their voices explain their perspective, and to understand why they chose to do what they did.

But I would never have a conversation with them again, never have a chance to reassure them that no matter whom I met in Chicago, blood or not, or what truths I uncovered, everything would work out. They were still my parents after all, regardless of our fraught past.

I won't lie: My adoption revelation had wounded me deeply, leaving my emotions as unstable as soda in a can, shaken up and ready to spew. I needed a lifeline to cling to, an anchor to keep me from spiraling into the cosmos. It arrived in the form of a quote.

The truth shall set you free. I'd seen these words on bumpers stickers, read them on inspirational memes, and heard them from the mouths of sages, countless times. I decided that knowing the truth of my identity was preferable to believing in a fabrication, even if this protective cocoon was all I had ever known. As long as I lived in a lie, I would never be complete.

CHAPTER SEVEN

A Curious Case of Synchronicity

AS A YOUNG CHILD, I was easily lulled to sleep by the hypnotic movement of a driving car.

I still am.

Albuquerque International Sunport lies an hour south of Santa Fe. The vistas along the highway are vast, sparse, and dusty. For me, driving across this stretch of Route 66 feels like taking a sleeping potion. Just out of Santa Fe, my eyelids flutter, followed by drowsy head nodding. Usually, I remedy my drowsiness by singing loudly with FM radio or listening to engaging podcasts. But none of that was necessary today. I may have been cruising at the speed limit, but my overwhelmed mind was racing well beyond that.

Ken asked if I wanted him to accompany me to Chicago, but I told him I was okay on my own. Since Lilly's bombshell, we'd talked about little else, so I was glad to give him a break from *the story*. I suspected that when I returned home, we would talk about it all over again.

Lilly also volunteered to join me on my flight east. "For moral support," she said.

"Thanks, but I really need to do this myself."

"You won't even know I'm there," she insisted. "I'll stay in the hotel room. I don't even have to meet Martha if you don't want me to." Lilly was a mother squirrel protecting her young, trying to keep her little sister safe from a storm Mom had warned her would wreak havoc on my life.

"I appreciate it, Lilly, really, but this is something I need to do on my own."

"Okay, but if you change your mind, I can just hop on a plane . . ."

"Thanks, Looscious," I said, hoping my use of her nickname would make her giggle. For once, it didn't.

I would have relished my sister's company at any other time, but I knew this undertaking was best faced alone. To understand the past, I had to experience the events ahead through my own lens, to hear people's words without others' assessments, and to draw my own conclusions. Like the scarecrow in *The Wizard of Oz* whose innards were decimated by crows, I needed to put *myself* back together again. No one else could do it for me.

"Business or pleasure?" the shuttle driver asked.

I looked up and spotted his eyes in the rearview mirror as we drove from the airport parking lot toward the terminals. My mouth opened to respond, but I was unsure how to answer. There was no category for this trip.

"Neither," I said with a smile, then resumed looking at the photograph of my adoptive mother, Mary, on my cell phone. The previous day had been the seventeenth anniversary of her death. As was my custom, I'd taken the physical version of this photograph, the one I kept in our bedroom in a wooden frame, and set it on our dining room table for the day. It was a glam shot, taken at a beautician's conference on Catalina Island. Mom sat in a restaurant, dressed in her white uniform, cocktail in hand, face wistful. She reminded me of a movie star caught by a paparazzi's flash. I'd placed a tea candle in a dark red votive holder in front of her image and—with a strike of a match—lit the wick.

In my early years, I witnessed Mami perform this same ritual of photograph and candle as her way to honor the dead. Paying homage to the departed was one of the few things from my childhood I'd carried into the present.

Now, on my cell phone, I again looked into Mami's gaze, her dark brown eyes always watchful, often judging, ever vigilant.

The bus braked; its groan interrupted my thoughts. As soon as the doors swung open, I climbed down the stairs, pulling my purple suitcase behind me as I headed toward the terminal. Trepidation nagged at me; a fear of the unknown was taking hold. On autopilot my feet walked forward, spurred ahead by the memory of my parents, who had shrunk from nothing. With barely the clothes on their backs, they immigrated to a foreign country. So, what was a journey across a few states? Today, I'd borrow their courage. Fear would not steer my ship.

Like most people over the age of ten, I've traveled through countless airports. But this time, as I made my way toward the security lines, I was struck by the many forms of baggage scurrying back and forth toward unknown destinations. Ahead of me, a flock of flight attendants in matching outfits gabbed while pulling identical black rolling suitcases behind them. A couple of young hikers in fleece jackets and torn blue jeans carried their belongings in weathered packs on their backs. Hunched tech nerds with computer bags slung over bony shoulders shuffled by. By chance, I caught the eye of an elderly Indian woman in an orange sari who was frowning as she clutched a cardboard box secured with twine tightly in her arms. I smiled, and her grimace softened. I wondered what was inside her box, the hiker's backpacks, and the sea of suitcases surrounding me. But more so, I felt curious about the baggage I couldn't see—the invisible pieces we all gather over the years and tote in mind and heart, adding extra weight to our lives.

After clearing security, I found a flight information display board and pulled out my boarding pass to double-check the gate number and departure time.

"What the . . ." I said out loud, adjusting my glasses to make sure I wasn't hallucinating. "What?!" I brought the document closer to my eyes.

The businessman beside me looked up, gave me a perplexed look, then walked away.

My heart beat rapidly, its waves pulsating in my ears. I scrambled for my cell phone with clumsy fingers and quickly phoned my sister.

She picked up on the first ring.

"Are you okay? Are you at the airport? I'm making fig jam," she said, out of breath. I heard a metal spoon clank against the side of a pot.

"Guess what my flight number to Chicago is?" My voice struggled to steady itself.

"I don't know, what?"

"4619," I said.

The spoon stopped clanking.

"I have to sit down," Lilly said after a long pause. "This is all just too much."

While I waited for my sister to compose herself, I pictured the beige rotary phone that lived outside my bedroom when I was a kid. It sat on a shelf over a tarnished silver tea set. At its center, penned in black ink, were the numbers: 684-4619. For fifty-seven years, our home number ended in 4619. These digits that I had lived with for so many years, numbers that I had given away to countless people, and that I had dialed thousands of times, were part of my genetic makeup. Saying them aloud was a spell that conjured up my youth.

Since the day Martha contacted me, there had been several strange synchronistic moments related to numbers and dates. The day my DNA results arrived in my inbox was also Martha's birthday. A week later, when I called my new half-sister to share my findings, it was Valentine's Day. March 30 was the date stamped on my half-brother Robert's death certificate. March 30 is also my birthday. I was flying east on the day after the anniversary of my adoptive mother's death. And now, four unexpected and deeply meaningful numbers—4619— were on my boarding pass to Chicago.

When I shared my adoption story with my friend Chandra, she said, "Seems like the divine hand is at play in your life, watching over you."

These numbers confirmed her notion. I was flying into the uncharted waters my parents had feared, but they were right here, swimming alongside me, on this journey. *4619* was their way of letting me know this.

Standing in front of the giant board, staring at the four familiar numbers, it was suddenly clear to me that traveling forward in search of the missing answers to my adoption also meant journeying back in time. The keys to my mystifying origin story might live in Chicago, Illinois, but they also were buried in Carpinteria, California—hidden in the folds of my past, where childhood memories I once took for granted could no longer be taken at face value. I dug through my backpack and found a notepad and a pencil with a dull point; instruments I would use on the flight to record the downpour of past events besieging my mind and demanding to not only be heard but also rewritten from a new perspective.

"Take a nap and save me some fig jam, okay?" I said to Lilly. "I love you."

"I love you too, Carboonish."

I hung up the phone and took a final look at the flight board. The numbers had not changed. I slid my boarding pass inside my jacket pocket, made my way through the crowd, and boarded flight 4619, headed to Chicago and into the unwritten pages of *my Unexplainable Knowing.*

PART TWO

"In the midst of hate, I found there was,
within me, an invincible love."
—Albert Camus

CHAPTER EIGHT

Life on Escondido Road

SATURDAY, my most cherished day of the week, never came soon enough when I was six years old.

In a faded pink room that I shared with my sister, a lyrical snoring belonging to neither of us woke me. The alien snorts emanating from beneath my blanket belonged to our dog Orange.

Dogs were absolutely verboten inside our house, so I sneaked Orange indoors each night after everyone was asleep. I had two dogs, but could only fit one onto my bed. Since Orange always beat Bandit to the back door, he was the lucky recipient who shared the bottom bunk with me.

That morning, I scratched fiercely at my flannel pajama top. When I lifted my shirt, small dark flecks jumped off my skin and onto the blanket. A black snout dug its way from under my covers, then the rest of his muscular body emerged and stood on the bed. Shaking his massive frame, Orange shed a few more fleas before jumping off and landing on the linoleum, whose red-black design resembled amoebas under a microscope.

Purposeful footsteps made their way through the dining room and into the bathroom, cueing me to grab Orange's chain collar and silence its jingling. When a plastic lid slammed against the rear of the toilet, I knew the coast was clear. Orange and I slinked toward the kitchen, past a partially open door where my father, wearing a white V-neck T-shirt and khaki pants, prepared his razor for his morning shave.

Quietly, I unlatched the back door, then whispered into my beloved dog's ear, "See you soon, Buddy."

I kissed the top of Orange's sizeable block head, sealing our friendship, before he escaped into the yard in search of Bandit.

At breakfast, I ate cereal while reading the backside of a cornflakes box. Every now and again, I'd glance at my mother—a five-star general assessing the rooms in our cramped house before she left for her job as a hairstylist in nearby Montecito. Mami's impeccable white uniform dress, statuesque posture, and *do-not-mess-with-me gaze* supported her absolute sovereignty in our home. Lilly followed behind her jotting down Mom's commands with her perfect printing on a yellowed pad of paper. My sister was a dutiful daughter who never complained about the long list of to-dos our mother assigned, but her somber expression and hunched shoulders told me that today's tasks would cut short her afternoon rendezvous with *American Bandstand*, her favorite TV show.

I came next on the list.

"Take a cookie from the jar." Mami nodded toward the transparent red plastic container behind me. I shot a look at the vanilla wafers, my mouth watering, but her tone, curt and brimming with authority, made me wince. Even when Mami said a statement as innocent as "the milk is in the fridge" or "here's your lunch," my tomboyish body braced itself for her oncoming disapproval; from an early age, I'd harbored the presumption that Mami's terseness stemmed from something I had done wrong.

I reached deep into the canister, took the cookie, and slipped it into my mouth. Then, when she wasn't looking, I slipped a second wafer into the pocket of my knee-length shorts. With the biscuit dangling from my lips, I picked up my bowl and edged past The General and her assistant to get to the kitchen, where I ran my dish under a stream of cold water and then laid it on a corroded drainer whose one short stump made it seem like it held its leg up to pee.

The sun filtered through a crumbling screen, emphasizing a streak of yellow paint and a layer of dust that lived permanently on the glass. As I munched on my cookie, I lifted my face toward the sunlight. Its warmth was heaven on my skin.

Even in the summer months, our house was damp and dark. During the day I searched our yard for sunny spots to lie on—a piece of sheet metal, a wooden plank, or even a clear space on the cement driveway. I spread my lean frame across these heat conductors like a sea lion over the rocks. The sun's rays penetrated deep into my bones and felt more delicious than chocolate could ever taste.

My mother glanced at the slim gold-plated watch on her wrist; her grimace betrayed that she was running late. Mami worked six days a week, including Saturday, as a beautician in Montecito, the stunning Mediterranean enclave just north of Carpinteria. With its manicured hedges, elegant mansions, and exclusive boutiques, Montecito would one day become home to Oprah Winfrey, Ellen DeGeneres, the Duke and Duchess of Sussex, and other celebrity notables who could afford life in one of the most expensive places in the United States.

In contrast, Carpinteria's ranch-style homes, beachside apartments, and quaint bungalows housed a diverse populace of white and blue-collar workers. With its self-proclaimed World's Safest Beach and infamous Rincon Point, the community drew surfers like the pope attracts believers. The town's sprawling avocado and lemon orchards offered jobs to Mexican immigrants who had been arriving there with their families and dreams since the 1800s.

In the future, Carpinteria would gentrify and reign as the avocado capital of the world. But for now, *Carp* was Montecito's country cousin. And our house, on a dirt road that mutated into a muddy swamp after the winter rains, was an even poorer relation.

Mami peeked into our bedroom. Her lips pursed as she scanned the disheveled bunkbeds and clothes scattered throughout the nine-by-nine-foot space.

"Clean your room," Mami said to Lilly, who gave me an accusing look since it was mostly my clothes littering the floor. I crossed my fingers behind my back, hoping my mother would miss the tiny black specks leaping across the white sheets on my bed.

As Mami examined our room, I studied hers. Her kitchen was a narrow, L-shaped space with dull yellow cabinets and a peeling linoleum floor revealing patches of substrate. Stacked one on top of the other were dented pots, pans without handles, and copper-colored gelatin molds. Streaks of grease—refugees from various cooking experiments—glued hanging cobwebs against the anemic yellow walls, creating arachnoid-like works of art.

Mami's kitchen was not the only room in our home suffering from disarray. Brimming from every closet were secondhand clothes we never wore. Glass baubles cluttered the tops of cabinets. Cardboard boxes with outdated magazines competed with us for space on the world's most uncomfortable sofa. Old, unwanted, and forgotten miscellany blocked the outsides of windows, making our tiny sunless abode even gloomier. As Mami criticized our messy bedroom, I wondered what the difference was between that and the rest of her house.

I didn't wait to find out. As quickly as my sneakers would carry me, I headed toward the front door. But before I reached it, I stopped in the doorway of my parents' bedroom and peeked inside.

In front of my mother's vanity was a shiny wooden chest that would have been the prize of any antique store had its beauty not been hidden by the weight of several overloaded suitcases piled on top of it. Two twin beds covered most of the space. Mami's bed had the best view of the house, looking into the living room and directly onto the TV sets. When she wasn't home, I lay on her bed and watched my favorite shows on our double-decker television system. The top TV displayed the picture in black and white. Below it, a second television with a broken screen played the audio.

What intrigued me most in my parents' room, however, were the images adorning the walls. Over my mother's bed hung a painting of St. Anne with her daughter Mary, a girl slightly older than me, known to Catholics the world over as the Virgin Mary. Her large, sorrowful eyes looked toward heaven, as if understanding that one day an agonizing burden would rest on her delicate shoulders. Did Mami lie here at night thinking about this girl, her namesake, and the secret she held deep in her heart?

Mami congested the interior of our home with garage sale treasures. But the outside was my father's jurisdiction, and he picked up where Mami left off.

That morning, with cornflakes and a vanilla wafer filling my belly, I embarked on my Saturday expedition with Orange and Bandit. After splitting the extra vanilla wafer I stole from the cookie jar between them, the three of us trekked behind the house, passing stacked lumber draped with plastic, piled mattresses and a family of forty porcelain toilet bowls. Eventually we ended up inside my mother's faded charcoal gray 1957 Volvo Sedan.

There were plenty of clunkers on our property, but Mami's Volvo was my favorite. I climbed into the driver's seat and held the wheel, while a pencil—my imaginary cigarette whose butts I tapped on the wind wings—stuck out the side of my mouth. Orange sat in the torn seat beside me, grinning.

Mami found me there a few minutes later.

"Be a good girl and do everything Lilly tells you," she said, opening the car door quickly to let me and Orange out. I wrapped my arms around her neck and kissed her cheek; her skin smooth and warm, like a velvet scarf you can't stop caressing.

"I will," I said with absolute zero intention of doing anything my sister asked of me.

My father, attentive to Mami's tight schedule, rolled open the immense forest green gate at the end of the driveway as Mom backed her car out. Once the Volvo disappeared down the street, he pushed it closed again to keep the external world from looking inside.

With Mami off to work, I beelined to my next favorite place on the property: Lilly's gypsy caravan, a life-size wagon perched on an oxidized frame.

After climbing over a flat tire that made the dilapidated structure tilt to one side, I reached the front of the carriage. When Lilly was younger, this had been her playhouse, a home for her many toys—a trove of riches she'd abandoned now that she was a mature fourteen-year-old who watched *American Bandstand*. The caravan's crusty green paint, the holes in its flimsy frame, and the smell of mold didn't impede my imagination as I pretended two jet-black horses were pulling Bandit, Orange, and me through Robin Hood's Sherwood Forest.

Every Saturday I discovered new treasures inside the wagon. Today was no exception. Rifling through mildewed boxes, I found a crimson vest three sizes too big, a straw hat with a fist-size hole that I could slip one of my pig tails through, and a silver pot missing its lid—all useful for a tea party held with my stuffed animals. After imaginary refreshments and conversation, I entertained my animal guests with tunes from old Disney movies that I played from vinyl 45s on a hand-cranked record player that folded into a small pink suitcase.

Time passed quickly in my fanciful world and soon my brother Art poked his head into the caravan and said three words:

"Yo, Carlyn—lunch."

Lilly was a splendid and diligent teenage chef who transformed egg salad sandwiches into perfect bite-size squares and made canned vegetable soup fun by sprinkling broken soda crackers over its surface.

We ate our meals quickly, but never in silence.

"How come you're so short?" Art teased me as he stole my sandwich off my plate then took a big bite before putting it back. With his typical grin, he ignored my protests.

"Daddy, Art says *que soy short*." Lip quivering, I turned to my father, my face lined with indignation.

"*No se deje, Chiqui, no se deje!*" Dad bolstered my courage, encouraging me not to wimp out and give in so early in the match. With my finest impression of a boxer in the ring, I faced Art, defiantly holding my chin up, and gave him my best verbal shot.

"Well, you're so . . . so . . . so tall!" I said, mimicking Mami's sternness.

"You're not short, Carlyn... you're just uuuuugly," Ray said, breaking into a low, rumbling laugh that shook his lanky frame so much that his eyeglasses nearly fell off his face.

Art and Ray, peas in a pod, always sided together.

"*Verdad que sí, Jefe?*"—Right, boss?—Art asked my dad, who was already pushing his chair back, making room for me to crawl onto his lap and hide my frustrated tears against his powerful chest.

"*Sana, sana, colita de rana*"—Heal, heal, little frog tail—Dad's pale green eyes sparkled with mischief even as his chiselled arms tried to console me.

Playful teasing, raucous laughter, and a smorgasbord of Spanish and English shouted across the table punctuated our family meals. Our gabfest consisted of half sentences and partial jokes started in one language and finished in another. My parents spoke English as their second language and insisted that whenever we spoke to them, it must be in Spanish. But when my siblings and I spoke to each other, we only conversed in English.

After lunch, I collected the plates and brought them into the kitchen, where I begged Lilly to play my favorite game: Mrs. White and Mr. Really. As she washed the dishes, I imagined I was a Lilliputian-size man wearing a blackish top hat and carrying an attaché case who arrived at the door to sell her life insurance.

"Hello, Mrs. White," I said pretending to take off my hat before bowing dramatically.

"Hello, Mr. Really," Lilly answered.

"Is your husband here?" I asked.

"No, he's dead," Lilly said, deadpan and without skipping a beat.

"So, he won't be needing any life insurance, then?" I giggled.

"Wheeeeet whoooooo," Pepe, my mother's myna bird, interrupted us.

Pepe lived in a cage. At night, Mami set it on a tall chair beside the kitchen door, but during the day she hung it on a hook outside in the shade, so Pepe could overlook the comings and goings of life beyond our fence. Every afternoon, this shiny black mischief-maker with a sharp yellow beak sounded the alarm with his whistle. But this was not just any whistle: Pepe's alert was a piercing, two-note *wolf whistle*—a signal that had only one outcome.

Quickly, Lilly and I shed our Mrs. White and Mr. Really roles and shot outside. Lilly climbed onto the cement foundation that supported the forest green plywood fence surrounding our property and claimed the upper peep hole in the wood. I, meanwhile, stared through the lower slit between the bottom of the wall and its concrete base.

Next door to our house was St. Joseph's Catholic School, where Lilly attended and, soon, so would I. With our hands clenched over our mouths to contain our giggles, Lilly and I peeked through our respective spots as three Immaculate Heart of Mary nuns, wearing black-and-white habits, walked past us. Side by side, hands pressed together in front of their sternums, the trio glided across the pavement praying in synchronized whispers until . . .

Wheeeeet whoooooo!

The sisters' habits whirled in our direction like dark tornadoes as they searched for the ungodly offender. Then, as if they were the ones caught in a crime, the nuns quickly composed themselves and returned to their prayers. But sometimes I noticed a brief smile on their saintly faces.

That Pepe, he sure could make us laugh.

"Want to surprise Mami?" Lilly asked once we got inside. "Let's organize the kitchen before she gets home from work."

"What about *Bandstand*?" I asked.

Every Saturday afternoon, my sister stood in front of the giant mirror over her piano, brushing her waist length hair, and adding a touch of strawberry gloss to her lips before shooing me outside. Then she confiscated our double-decker television system for one hour so she could dance with the ironing board while watching the favorite show of all teenie-boppers across America: *American Bandstand*.

"Why don't we clean the kitchen instead?" she asked.

I surveyed the surplus of tin cans, empty and full, littering the tattered laminate counters. When we visited our relatives, their houses were different—better organized, and not so cramped. The idea of a spacious kitchen excited me. Maybe, once we cleared it, it would come to resemble the modern kitchens I envied on television commercials.

I dared to dream bigger. What if after we finished the kitchen, we tackled the living room? And what about my parents' bedroom? Wouldn't it be wonderful for Mary and St. Anne to enjoy the sunshine once we removed the soda pop crates and decaying boxes blocking the outside of the window?

Energized by our adventure, Lilly and I gathered unused plastic lids, glass jars, and Teflon cookware and packed them into any cardboard boxes we could find. With her enviably neat printing, my sister clearly labeled each box with a marker and listed its contents. I helped her carry what I could lift into the garage, where we miraculously found an empty wall to stack the cartons against.

Two hours later, our kitchen was transformed. Lilly and I looked proudly at the streamlined kitchen devoid of clutter; a room that I could swear was now breathing. I pictured my mother, a woman reluctant to smile, unable to contain her joy when she came home.

To celebrate our success, Lilly made chocolate chip cookies. I waited on the couch for Mami to come home, licking the sweet, dark goop off the mixer's beaters.

An hour later, the screen door swung open and Mami stepped inside carrying two paper bags full of groceries that she set down on a chair. Eagerly, I stood in the dining room doorway, awaiting her look of surprise and the gratitude in her forthcoming words. I expected that Lilly and I would soon receive our induction into the Extraordinary Daughters' Hall of Fame.

That ceremony never happened.

Mami's anger was never a tornado; it was a volcano. The eruption this time was silent, but its heat was so intense that it radiated beyond the skies and seas.

Being older, my sister got the full impact of Mami's fury. It began with a look perfected by angry Latinas the world over: *the hairy eyeball*, two creases furrowed deeply between Mami's eyes, announcing her displeasure.

"Bring my things back *now*," Mami said in a quieter voice than usual.

Not a daughter to argue, Lilly immediately headed to the garage—shoulders stooped, cheeks flushed, tears brimming.

"Can I help?" I asked my sister, somehow sensing I could not.

Lilly shook her head and averted her gaze.

As my sister brought back box after box from the garage, Mami emptied them, returning the exiled contents to their former glory. The kitchen grew fat again as the plastic lids I'd sorted so carefully by size, color, and worthiness crowded the counters next to burned pots and empty cans of coffee.

Mami's reaction confused me. I felt bad for Lilly, and disappointed that a modern kitchen was not in our future. Weeks would pass before Mami's cold shoulder thawed and she engaged in a normal conversation with Lilly again.

I slipped into my parents' bedroom and sat under the portrait of the young Virgin Mary, captivated by the look of sorrow in her upturned gaze. I wondered if Mary's mom ever gave her the hairy eyeball. But St. Anne's sympathetic face told me she had been a softer mother who kept an orderly kitchen, filled with sunlight, where myna birds flew free and didn't whistle at nuns.

CHAPTER NINE

Surviving Tia Petra

WHEN MY FATHER'S OLDER SISTER ARRIVED FROM MEXICO, it was as if The Wicked Witch of the West had landed in Carpinteria instead of in Oz.

Tia Petra carried a scuffed suitcase in one hand and a strand of black rosary beads in the other. Beneath the waistline of her floral dress, protruded a hard round belly, which from my vantage point looked like it could come in handy as a dinner tray.

Our rift began with red poinsettias. In Mexico, Tia Petra specialized in the making of crepe paper flowers for neighbors and friends to sell during the Christmas holidays. Our garage was filled to the hilt, but Daddy worked his magic and cleared away crippled bikes, a busted refrigerator, and impaired furniture from one end of the room to the other. In no time a six-foot rack, a square card table, and two folding chairs had become a poinsettia workshop.

Before breakfast, Tia Petra usually took a stroll around the perimeter of our property, her rosary beads swiftly moving through porcelain fingers as she recited her prayers out loud like a lost spirit haunting the junkyard. My mother forbade me to interrupt Tia Petra's communications with The Almighty, and I was happy to oblige.

When I wasn't exploring the hidden wonders of our yard with my dogs, I was Kareem Abdul-Jabbar, Los Angeles Laker, dribbling a basketball bald from wear down the cement driveway. Approaching the rim, I'd take two giant steps, my compact body stretching high before shooting a lay-up into a basket of galvanized steel my father had designed. Like fine chain mail, the hoop's metal rings formed an hourglass figure just wide enough for my ball to whoosh through.

If my basketball bounced off the rim, it could go one of two ways: left and over the industrial-size freezer sitting next to our front door, or right and over the rusty patio furniture stacked above a stockpile of wooden beams. If it was the latter, the ball would roll into a dark corner inhabited by *niños de la tierra*—children of the earth, otherwise known as potato bugs—whose beady stare and sinister smiles instilled a fear of insects for many years to come.

As I retrieved my ball from beside the fence one day, I glimpsed the pristine basketball courts with real cloth nets and large backboards lying on the other side of the wire mesh, and my eyes filled with envy. In thirty seconds, I could walk over to St. Joseph's School and play basketball on those gleaming courts. But Mami wouldn't let me leave the borders of my home alone—not now, at seven years old, or in the future, not even when I was seventeen.

From the sidelines, I took my shot. *Swish!* Nothing was more delicious than my ball slipping through the basket like a bullet soaring through metal silk. The roar of an invisible crowd, led by Kareem Abdul-Jabbar, fed my dreams of athletic stardom.

Tia Petra did not share my vision. She was a child of an ancient order who believed girls should learn to cook, sew, and clean. And if such a girl was especially lucky, she excelled in the art of making crepe paper poinsettias.

My basketball hit the rim; the backboard's vibration was Tia Petra's cue.

"Carlyn, *ven aqui!*" Her shrill voice summoned me from the bowels of the garage.

I feigned deafness and took another shot. The ball ricocheted against the rim and sailed right, toward the land of the potato bugs.

"Carlyn!" her voice insisted.

Reluctantly, I trudged into Tia Petra's poinsettia shop of horrors.

. . .

My aunt sat in front of her table. Across from her was an empty chair. Her nod made it clear that this seat awaited me.

For the next few hours, Tia Petra showed me how to wrap green crepe paper over six-inch slices of coat hanger, transforming them into stems. Next came leaves created from red crepe sheets folded over wire loops. Infinitesimal specks plucked from cotton balls bloomed into flower buds. As I watched her fingers turn paper into plants, my eyes drifted to her wiry gray hair, secured into submission by hairspray. The sharp aroma of the spray competed with the sweet scent of Elmer's glue.

Tia Petra smiled as she worked. I yawned as I picked at a cotton ball, and daydreamed of Kareem until lunchtime.

After lunch I settled onto the sofa to watch *Johnny Quest*, a cartoon portraying the adventures of a boy and his dog. The moment my bottom touched the frayed fabric, Tia Petra handed me a crochet hook and a ball of red yarn.

"Whenever you watch TV, you need to make something," she said, before turning the channel to her favorite Spanish telenovela. I sighed; I didn't like her new rule, but I did love television. So, I learned how to crochet a chain of stitches, and then started putting them together into what I was sure would become fabulous creations, the envy of my family.

But my polyester productions were not masterpieces. Far from it. The lines were rarely straight, the stitches were mostly uneven, and the colors I chose were fit for a clown. For Christmas, I made beanies for Ray and Art and a little cap for my teddy bear, Happy. I also crocheted a chocolate brown scarf with green trim for my father and a festive pastel blend for my mother.

As we watched *George of the Jungle* on our double-decker TV, Lilly studied my latest handiwork, a cavernous blue beanie with rainbow trim.

"Is this for me?" she asked, giving the beanie's bright green tip a sturdy flick. Presuming she admired my talent with the hook and yarn, I couldn't help but allow a dollop of pride to mix with my smile.

"Yup!" I boasted.

"Really, you shouldn't have," Lilly said, then stole the hat from me and pulled it down over my head, pretending to suffocate me, until I begged for mercy.

When Tia Petra's fifty-second birthday arrived, I grew nervous. What could I gift her? My mind drifted to her poinsettias in the garage, sitting on paper plates, trapped in clear plastic wrap like rejected Christmas cookies. If my aunt could create something out of nothing, maybe I could too.

That morning, Orange, Bandit, and I embarked on a reconnaissance mission through the yard. In short order we returned with a handful of palm-size rocks from my mother's garden. I borrowed the Elmer's glue from my aunt's workshop, then stopped by the kitchen, where I appropriated some used aluminum foil from a drawer.

While Tia Petra took her morning walkabout with Jesus, I put together her birthday gift. One by one, I shrouded the five stones in tin foil, then I painted each of them in their own unique color with Magic Markers. I knew Tia Petra's god approved when a shard of light made it past the corroding furniture piled outside my window and shone onto the blue, green, purple, and pink aluminum eggs, making them glitter like sea glass touched by heaven.

With a dab of glue here and another there, I bound the rocks together. Soon, the bodies of a dog and a pig came into being. After adding a cotton ball for the piggy's tail and toothpicks for the doggy's whiskers, I assessed my work. I had made something truly beautiful for my aunt; surely the best gift anyone would give her tonight.

Mami served a fabulous dinner that evening: red enchiladas, aromatic calabaza squash, perfectly textured refried beans, guacamole sprinkled with cilantro, and a large platter of Spanish rice garnished with peas.

My father was in fine humor, and in the middle of the meal he asked me to bring him a glass of water.

"Sure!" I said eagerly, proud that he'd chosen me, rather than Lilly, for this task.

When I got back from the kitchen, my enchilada was missing off my plate.

"Hey, where's my enТHilada?" My lisp from a missing front tooth competed with my family's bilingual cacophony.

"You must have forgotten you ate it," Ray said, trying not to laugh.

"No, I didn't," I said with righteous indignation. "It was right here when I left. Right here!" I pointed to red streak across my plate that looked as if the enchilada was dragged away against its will.

Feigning innocence, my siblings stared at me, then at my parents, and then at each other.

"Go get another one," my father suggested.

When I returned from the kitchen with my second enchilada, I discovered that the missing hostage had reappeared on my plate—*half eaten*. I looked at my family for an explanation but they kept eating as if nothing was amiss.

I'd learned by then that Dad had a tell. When he wasn't being completely honest, a slight twitch seized his upper lip, as if the truth was trying to escape the corners of his mouth. Tonight, his lip was definitely twitching.

After the Happy Birthday song, Tia Petra blew out her candles. It was time for chocolate cake with a scoop of Neapolitan ice cream, followed by gifts. Mami gave my aunt a scarf from one of her thrift store excursions, and Dad offered a bottle of perfume. Even at my young age I knew the fragrance came from my mother, since Daddy rarely shopped for anything other than tools.

Lilly gifted Tia Petra a Christmas ornament she'd baked and painted herself. My sister was the most talented person I knew. Not only could she craft ornaments but she could even play Fur Elise on her spinet piano without making too many mistakes. Still, I knew that when it came to presents, my dog and pig rock animals would be pretty hard to beat.

When it was my turn, I proudly handed Tia Petra a shoebox, formerly the home of a spider family that lived under my bed. When the lid came off the carton, I waited for Tia Petra's gasp of surprise and big smile to replace her pouty pink lips. I even wondered if an extra piece of birthday cake would be my reward for showing such industry.

She tilted the container forward for all to see. But like a magician opening his disappearing box, my precious creations had vanished. Instead of a pig and a dog, what remained were just rocks wrapped in colorful foil. Elmer and his glue had failed me.

Tia Petra's lips grew tighter and her cheeks reddened as my siblings split a gut. Mami silenced them with a flash of her hairy eyeball. I was not offered another slice of cake.

Later that night, as my family got ready for that week's episode of *Star Trek*, I sat in my room, disappointed that my painstaking efforts had fallen apart.

Tia Petra burst in, jarring my thoughts.

"Everyone gave me beautiful things," she said as she shoved Mom's scarf near my face. "From you, what did I get? *Piedras! Rocks!!!*" she shrilled, her body trembling.

I looked at the little stones in their motley outfits. Every time she said the word *piedras*, the spell faded, and soon I no longer saw magical creatures—I too saw only rocks.

But then I thought of Tia Petra's poinsettias. What were they but crepe paper, wire, and glue? Were they so different from my rock animals?

While she muttered and paced, I sat on my bed, watching her belly jut out from her dress. I wondered if she was going to have a baby. As I looked at my own babies in the shoebox—dismembered, abandoned, and unloved—Mami poked her head into the room. Tia Petra's lips pressed tightly together like a hyena's grin.

"Is everything okay?" Mami asked, glancing from me to my aunt and then back again.

Tia Petra grabbed her gifts, all except the shoebox, and brushed past my mother, exiting the room. Mami looked down at me. I looked up at her, feeling a bit like a toad perched on a stool. Her hairy eyeball materialized. But tonight, it wasn't meant for me.

When I was alone again, I whispered to my rock animals, assuring them that whatever form they took, be it mineral or animal, they would always have a home with me. I closed the lid and slid them under my bed—not very far, since a thriving ecosystem of clothes, clogs, candlesticks, and cookery already lived there.

The next day, Tia Petra added knitting to my repertoire of feminine talents. Maybe there were other girls who enjoyed knitting a blanket or crocheting a scarf. These girls might find excitement in the secret art of flower creation. But I was not one of them. I wanted to shoot hoops with my basketball and hang out with my brothers, who let me turn on the ignition and push on the brakes of old cars as they worked on them. I wanted to go back to the Saturdays when Lilly and I played Mrs. White and Mr. Really and Pepe the myna bird whistled at pious nuns. I missed running free with my dogs in the junkyard, searching for hidden treasures in the tangle of rust and rubble.

But I was a kid with no power, no voice, and no choice. I took the fat knitting needles and garish yarn from Tia Petra's age-spotted hands.

My aunt flopped beside me on the sofa and showed me how to knit a garter stitch. As I watched her fingertips navigate masterfully over the yarn and listened to the needles click like a woodpecker with a steel beak, I thought of the precision with which her rosary beads sailed through her short fingers. Tia Petra's hands were always moving, whether she was cooking, cleaning, knitting, crocheting, or praying. I wondered what would happen if they just stopped.

When Mami arrived from work, she found me sitting on the couch, stabbing the ball of yarn with a knitting needle. I didn't bother to get up and hug her as I usually did when she came home in the evening.

Mami peered at the television, which was turned off.

"Why aren't you watching TV, *Mija*?" she asked.

I shrugged and made an obnoxiously elongated stitch.

She took the knitting needles and yarn out of my hands. "Go out and play," she said.

Her stern voice implied that I had no choice other than to obey. Like a prisoner released from solitary confinement at the Knitting Penitentiary for Wayward Girls, I kissed her velveteen cheek and burst outside, my pig tails almost catching in the screen door as it slammed behind me.

I sat on the stone stoop in front of the front door, tossing a saliva-soaked tennis ball to Orange. Mami and Tia Petra's voices carried through the house and just far enough outside for me to eavesdrop.

"How is she ever going to get a husband if she doesn't know how to sew or cook or clean?" Tia Petra's shrill escalated to a new high with this line of questioning.

"I don't care if she ever learns that," Mami said, defending me in a way I had never heard before. "She's a child, she needs to play. I never want you to put another crochet hook or knitting needle into her hands again." Mami's tone was firm, uncompromising—and, like a judge's verdict, absolute.

Tia Petra fell silent, her voice down for the count.

It didn't matter if you were the Pope of Rome, the Queen of England, or Captain James T. Kirk of the *Starship Enterprise*, no one could ever win an argument against my mother when it involved her children.

Maybe Mami had come to understand the futility of knitting warm clothing in our Southern California climate; perhaps she'd had her fill of her sister-in-law exercising a staunch hand over her kids; or maybe she remembered that once upon a time she too had been a headstrong child who loved to climb trees and play with dogs. Whatever the answer, I didn't care. At long last, I was free of Tia Petra.

After my aunt left California, Mami stuffed her flower-making materials into a box and relegated them to the back of the garage. Lilly, in control of the kitchen again, baked chocolate chip cookies. And my free throws were getting so good that I laid bets with my brothers that I could make the shot whenever they walked by. (I lost as often as I won.)

In no time, I forgot how to knit a garter stitch and Tia Petra's long needles became spears that my stuffed animals held in their paws for protection. I suspected my parents and siblings were relieved to no longer be recipients of my handmade hats, scarves, and blankets.

Mami released me from Tia Petra, and I loved her for it. Yet my child's adoration, pure and tender, would eventually fade into a limbo of silence. In time I would grow into a caged animal hoping for a glimpse of the sun, and my love for my mother, once innocent and childlike, would twist and contort.

Soon, it would become unrecognizable to both of us.

CHAPTER TEN

A Doll's Story

ON WEEKDAYS, Mami dropped me off before kindergarten at Abuelita's bungalow near the train tracks on the other side of Carpinteria, before heading for work.

Abuelita's house was a feast for the senses. The vibrant hues of purple-blue hydrangeas, a burst of fresh sea air wafting in from the beach, and the occasional train whistle greeted me as Mami and I walked toward the front porch where my poker-faced grandmother waited.

Mami and Abuelita, evenly matched in size and temperament, exchanged few words. I glanced up at their faces and wondered why neither smiled. Weren't they glad to see each other? When Mami came home from work, I often jumped off the couch, flew into her arms, and, in record time, blathered all that had happened in my day. Feeling her arms wrapping around me, hearing her chuckle when I said something I didn't realize was funny, and inhaling the sweet garden bouquet on her skin—these moments filled my heart. Wasn't that true for Mami and Abuelita?

Once Mami left, Abuelita and I watched cartoons on her television; a single box with rabbit ears, not quite as extravagant as our double-decker set. My mother taught us never to ask for anything from anybody but Abuelita was a mind reader; she always knew my deepest desires. At 10:00 a.m. every day, she got up from her recliner and shuffled across the tile in her navy blue slippers toward the kitchen. When she returned, a snack-size bag of Fritos was in her outstretched hand.

Next to Orange licking my face and sinking baskets through my hoop, the taste of salty corn chips was the best thing in the universe. My mother insisted on good manners and had ingrained the words *thank you* into my vocabulary. I took the offering, thanked Abuelita, and showed my gratitude with a huge hug, which gave me the chance to stroke her Adam's apple, the lump in her throat that bobbed while she swallowed. I found this part of her anatomy endlessly fascinating.

Mami always picked me up after work, but one day my father pulled up in his pickup truck instead. I waved from the window and waited for him to come inside to get me, but he didn't. Instead, he sat in the idling Chevy, facing forward like a cabbie awaiting his fare. Abuelita watched from behind the lace curtains—a panther spying on a rabbit.

"Go to your father."

Abuelita spoke in even shorter sentences than Mami did, but unlike Mami's voice, hers didn't make me wonder what I'd done wrong. I adored Abuelita and was grateful for her unlimited supply of Fritos.

I hugged my grandmother goodbye, lightly tapped her Adam's apple with the tip of my finger, then bounded down the walkway and jumped into Dad's truck. I kissed him on the cheek, his five o'clock shadow sandpaper to my lips, then settled into my seat. As we left the curb, I waved goodbye to the figure behind the curtains.

"How come you didn't come inside, Daddy?" I asked.

"*Una gallina nunca se junta con un coyote*," he answered as though he were a priest lecturing his flock.

My father often spoke in *dichos*—short Spanish sayings with deeper meanings than the actual words themselves. I found this way of communicating perplexing. I was a kid who loved jokes but hated riddles. Why did I have to figure out what he was talking about? Why couldn't he just talk like normal people? *A chicken never befriends a coyote*, Dad said. What did this have to do with going inside Abuelita's house? My grandmother didn't own chickens, and I had never seen a coyote except Wile E. Coyote on TV. Abuelita didn't even have a dog.

I didn't know it then, but Abuelita and my father's relationship was as cozy as a glacial wind in winter. After my grandmother's kidnapping caper tanked, a truce had ensued. On the rare occasions that Abuelita came to our house, Dad disappeared out the back door and into the yard. He, meanwhile, never visited Abuelita's house except to pick me up or to fix her plumbing when Mami insisted. At gatherings, while our family laughed and music played, Dad and Abuelita sat apart, never saying more than a few words to each other. They kept to their respective corners, and maintained the peace.

I didn't question the behavior of the adults in my life; I accepted it. When Mami and Dad spoke in hushed tones, then noticed me in the room and suddenly stopped talking, I understood there were secrets that only grown-ups were privy to. When they wanted to share their stories, however, I was all ears. Especially when the subject was their love story, which I begged Daddy to tell over and over again, as if it were the first time I had heard it.

One day I pleaded for this story until my father acquiesced and heaved me onto his lap.

"Years ago, when I was young and living in Mascota, I was working on a scaffold with a construction crew. I was painting the side of a building, when I saw a beautiful girl in a sundress and high heels walking towards us."

This is how his story began. He told me the young woman carried an umbrella for two purposes: to shield her from the rain and to protect her face from the fierce summer sun.

"Who's that?" Dad asked his friend who was working on the platform beside him.

"A girl from America," the friend answered. "They call her La Morena."

Dad winked at his buddy, then grabbed his jacket and sped down the ladder. Once his feet touched solid ground, he ran across the cobblestone street that had been soaked by an earlier thunderstorm. With a dramatic sweep of his arms, he lay his threadbare jacket over the muddy sidewalk just as Mom's pretty shoes reached it.

"*Pase la reina!*" he proclaimed with a chivalrous tone and a hint of sarcasm.

Some women might smile and say thank you to a dashing young man who offers his only jacket to prevent her new shoes from ruin. Other women might find it flattering when a good-looking guy singles them out and says, *Pass, my queen.* Some might even blush when they realize the galant young man with the mischievous green eyes and unforgettable dimples is a dead ringer for the 1950s heartthrob, Richard Egan—*but not my mother.*

Mami took one look at the sweaty laborer dressed in splattered overalls and said, "Humph!" Head held high, she stepped off the brick sidewalk, bypassing Dad's garment, and trampled through the muddy street. Mom's rejection of my father's overture sent the construction crew howling.

"*Pase la reina,*" they joked among themselves as one of them pretended they were Dad and another the girl marching through mud. Deaf to their heckles, Daddy watched Mom disappear down the street. Who can hear anything when they're smitten?

A few weeks later, a good friend invited my father to Sunday lunch. There she introduced him to her cousin, an olive-skinned beauty who was originally from Mascota but was now visiting from America. The young woman was my mother. Mami and Dad laughed, realizing they had already met in the muddy streets a week before, and soon romance blossomed between them. My father fed their courtship by serenading Mami outside her window with his twelve-string guitar and stirring voice.

I like to think of my parents in those early days—a time when their love was fresh, unstoppable, and defied all obstacles. As they grew to know each other, they found common ground in their dreams—not of money or success but of family.

Years later, after they realized those dreams, Mami would rule with an iron hand. Her love for her children, fierce and uncompromising, was clear. But her brand of justice was not one I easily understood.

. . .

Melanie appeared on my father's bed, laying over a stack of thrift store garments. The blond curls and her sapphire eyes, the color of an African lake I had seen on the cover of a magazine, mesmerized me. Despite the D battery–size hole in her upper back showing she'd once had the power of speech, Melanie was the most perfect doll I'd ever envisioned.

I wasn't partial to dolls. I preferred the stuffed animals I curled up in bed with every night. My sister had Barbie knock-offs living in her gypsy caravan, but I didn't care about them. Those figures with their hourglass bodies and strange orange skin were only useful for tea parties. They did not touch my heart as Melanie, with her dimpled smile and rose-colored cheeks, did.

For months I played with this doll at every opportunity, whispering my secrets into her ear and promising her that she would always be mine. Perhaps my mother had mentioned that the doll wasn't meant for me and that she planned to give her away. If she had, I'd dismissed it. Love had made me deaf to anything else.

July arrived, signaling our annual trip to Mexico. Every summer we climbed into The International, my dad's behemoth truck. Like my father, this rig was rock-solid, resilient, and built with one purpose in mind: to see us through any calamity on our journey through the Sonora desert.

Mami loaded the camper with secondhand goods she had collected the previous year. Boxes of used kitchenware, electronics, hardware, and clothing quickly filled the compartment—castoffs that would find new homes with people south of the border who had less than we did. When I climbed inside, I found Melanie lying across the plastic-covered seat waiting for me.

Our three-day trip through the hottest, most arid landscape in Mexico was taxing. Temperatures were in the low one-hundreds. In the back cabin, I sweated and slept, but holding Melanie on my lap made the journey more bearable. Through the jalousie windows' vents we watched the endless armies of Saguaro cacti sweep past our speeding truck.

On these long drives, my father was in his element. His tanned, muscular arms gripped The International's steering wheel, forcing its vibrations into submission, as he drove long hours across vast stretches of desert. When we got a flat tire, he fixed it. When the engine over-heated, he had it up and running again in no time. My mother rode shotgun, keeping watch over Dad in case he nodded off from lack of sleep, the scorching sun, or mere boredom.

One night, after a grueling twelve-hour drive en route to Mazatlán, The International groaned to a stop. I sat up in the rear cabin and looked through the glass panes at my father sliding a nozzle into the truck's gas tank. The smell of fuel mixed with fried street food reached me as Mami opened the back door.

Her arm stretched toward me. I was about to reach back when I realized it wasn't me she wanted; it was Melanie.

"*Dámela*," she said.

I gripped Melanie tighter.

Mami repeated the word slower, as if I hadn't heard her the first time. "*Dá-me-la*."

Asking *why*, saying *no*, or refusing my parents was never an option. I did what I was told: I handed her Melanie.

As my mother closed the cabin door behind her, the cool feel of Melanie's chubby plastic legs lingered on my fingertips.

I scrambled to the window and watched as Mami approached a dark-skinned woman standing barefoot on the side of the road. Her parched face looked weary, as if attempting to smile would leave her exhausted. A little girl about my age, a smaller version of her mother, stood in front of her, her smile gappy and bright.

I couldn't hear what Mami said to them. But in the end, it wasn't necessary. When she handed Melanie to the girl, I knew my mother was giving her my child.

The gas cap clunked into place, alerting us it was time to get going. Mazatlán, with its crystal waters and poolside cabana, awaited. Lilly sat in the front cab mouthing the words to a song on her transistor radio as Ray and Art tried to beat each other into the truck. My father jumped inside as if the full tank of fuel had rejuvenated him as well as his vehicle. The International rumbled to life with a twist of the key. Mami climbed in beside Dad, her face devoid of emotion.

I peered through the window panels at the little stranger cradling my doll as if she were hers. *She is hers now,* I realized. Melanie looked at her new mom with the same frozen smile and blue gaze that had won my heart. I wondered if there were tears in Melanie's eyes as there were in mine.

Even at my age, I knew that this girl was poor and that my life in America was better than hers. I could have been happy for her, or admired my mother for her benevolence. But I didn't.

Instead, as I watched Melanie's new mommy disappear past the steam emanating from the food vendors' carts, I questioned my mother's love. Like a vase knocked from a mantel, a crack formed in the foundation that had once bound us together. Mami and I were not yet broken; the true rupture would come later. But today, something unfamiliar found its way under my skin into the place where love had once lived: seedlings of resentment took root in my heart, and there they gestated, eventually growing into shoots of hate waiting for the next time my vulnerability called on them to emerge.

CHAPTER ELEVEN

The Sweet Wisdom of Bees

LIKE THE MIGHTY SAGUARO CACTI, which stood impervious to rain, heat, and wind, my parents survived life's challenges through sacrifice, hard work, and their commitment to family.

While my mother washed and styled women's hair at a beauty salon, my father worked as the superintendent of buildings and grounds at the Cate School, a prestigious boarding academy about a mile from our house. But on Saturdays he spent his day in our yard, working on a myriad of projects that required sweat, ingenuity, and imagination.

Dad was a wizard. He was a self-taught master electrician, adept at repairing damaged radios, a skilled plumber who could fix a whole host of bathroom misfortunes, and a mechanical whiz who could resurrect the corpses of dead automobiles. Once, when I saw a bubbly blonde majorette on TV catch a baton midair and begged for a baton of my own, Dad fabricated one for me from a discarded black aluminum pipe and then popped two gray Superballs on either end. The baton may not have looked as fancy as the one belonging to the majorette but at least it was perfectly balanced.

"Daddy, do you want some water?" I asked him one warm day when beads of perspiration slid over the creases on his forehead and dripped onto his shirt. Usually he answered *no*, but this time he must have been really thirsty because his dimples emerged on either side of his winning smile and he nodded.

I ran inside the house and filled a glass to the brim with cold water from our dispenser. On the way back I tiptoed gingerly, so as not to spill a drop, while Orange leaped ahead of me as if metal springs powered his back legs.

When I arrived, I proudly handed Dad the glass.

"What took you so long?" he asked after gulping down the last trickle of cool liquid.

"Did it?" I said, looking back at my footsteps, wondering why he thought that. "It's just how long it takes to walk down the path."

"But why didn't you just go down the trail that leads to the kitchen?" he asked.

"Because of the bees," I answered.

Two large beehives stood on either end of the dirt path that ran parallel to the back fence of our property. My father collected the honey, and we enjoyed it over peanut butter on toast or pancakes on Sunday mornings. Except in the early hours and at night, the winged inhabitants of these white crates flew in and out of the hive entrance, swarming across the path. There was only one of me and an army of bees, so I always gave them their space and walked the long way around.

"The bees?" Dad asked, surprised by my response. "Why don't you just walk through them?"

I couldn't answer him because I didn't know why. Countless times I'd watched my parents, siblings, and even my dogs trot through the swarm as though it was invisible. It had never dawned on me I could do the same thing. Walking through a cluster of bees was a superpower I hadn't been born with.

I looked at Daddy and said nothing. I didn't need to. He saw the troubled look creep across my face and recognized it as fear.

Like a chef preparing his signature meal, Dad slipped a rag off of his shoulder, wiped his greasy hands as clean as possible, then beckoned me with his forefinger.

My dogs and I followed him down the dirt path, past the boysenberry bushes whose red dimpled fruit was verging on ripe.

At the base of the vines was a low cement wall Dad had built to keep the soil contained. Engraved in the concrete were familiar names—*Lilly*,

Art, Ray, Vincent, and *Mary.* Also immortalized in the plaster were *Rose* and *Ralph,* the names of Lilly's now-deceased chihuahuas. *Orange* and *Bandit* were also there beside two paw prints, ensuring that curious visitors knew that these were not the names of my parents' children.

My name was also etched into the cement, though it was spelled *Carlin* instead of *Carlyn.* For some inexplicable reason, Dad often misspelled my name, using an *i* instead of a *y.* Sometimes he called me Carlyn Marie; sometimes he wrote my name as *Carlin Maria.* He never misspelled Ray, Art, or Lilly's names; I wondered why he had such a hard time with mine.

As we walked, I came across a boysenberry splattered on the cement. Honeybees hovered over the mush, their striped bodies inspecting the contents. Unfazed, Dad stepped past them, followed by Orange and Bandit, who also wandered over the berry puree without a care. I trailed them, giving the flying insects a wide berth.

The buzzing intensified as we approached the apiary. Goosebumps seeped above and below the surface of my skin, betraying my unease. Dad paused at the edge of the swarm. His hand settled on his hip while the back of his other arm wiped the sweat from his brow. I didn't need to see his expression to know which one he was wearing. It was the same gaze he had when driving across flooded creeks and overflowing rivers on our long-distance adventures to Mexico.

My father and The International became one being—half man, half steel—when faced with those formidable currents, a byproduct of the torrential rains unleashed during the summer months. With unwavering determination and force of will, Dad grabbed the knob on the manual transmission, forced the grunting truck into overdrive, and, with great care and calculation, steered the metal monster and those inside it forward. As the cab descended deeper into the current, the water pressing against its doors rose higher. I'd nearly drowned in a swimming pool as a baby, so deep water was not my friend. As we ventured into the current, I squeezed my eyes closed and held my breath, hoping against appearances we would make it to shore—which we always did. Dad

didn't retreat from fear, and he expected his children to be just as resilient. Fear was not an emotion that people made of Saguaro tolerated.

My father was not asking me to drive into an overflowing river on
this day, but he may as well have been. "Just walk through it," he said,
tilting his head toward the swarm of bees.

My seven-year-old brain could not compute this. If I stepped into
the bevy, I thought I might die. But defying my father would ensure a
fate similar to death.

The colony buzzed intensely, as if confirming I was not worthy.

"They'll bite me," I told Dad, not understanding the difference
be-tween a sting and a bite, just knowing that both hurt.

Dad's dimples surfaced. He turned, faced the swarm, and walked
through the mass as if it were a bedsheet hanging from my mother's
clothesline.

When he returned, it was clear he expected me to do the same.

"Now you, *Chiqui*," he said, using his favorite nickname for me.

Chiqui was short for *chiquilota*. As a kid, I thought this was the name
of an enchanted bird; I imagined a glorious *chiquilota* soaring over
Escondido Road, its plumage resplendent. But as an adult, I'd learned
that regardless of how endearing *chiquilota* sounded, no such creature
existed. My father's moniker for me was just another word for *pipsqueak*.

Daddy crossed through the bee swarm unscathed. But my feet
remained planted in the dirt, unconvinced I could do the same. Orange
seemed to understand the value of this teaching moment. Casually,
my dog ambled through the mass, tail wagging, and disappeared on
the other side.

"See, Chiqui? Even the dog can do it."

I took Dad's words to mean I was a failure. Stung by shame, my eyes
watered. Why wasn't I like everyone else? Why couldn't I be brave?
What was wrong with me?

Daddy's knee bent to the pavement until we were the same height.
"I'm going to tell you a secret," he said. "The bees know you're afraid.
Fear isn't a smell they like. When they smell it on you, that's when they

sting." He poked my arm for effect. I rubbed the spot as if it actually hurt. "The secret is to walk through the swarm believing you *aren't* afraid—then they won't hurt you."

I looked at Dad's face, his light skin browned by countless hours under the sun, and borrowed a little of his courage.

He added a dicho: "*Dando y dando, pajarito volando.*"

I understood this saying without having to think about it too much— *Try, try, little bird.*

Bees sense fear. It took a few breaths to register the power of this knowledge. But soon the truth spread through my body and, taking control of my legs, it ordered them forward.

Before I knew it, I was inside the swarm. There I became conscious of the bees teeming over my skin, sweeping across my arms. Teensy feet caressed my face, gently baptizing me with their tickle.

I'm not afraid, I'm not afraid . . . I lied to myself.

Then it was over. I was on the other side. I wasn't dead.

I opened my eyes and scanned my exposed limbs. Not one bee had landed on me. There were no stings except for the memory of Dad poking my arm. Emboldened, I turned around and again walked through the swarm. The colony accepted my back-and-forth movements with patience as the thrill from conquering fear seeped into my cells.

As worry faded, something took its place: connection. I studied the bees, mesmerized by their wiggling black-and-yellow bodies and the gleam of dark fuzz on their delicate legs. Their ability to linger in the air and then fly away at will impressed me. More so, when I dared look into their faces, individuals looked back—an understanding that filled me with an indescribable joy.

"*Poco a poco, se anda lejos, Chiqui,*" Dad said with a parting wink. *Little by little, one goes far, Pipsqueak.* Dad returned to his engine block, leaving me to ponder his words.

Orange, offering a fanged smile and muddy snout, dropped a recently unearthed bone at my toes and then stepped back, awaiting my praise.

"Good boy, what a good dog!" I said, rubbing his broad neck with vigor. With all my strength, I tossed his offering into the middle of the junkyard.

He bolted after it. Bandit watched him go, then dismissed us both with a flick of his tail before dropping back onto his side and resuming his nap.

I paused a while longer near the cement wall autographed with our names, eating boysenberries off the vine, and watching my new friends buzz in and out of their skep. My father had shared a brilliant secret with me—a revelation that cloaked me with a coat of new confidence. I wondered if my father had any more secrets as powerful as this one. And when I would be ready to learn them.

CHAPTER TWELVE

What the Poet Said

AT THE END OF SECOND GRADE, the grammar school on the other side of our fence closed its doors from lack of funding, and the Dominican nuns Pepe delighted in whistling at became a memory. Although it was more expensive, and farther away, my parents sent me to Our Lady of Mount Carmel Catholic School in Montecito for the next six years.

Five days a week, in the parking lot of St. Joseph's Church, I gathered with the other local kids whose folks insisted on a religious education. We entertained ourselves with kickball, tag, and tetherball until the yellow bus with black lettering pulled up to take us to school.

Sometimes the doors swung open and Mr. Griggs, the church's crotchety caretaker, sat in the driver's seat answering our cheerful good mornings with a grumble. But once in a while, my brother Art drove the bus instead.

Both my brothers were in college by this point. Art was studying photography and Ray, who had flipped a coin to decide between medicine and law, was studying to be an attorney. By driving the school bus, working at the local gas station, or doing landscaping, my big brothers earned extra cash.

I made some pocket money too. The Top Knot Beauty Salon, where my mother worked, was only a ten-minute walk from Mount Carmel. On the days that I would not go home on the bus, I walked along the tree-lined trail beside the main road to the salon, a quaint little shop resembling an elfin cottage nestled under the shade of a sprawling oak.

One day I pushed the heavy wooden front door open, setting the cowbell jangling, and found my mom's boss, Dorothy, a giant of a woman with short curly brown hair, hunched over a massive appointment book.

"Hey, Dorothy," I said, wrestling with the door as I juggled my school books.

"I've got something for you," her voice boomed, though I was just three feet away.

She winced as she stepped out from behind the desk, her right hip gliding unnaturally high with each step. Her exaggerated gait reminded me of gunslingers in Westerns.

Dorothy bent over, meeting my height, and opened her hand. A shiny quarter looked up at me.

"Thanks, Dorothy!" Eagerly I took the coin from the center of her palm as if it were a gold nugget. I glanced at the photograph on the wall behind her. A much younger Dorothy smiled from the cockpit of a two-seater plane. I'd once overheard Mami tell Lilly that years earlier, Dorothy worked as a pilot until an aircraft she was navigating crashed and ended her airborne days. Her wide swagger was a result of the accident.

Although she wore a white polyester dress similar to Mami's, I could only imagine Dorothy truly at home in a khaki green jumpsuit aboard a Cessna. Art drove my school bus from time to time but Dorothy commanded the skies.

In the Top Knot's kitchen, I struggled with my math homework and was glad to abandon it when my mother poked her head in the door and summoned me to come with her.

Mami's workstation was in the shop's rear. To get there, we walked past the booths where the handful of female employees worked. Fingernail polish, hair-styling chemicals, and perfumed lotions thickened the air. Irena—tall, curvy, and marble-eyed—smiled at me with pouting lips highlighted by nude lipstick. Carol, a redhead with matching freckles, waved at me with a pair of scissors in hand. Madge the manicurist, a single mom with creases around the sides of her mouth, spoke my name in a neutral tone as I passed her door.

At my mother's station, an elderly lady with powder blue hair sat on a hydraulic chair in front of a giant mirror.

"This is my daughter, Carlyn," Mami said, taking a hard-plastic rod and a mini white tissue from a tray. She rolled a section of the woman's hair between them.

This wasn't my first introduction to a client of my mother's. I was used to their examinations. From my gray uniform skirt down to the white bobby socks inside the green-tan bowling shoes I begged my mother to buy, they scanned me from head to foot. I assessed them too, these ladies of means in their second and third acts, their hair various shades of platinum, gray, or blue who came to Mami to give brio to their manes and have their troubles heard.

"Read me something," Mrs. Waters insisted in a raspy voice reminiscent of crinkle wrap. "Start where the bookmark is." She handed me a book of poetry.

The book's frayed brown cover and worn binding looked antiquated. Its musty fragrance brought dentures soaking in a glass to mind.

I glanced at my mother. Her stern eyes demanded that I *read* and that I do it *now*.

I opened Mrs. Waters' book, unleashing a wave of mustiness.

"The woods are lovely, dark, and deep and I have promises to keep—"

"Are you in a hurry, dear?" Mrs. Waters asked, stopping me mid-sentence.

I shook my head, knowing this was a lie but the correct answer for the occasion.

"This time take a pause, feel the words as you say them," she instructed.

Slower than before, I repeated the same line. But what I didn't understand was how I was supposed to *feel words* written on paper. I tried again.

"No, no, no, not like that," Mrs. Waters said, her voice taking on a nasal quality. She took her book back and stared at the page. "The woods are lovely, dark, and deep, but I have promises to keep. And miles to go before I sleep, and miles to go before I sleep." She finished her sentence sadly, wistfully, and with a reverence I couldn't comprehend. I stifled a yawn, hoping our poetry session was over.

Mami rolled the last wisp of Mrs. Waters' fine hair into a rod and assessed her work in the mirror. The blue cornfield was now home to several tidy rows spaced between paths of pale pink scalp.

"Time to dry your hair," Mami announced, pushing Mrs. Waters' chair under the standing hairdryer. She bent its metal neck forward, then set the clear plastic dome over the blue cornfield.

But Mrs. Waters wasn't done with me yet. She beckoned me closer with her forefinger.

Reluctantly, I trudged toward her.

"Get me my purse, dear," she said.

I handed her the leather bag lying on a nearby stool.

Mrs. Waters reached into its mouth and pulled out a five-dollar bill, which she set inside the poetry book before handing it back to me.

"It was nice to meet you, Caroline," she said.

I didn't bother telling her my name was *Carlyn*, pronounced like a person leaning out of a car. I just thanked her, took my gift, and headed back to the kitchen and my math homework, which I'd decided was infinitely more interesting than reciting poetry.

Mrs. Waters was one of many women who asked to see me when I visited my mother's work. They asked me mundane questions about what I learned in school, what my favorite sports were, and what subjects I was good at. For my efforts I had received a few dollars, candy, and a bookmark. My mother showed me off so often that my brothers began calling me *Charlie McCarthy*, after the famous ventriloquist's dummy who wore a top hat, tuxedo, and monocle and repeated whatever he was told to say.

What I did not know at the time was that these women were television writers, producers, authors, heiresses, mothers of famous musicians, dames, and other females of influence. Oprah Winfrey and

Ellen DeGeneres may not have lived in Montecito yet, but these were the crème de la crème of Montecito society during the late '60s and early '70s.

Mrs. Waters introduced me to poetry, and it was a tepid first interaction. But this was not the last time poetry and I would meet.

My second-grade teacher was Mrs. Sullivan, a sweet lady from the Midwest with horn-rimmed glasses and short curly auburn hair, whose daughter dated Art. Mrs. Sullivan not only thought the world of my brother, she seemed to like me too. This special connection between my teacher and me led to special privileges. At Christmastime, Mrs. Sullivan gave each of her students a small book, but not me. Instead, Mrs. Sullivan gifted me a doll with sun-kissed hair and a blue checkered dress like the one my Abuelita sometimes wore. And when my classmates misbehaved and she listed their names on the chalkboard, meaning detention awaited them after school—when I behaved badly and my name joined the list, Mrs. Sullivan would cancel detention and send us all home instead.

But my days of dolls, clemency, and being a teacher's pet ended when I arrived at Our Lady of Mount Carmel School. My third grade teacher, Mrs. Langley, was not Mrs. Sullivan. Stern and abrupt, Mrs. Langley's tight wrinkles creased at the edges of her infrequent smiles, adding to her severity. Mrs. Sullivan had been a fluffy pink sponge, soothing to the touch. Mrs. Langley was an unscented brillo pad forged of steel wool.

At Mount Carmel, the classes were harder and the kids smarter. I had no friends except the handful of students I rode on the bus with from Carp, who were having their own problems fitting in.

Not long after we arrived at the pink L-shaped stucco building, Mrs. Langley gave us our first assignment: select a poem, memorize it, and present it to the class the following week.

After school that day, I sat with Art at the dinner table, eating Lilly's chocolate chip cookies fresh out of the oven, while he read the newspaper.

"How was school, Mouth?" he asked.

"Mouth" was a new nickname he'd given me after deciding that I couldn't keep a secret. I hated it.

"Do you know any poems? I've got to pick one for school," I muttered in between bites of gooey richness.

With a dramatic look in his eyes, Art set down the newspaper, gazed beyond my shoulder, then lifted his arms like an archer holding a bow and arrow.

"I shot an arrow into the air; it fell to earth I knew not where," he said as he released the imaginary arrow into the distance.

I nearly fell out of my chair. Art teased me relentlessly, but he also made me laugh like no one else, and as far as brothers went, I thought he was pretty cool.

That evening, I remembered the book of poetry Mrs. Waters had given me, and I dug it out of a drawer. Miraculously, I found Art's poem inside of it—"The Arrow and the Song," by Henry Wadsworth Longfellow.

For a week I practiced reciting the lines—in front of my dogs, to my stuffed animals, and to anyone else in my family who would listen.

Then the day of our poetry recital arrived. Patsy delivered "Roses Are Red, Violets Are Blue" with conviction. Jack stammered through "The Cat in the Hat." And Shawn brought the class to tears with, "There once was a girl from Nantucket, who crossed the sea in a bucket . . ."

Mrs. Langley silenced us with a smack of her pointer on her wooden desk.

"Sarah Marchand," Mrs. Langley announced, referring to the petite, mousy-haired girl to my right.

Sarah walked to the front of the class, holding a wrinkled sheet of paper in her hand. She tossed her head, causing her deeply parted hair to slip down over her right eye. A small gap shone between her front teeth when she opened her mouth, just like the space that lived between mine. The moment Sarah spoke, I understood Mrs. Waters' infatuation with poets and their words.

Sarah's verse told the story of a soldier during the Vietnam War; the suffering he endured as his friends died around him and his heartache after coming home. She delivered the lament with an honesty that delved deep into my heart, planting seeds of compassion for the underdogs of the world. When she finished, the room fell silent, our thoughts captured in the poem's snapshot of time, regret, and despair.

"Who is author of that poem, Sarah?" Mrs. Langley asked.

"Me . . . I wrote it," Sarah answered.

A collective gasp seized us. It was clear from my classmates' reaction that I was not the only one who found it hard to believe that a girl my age could write something so profound.

"Carlyn, come up and read your poem," Mrs. Langley said as Sarah passed me on the way to her desk.

My heart sank into my bowling shoes. Henry Wadsworth Longfellow and his bow and arrow were no match for Sarah's poignant words about war, friendship, and loss. I slipped out of my seat and muddled toward the head of the room.

"I shot an arrow into the air; it fell to earth I knew not where." I held my arms out like an archer, as Art had, but when I finished the three stanzas no one applauded and no one chuckled—not even a grin emerged. The only laugh I got was when Shawn yawned with exaggerated flair from the back of the room.

My poem won third place. Sarah, beat out by Erin's dramatic rendition of "The Raven," came in second. She could have come in last for all I cared. All I wished for was to become friends with this extraordinary girl. Maybe some of her brilliance would rub off on me.

At lunch that day, my classmates gathered at picnic tables under the grapevines in the yard. The Carp kids sat on a table at one end, while the students who had attended Mount Carmel since first grade sat at the other. Sarah sat with her twin sister, Yvonne, and a group of other kids who didn't give us the time of day. Their casual closeness was intimidating, as though they shared mysteries between them we could never be a part of. But today, a swell of awe fueled my boldness.

Like a robot on a mission, I stood up, left the Carp kids behind, and approached Sarah's table.

"That was great!" I gushed. "Your poem, I mean."

Sarah smiled shyly. "Thanks, I liked yours too." She slid to one side of the bench, making room for me beside her.

This moment gave birth to a best friend. Sarah and I ate lunch together that day, and did so every day afterward for years to come. But like leather and lace, my new companion and I came from distant worlds. The chasm between us was not obvious yet to our innocent eyes, but it wouldn't be long until our differences came to light.

CHAPTER THIRTEEN

From Treasure to Junk

I WAS TEN YEARS OLD when Sarah invited me to her house for my first official playdate.

My excitement was a geyser threatening to burst through the top of my head. When Mami got home, I carried her groceries inside before I pleaded for permission to visit Sarah's on Saturday. She agreed.

The minutes trickled at a possum's pace until the weekend arrived. On her way to the beauty shop, Mami dropped me off at the Marchand estate—a sprawling, modern, single-story structure set under giant oaks on a private lane in Montecito.

Sarah and Yvonne, who at school were always well behaved, ran through the house screaming and yelling like untamed banshees. I followed them down their hallway, walking slowly and relishing the vastness that housed six brothers and sisters, a dog, a cat, and a house-keeper. Inside their kitchen, sliding glass doors filled an entire wall, turning the space into a sunroom.

What is it like to be a Marchand? I wondered. *Sitting at this table every day, eating cereal in the sunlight, and running around a grassy yard with a giant trampoline and swing set?*

Sarah and Yvonne's bedroom was paradise. New toys, a television set, and disheveled beds cluttered their room, and everything in it belonged to them, not to their mother.

Because this was my first trip to a friend's house, I wasn't clear on the rules, so I sat in a corner chair and watched a giant beach ball fly back and forth across the room.

"What's wrong?" Sarah asked.

I didn't know what to say. At school I was a Chatty Patty, but today I was Silent Sally.

"Here, do this!" she shouted and leaped onto her bed. Yvonne did the same. Like two chimpanzees freed from captivity, they jumped up and down on the mattress, hollering and laughing. A pillow smacked my face.

I set the pillow aside.

"C'mon!" the twins whined. I looked around the corner. Their mother, Mrs. Marchand, was nowhere in sight. I stepped onto the mattress and did a test bounce. It was springy and inviting under my feet.

At home, my mattress dipped in the center. The only way for my body to sleep straight was for me to scoot to the far edge and burrow into the space between the pad and the wall. In the morning, I was again in the middle of the bed, nursing a sore back.

Sarah's bed, in contrast, was the perfect trampoline. In no time, I was leaping up and down, shrieking with abandon, beating my friends with pillows as though I had done it my whole life. It was liberating— the best day a kid could ever wish for. And I never wanted it to end.

On my ride home with Mami, I begged her to let me invite the twins over the following weekend. She hesitated but I persisted, promising her the world.

"I'll clean my room and wash the dishes, and I'll pick up all the dog poop too."

I don't remember what else I pledged before Mom said the most magnificent word in the Spanish language:

"*Sí*"—*Yes.*

Early the next Saturday morning, Mrs. Marchand and her daughters pulled into our driveway in a blue Volvo Sedan. I raced out the front door to greet them. Sarah, Yvonne, and Mrs. Marchand stepped out from behind their respective doors like synchronized swimmers. But when I reached them, it was as if I were invisible. The Marchand trio stood immobilized, their doors acting like shields protecting them from an unexpected threat.

Sarah and Yvonne got over their shellshock. Their mother did not. She scoured the handicapped cars lining our driveway, and bit her lip when she saw the marooned silver Airstream trailer that had replaced my sister's gypsy caravan in the front yard. Orange barked from inside the kennel, flinging his sturdy frame against the wire fence like a mad beast. Beside him, Bandit jumped up and down like a pogo dog.

Mrs. Marchand reached into her pocket, pulled out a cigarette, and brought it to her pale lips, but she didn't light it. Escondido Road, it turned out, was an alien world compared to the Marchands' prosperous life in Montecito. She glanced away from the messy site and said something to the twins I couldn't quite make out.

"Mom! It'll be fine!" the sisters protested in unison.

"I don't know," Mrs. Marchand answered stiffly as she spotted my father and brothers engaged in their Saturday morning ritual of burning garbage in front of a smoky pit. Mrs. Marchand's wary expression left little doubt about her reluctance to leave her kids for five minutes, much less five hours, in this empire of forgotten things. But the girls knew how to work their mother. They whined long and loud until she surrendered.

"I'll be back at three," she said, getting behind the wheel.

"No! Four!!" the girls insisted.

The slight nod from their mother told me the twins had won this battle. I had never witnessed children with this kind of power before; I was now convinced that whining was an effective tool for negotiation, and decided to give it a try sometime soon.

The twins and I had a wonderful afternoon. My bed wasn't springy like Sarah's. I didn't own any new toys or board games like their expansive collection. But we played basketball in the crammed area outside the front door—being careful to shoot away from the Christmas lights that hung year-round across the front of the house—and Lilly was a hit with the twins. She made us a tasty lunch of peanut butter and strawberry jelly sandwiches and gave us vanilla ice cream for dessert, which we ate while watching cartoons on our double-decker TV sets.

After our meal, I suggested that we build a plane, sure that we would find all the necessary parts in the yard. The girls agreed and we got to work gathering plywood, bent rusty nails, saws, and hammers. None of us knew the first thing about building an aircraft. But our imaginations pretended we did.

Mrs. Marchand's disapproving eyes kept coming in and out of my thoughts. Her gaze said there was something wrong with our house— and me, by extension. If we built a plane, perhaps the twins and I could fly away from here and the uncomfortable knot in my stomach would fade. The fantastical thought filled me with a burst of possibility. I nailed the boards faster.

"This can go on the tail," Sarah determined, handing me a greasy rag she'd discovered in an old milk container.

"Look what I found!" Yvonne said, smiling from behind the corroded body of a long-dead Nash Rambler. She held up a rusted steering wheel as though she had found a lost relic.

We had only finished nailing two planks together when Mrs. Marchand's blue Volvo appeared in the driveway. She waved the twins toward her.

"Thank your mother for having my girls over, would you?" Mrs. Marchand asked before hurrying the girls into the car.

From behind the line of demarcation, a brick row in the cement at the end of the driveway that Mami forbade me to cross, I waved good-bye to my friends until their car disappeared. I set the plane's wings inside an old sink laying askance, then stepped into the dog kennel and locked myself inside.

As Orange licked my face and Bandit plopped alongside me, I lay on my back, lounging on their doghouse, reminiscing on the details of the day. Mrs. Marchand's face haunted me. She'd scrutinized our yard like I examined my least favorite meal; Spam and ketchup with a side of spinach. Imagining I was Mrs. Marchand, I studied the tangled, rusted, and decaying elements in our yard through her eyes. In short order, my fantasy evaporated. Sarah's home, and her family life, was a far cry from my world of never-ending clutter.

With the mirage that had colored my childhood in retreat, I no longer saw hidden riches, only scrapped toilets, dilapidated houses, and dismembered jalopies. Shame wrapped me in an all-encompassing blanket that I would wear for decades.

Orange scratched at the wire fence, anxious to get out. I wrapped my arms around him until he settled into me with a loud snort, more equine than canine. He and I were the same: junkyard dogs trapped in a cage.

Sarah, Yvonne, and I stayed good friends for years to come. But that day was the last time I ever invited them over to our house on Escondido Road—the look in their mother's eyes had seen to that.

CHAPTER FOURTEEN

Desperately Seeking Normal

AFTER THE TWINS' VISIT, I molted a layer of skin.

This shredded dermis, a protective coat that had for so long kept me safe on the banks of denial, provided me with a blissful respite from the glaring awareness that I, for all intents and purposes, lived in a field of junk and honey.

My new skin, invisible to the eye, had more exposed nerve endings than its predecessor. Like a pair of shoes too small for my feet, this foreign sheath left me with painful blisters.

After Sarah's visit, I never again invited another friend to my home until I was well into high school. The humiliation stemming from Mrs. Marchand's censure filled me with more shame than I could bear. A scarlet letter branded my house—and me. Just like the unforgettable sting of a man-o-war I'd encountered on a Mazatlán beach years before, this stigma remained ever-present.

It had happened without warning. One moment, I was playing at the ocean's edge, collecting seashells in my red plastic bucket and giggling as tepid waves crashed over my six-year-old body. The next instant I'd stood frozen, the sand holding me captive like wet cement, my eyes wide and fixed upon the bulbous blue creature clamped onto the side of my leg.

I would have stared at the cobalt-colored blob all afternoon if panic had not robbed me of breath. I swiped at its gelatinous tail, but my fingers slid off the slippery whip. Hundreds of harpoon-like teeth penetrated my skin, refusing to let go, its venom making its way through my leg.

Alarm set in, then panic. Across the sand, in our cabana, Mami stood behind the window, her eyes transfixed on the ocean, her mind elsewhere. I cried out, hoping she'd hear me, but the crashing waves drowned out my voice. Nearby, my brothers tossed a Frisbee back and forth. Ray saw me and waved, unaware I was in trouble, then flicked his wrist, setting the Frisbee free to find Art.

Finally, my fingers discovered a tiny gap between the animal's teeth and my skin; I pulled hard and the animal detached from my flesh, tearing like ripping cloth before I flung it into the sea.

Hysterical, I ran toward my brothers. They fled in the opposite direction, thinking I was trying to steal their Frisbee. My leg was on fire. I didn't know what to do. Exhausted, I collapsed onto my hands and knees—sobbing air, drool collecting underneath me in a pocket in the sand. Then two hands scooped me up. The last thing I remembered was jostling in Art's arms as he ran across the beach carrying me, moments before I passed out from the pain.

Even after the poison left my system, a trail of red bumps remained along the side of my leg. In time, it was replaced by a six-inch scar that faded over the years. That Saturday in the junkyard, Mrs. Marchand's disapproval stung me like the man-o-war's teeth. That scar, unlike the one on my leg, lived under my skin, a reminder to be ever vigilant of unknown dangers dwelling in unsuspecting waters.

Mrs. Marchand's visit wasn't the only blow to my fragile sense of self. As time passed, I felt an increasing awareness of, and sensitivity to, how different I was, not only from kids of my age, but even from extended family members.

In San Diego, my cousins lived in a two-story house a stone's throw from the freeway. Their home was a maze of rooms that housed six children. When we visited, we filled our days playing games and whispering secrets to each other under our bedcovers. But unlike at our house, these Montes de Ocas, who spelled their last name with a small *d* instead of a capital *D*, lived in a home without clutter. And they were not the only family members who did.

In Carpinteria's foothills, a ranch-style house shaded by a giant oak tree was home to another set of our cousins. Even with six rambunctious kids, their home differed from ours in two important ways: my mother's younger sister, Carmela, was as sweet as sun-kissed fruit, and their house was not a collection of exhausted appliances and breakable curios. I didn't care if my cousins were home or not when we visited; I was more than happy to pretend this spacious retreat with the tire swing hanging from the oak in their front yard was mine.

Uncle Benjamin, my mom's youngest brother, was an attorney living in an exclusive area of Santa Barbara overlooking the Pacific Ocean. Mami loved Benjamin, and he adored her. He also shared her talent for intimidation with a frosty brown gaze. What they did not share, however, was the gene for hoarding. Uncle Benjamin's house was modern and orderly, with a clear front lawn surrounded by birds of paradise. My mother and father had seven siblings each, and not one of their houses contained a graveyard of rust.

There was no explanation for why we lived the way we did other than it started from my parents' desire to help relatives who had less means than they did. Somewhere, this big-hearted behavior went from quirky to off the rails; from a junk drawer, to a junkyard kingdom; their good intents unintentionally branding me with shame.

When the bus dropped off the Carp kids in the St. Joseph's parking lot after school, the children who lived closer to the foothills walked home as a group. When we reached Escondido Road, I'd say my goodbyes to John, Vicky, and Tina and casually turn down my street, smelling flowers, gazing at the mountains, and finding reasons to search inside my backpack. Anything to delay time. If my friends slowed down to watch me, I'd saunter past my house and step onto our next-door neighbor's front lawn, acting as if I lived there. Then, peeking through the hedges,

I'd wait for the last school uniform to disappear before stepping beyond the gate and into our alien world.

Hoarding was not the only way Mom and Dad were different. They were also the oldest parents of all my school friends.

"How old are you, Mami?" I always asked her on her birthday.

"Thirty-nine," she said without missing a beat. Yet every year, she said the same thing. I excelled in most school subjects; math wasn't one of them, but I didn't have to be a genius to calculate that if Mami was born in 1917, that made her forty-four years old when I was born. My father was three years older than her, making him forty-seven. Most of my friends' mothers and fathers were in their thirties.

When I questioned my parents about being older when they had me, Dad would answer, "You were a surprise!" Then he'd fling open his closet door as far as it would go before banging into Mami's sewing machine.

Inside his wardrobe, a battered zither harp hung from a shoelace on a rack mounted on the door. Beside the instrument was a handful of neckties my mother had purchased from secondhand shops and that Dad seldom wore. Whenever the closet door opened, the harp clunked against the wood, its discordant groan echoing as if disturbed from a Rip Van Winkle slumber.

"Before you were born, you were in heaven with the angels playing this harp," Dad said. Transfixed, I gawked at the instrument, trying hard to remember being in such celestial company. I loved that story so much that I never questioned how the harp had crossed time and space to arrive on the earthly plane. Or how it ended up in Dad's closet. Or that I was probably too old to believe such nonsense.

My father's tale touched my heart and delighted my imagination. Even so, the relationship between my parents and I was growing increasingly fragile the older I got. We were ships sailing toward opposite horizons, carrying vastly different cargos. My parents' baggage held tradition and control. Shame spilled from mine.

And that wasn't the only way we clashed.

I did well academically; I excelled at sports; and my friends often laughed at my quirky sense of humor. These three strengths—academics, athleticism, and wisecrackery—helped me blend in with my peers. I wanted to be *normal*, and I tried everything to fit into that box. But in addition to living the life of a hoarder, there was one more way in which I felt apart—the one thing I could not ignore, run away from, or erase: my ethnicity. I could not free myself from my Mexican-ness. My parents were children of Mexico and proud of their rich culture, but living in an America where popular TV shows and magazine covers celebrated light skin and admired fair hair—I was not.

My natural tan did little to hide the redness creeping into my cheeks when my parents spoke Spanish in the grocery store line. It mortified me more when Mami insisted that I speak it in front of my school friends. In Spanish class, I talked with an American twang and pretended I didn't know a single word, even though Spanish was my first language. The other kids raised their hands high, hoping to be called on. But not me. I slid down into my chair, my fist lodged defiantly under my chin, glaring at our teacher, Sister Eliza, as if daring her to call on me. She seldom did.

Now that Lilly was older, and busy with school, I inherited her Saturday chore list. My precious weekend, once my *joie de vivre*, was now composed of sweeping, mopping, making lunch, and picking up dog poop.

"Carlyn Marie—get up!" my mother's voice insisted early Saturday morning. I stirred, giving the impression I was about to rise, but Mami was on to me. Instead of throwing ice water on my head, she did the equivalent to my ears. Mariachi music blasted into my room from the radio on the kitchen shelf, sending shock waves through my comatose body.

Her tactic achieved the desired effect. I leaped out of bed and dressed quickly.

When Mami left the kitchen for her bedroom, I saw the chance to end my torture. I sneaked into the kitchen and turned the dial on the radio until it landed on static. When Mami returned, I was an obedient daughter pouring cereal into a breakfast bowl, giving the impression that I was unaware her music was no longer playing over the airwaves. She glanced from the radio to me, then back to the radio again before turning the dial to its former glory. Then, to make it crystal clear who'd won the radio war, she raised the volume loud enough for the neighbors to hear, launching my shame into the stratosphere.

The only place I felt at peace was in the kennel: sprawled on top of the doghouse, staring into the skyscape, flanked by two canines. *This can't be my life*, my mind insisted as I daydreamed of parents who would one day come and rescue me from all of this.

That afternoon—after I rinsed the dishes instead of washing them with soap; after I swept the dust under the carpet rather than collected it into a dustpan—I walked outside with a new purpose. I wondered if my dad would notice a missing toilet, should I put one in the garbage can. If I took an oxidized piece of scrap metal, an errant pipe, or a plank of rotted wood from the yard every day and fed it to the trash bins at the school next door, would my parents be the wiser?

The thought thrilled me. If I did this, how long would it take before our house looked normal?

As I contemplated my wild scheme, I found myself in front of *la otra casa*, a dilapidated shack that stood beside our garage. *The other house* was the original one-bedroom home that had been on the property before *the house that moved* arrived to keep it company. Abandoned by humans but saturated with chattel, this dwelling contained the over-flow of stuff my mom could not find space for inside our house. Here, my father's tools had been accumulating over many years, cramming cartons, lining the walls, and filling up a myriad of toolboxes. Clones begetting clones of screwdrivers, wrenches, and measuring instruments; all lived in the moldy confines of this ramshackle structure. The rear of the shack, originally a narrow kitchen, held vintage Coca-Cola crates stacked from wall to wall. Arranged within each were armies of baby food jars housing thousands of screws, bolts, and washers.

In what was once a living room, a broken jukebox, crippled bar-stools, and a hoodless salon hairdryer guarded a wall-size bookcase. The Encyclopedia Britannica minus a volume, radio repair mail order manuals, and dozens of paperback books lured me from their dusty shelves. Like an eager climber ready to discover virgin land, I scrambled over the stacked furniture and decomposing boxes. Daddy long-legs spiders scattered as I slid down onto the other side, finding the hair-dryer's cast-off head on my way. Once my feet landed on the sleeping floorboards, I came face to face with my salvation.

From the closest shelf, I removed a small paperback book—accompanied by a dust cloud. For the next few minutes, I sneezed uncontrollably (something I was becoming more prone to do because of our dusty and damp surroundings), but once I was past the worst of my sternutation and only bothered by watering eyes and an itchy nose, I examined the red horse on the book's cover, then the golden letters of its title, *The Catcher in the Rye.*

I whispered these five words to myself, wondering what red horses had to do with baseball. Like a priest standing with his Bible before God, I revered this sacred book before I ever even opened it.

"… the first thing you'll probably want to know is where I was born, and what my lousy childhood was like, and how my parents were occupied and all before they had me, and all that David Copperfield kind of crap . . ."

Holden Caulfield, the book's hero, had me at "lousy childhood."

I carried *The Catcher* outside and into the sunlight, freeing it from the shack's gloominess, the ever-present blanket of powder, and the rat poop I found smooshed on page eleven. Together, we walked the few yards toward the dogs' kennel and stepped inside to where Orange and Bandit lounged on the dirt, imprisoned that afternoon for the crime of being born canine rather than human.

I began to read . . . and could not stop.

· · ·

Later that same night, under the sheets of my bed and accompanied by a flashlight, I finished the book. Holden was older than me, and a lot cooler. But unlike Holden, who did not seem to mind being a black swan among a flock of ducks, I did. I wanted to quack exactly like everyone else.

The next morning, I hurried into *the other house* and took a second book off the shelves: *To Kill a Mockingbird*. Once I finished reading this masterpiece, I longed to change my name to Scout after the book's heroine. I even wrote the name *Scout Montes De Oca* across my Pee Chee folder where I kept all of my school assignments.

Mami vetoed the Scout idea, and my brothers teased me about it until I cried. But I yearned to be Scout and to have an elegant father like Atticus Finch, who defended the underdog. If Scout's mom had been alive, I was certain, she would never have resorted to playing mariachi music at full volume to wake her child up from a restful sleep.

I might have wished I was Scout, but in our ramshackle home on Escondido Road I was more like Boo Radley, the wacky neighbor who lived in a rundown house and was mocked by all the townspeople.

Despite the turbulent sneezing spells that seized me whenever I entered *the other house*, I pulled yet another book off the shelf and read, reread, and triple-read its brown-tinged pages. After completing *A Childhood's End*, there was no returning to the child I'd once been. In this short book, Arthur C. Clarke introduced me to the notion of human evolution and the astonishing future of humanity. It was a mind-bending idea that would forever fascinate me and feed my imagination.

Books offered a temporary escape from my junkyard kingdom. But reading about faraway places and tormented characters could not eliminate the growing pains of my aberrance. Try as I might to be normal, my freak flag only got bigger. As I grew older, I scowled more than I laughed, complained more than I obeyed, and pulled away from my parents instead of seeking comfort in their arms. But the more freedom I desired, the more Mami kept it from me. For reasons

I didn't understand, she even forbade me from befriending the other kids on the block.

Hearing laughter beyond the fence, I formed a ladder with empty cans, blocks of wood, and several bricks, then scampered onto it. From there I watched the neighborhood come alive with kids riding bikes, playing hopscotch, and dashing in and out of each other's homes.

I longed to be part of the melee—but while my school friends went to matinees, gathered together at ball games, and got ice cream after school, I stayed home, protected behind a forest green fence. Like a bonsai tree, my branches were clipped to keep my shoots from spreading.

My dogs fared worse than I did.

"Can I walk Orange for just ten minutes over to the school?" I asked Mami one day.

"No," she said as she folded my dad's white T-shirts, fresh from the dryer.

"Why not?" I pleaded. Outside, Orange's incessant barking and Bandit's desolate howling spurred me on.

"*Porque te dije que no*"—*Because I said so*—Mami said, then picked up a silent dog whistle and brought it to her lips. The whistle silenced all of us with one blow.

What I never saw at my young age when I looked over the fence, longing to be part of the lively world on Escondido Road, were the drug dealers down the street and the alcoholic living next door—people my parents did not trust near their children. Thirty years later, the denizens of Escondido Road would consist of different occupants who could afford the skyrocketing real estate, but until then this neighborhood on a potholed dirt road would wait out the years, a home to a questionable cast of characters.

Regardless of my age, Mami didn't allow me past the line of demarcation unaccompanied. To spite her, I'd ride my bike down the driveway toward it, maneuvering past the sideview mirrors that jutted from our parked cars. When my front tire reached the brick delineation, I rolled a few inches over it, thwarting her command.

Embracing my defiance, I was Scout, I was Holden—I was unstoppable. I was a hawk in flight, soaring on the cool breeze that washes over barren sand dunes. One day, I vowed, I'd leave this place and take my dogs with me. One day, I'd have enough money to get a ride on that jet plane, piercing the dragon's eye and, like *Johnny Quest* and his dog Bandit on television, Orange and my Bandit and I would embark on marvelous adventures. One day, I would be free from all of this. Free from my mother's laws.

I would finally be what my soul longed to be: *normal*.

CHAPTER FIFTEEN

The Girl in the Necktie Dress

EVERY SUMMER an invasion swept through Santa Barbara County, infecting its residents with a fervor resembling the zombie apocalypse. *The Fiestas* honored the county's Spanish roots by transforming downtown Santa Barbara into a five-day, city-wide jamboree of street dancing, parade watching, and festive feasting.

Man-o-war stings and mariachi music were memories I preferred to forget. But neither came close to the agitation that consumed me as the first week in August approached. If I could have crawled under my bed and disappeared, or hung in my closet like one of my mother's coats, or mutated into a swath of rubber shredded from a flat tire in our yard—I would have welcomed any of these possibilities rather than face what was to come.

I prayed to Our Lady of The Perpetual Green Light—the name I'd given the plastic statuette of the Virgin Mary that stood behind a glass nook on the wall across from my bed. A fluorescent night-light illuminated her hollow figure below, inundating her with a neon green brilliance that spilled from her outstretched hands into the rest of the room. Because the glow was so bright, my bedroom never totally darkened. Often, the light kept me awake late into the night.

Years before, my mother, pregnant with Ray, had promised the Virgin Mary that if she let her son live, she would keep this light lit in her honor for as long as she lived. I was glad Ray had survived the car accident that had almost taken his unborn life, but I couldn't help but blame him a little when I yawned so much during the day.

Tonight, I implored the Green Virgin to wipe Mami's memory clean so she would forget the fiestas this year. Perhaps I'd used up my allotment of prayers or had not fulfilled my promises in the past, but whatever the reason, no matter how hard I prayed, my appeals went unanswered.

The amount of time Mami spent with her foot pressed against the pedal of her sewing machine during the month of July suggested she was as eager for Old Spanish Days to arrive as I was to avoid them. My attempts to tamper with her radio and silence the blaring mariachi music on Saturday mornings may have failed, but I managed—motivated by desperation—to devise a new way of throwing Mami off the fiesta scent.

At 5:00 p.m. each evening the newspaper flew over the green gate, slamming into my mom's Kenwood station wagon before falling onto the cement. Orange, who clearly thought this UFO needed a lesson in earthly manners, grabbed it the instant it landed, then gave his head several vigorous shakes before running at high speed and dropping it on our front doorstep. For the next three days, I caught the paper before Orange's teeth did and hid it at the bottom of the trashcan in the hopes that Mami would avoid seeing any articles about the fiestas.

After dinner, Mami discovered our newspaper was MIA and went in search of it. I cracked the screen door wide enough to get a good look as she scoured the driveway. She checked under cars, peeked behind empty crates, and asked our neighbors if our paper was in their yard before returning empty-handed.

"Have you seen the paper?" she asked after coming back inside.

"Maybe Orange took it?" I suggested and pretended to search under Lilly's piano bench as Mami dropped to her knees and looked under the couch. Our dog had a history of not only collecting our nightly newspaper but also rounding up all the neighbors' papers too.

"*Perro maldito*," Mami swore at Orange under her breath.

A pang of guilt informed me I was throwing my friend under the bus. But like a condemned man awaiting execution, I was capable of any deed.

I believed Our Lady of the Perpetual Green Light had answered my prayers when Friday arrived and Mami had not yet mentioned the word *fiesta*. Perhaps this was the year I would finally be exempt from the fandango. For some people, watching parades, viewing flamenco dancing under the stars, and eating greasy tacos is their idea of fun. If that had been my experience at the Fiestas, I might have had a good time as well. If my indignity had merely been wearing a brightly colored peasant blouse, a swishy Spanish-style skirt, or a fire-red jumbo plastic flower in my hair, I could have lived with that. But it wasn't. My mother took fiesta fashion to dizzying levels, insisting Lilly and I dress from head to toe in garb rivaling that of the most hardcore of Mexican fiesteros.

The next morning, lying across Lilly's bed, was the outfit Mami had decreed my seventeen-year-old sister, a junior in high school dealing with teenage insecurity, must wear. Lilly did as she was told, and in short order the cream-colored cloak with red geometric designs changed my big sister from an everyday girl into an Indian princess. With a beaded headband across her forehead and her long, thick black braid draped over one shoulder, Lilly was ready to step onto the streets of fiesta central.

I sat on a beanbag chair, watching the Indian princess apply a touch of lip gloss in the mirror. *How lucky is she?* I thought. When watching Westerns on our double-decker television, I always sided with the Indians who seemed way cooler than the fellas with cowboy hats. If I had to dress up, I would have preferred wearing my sister's indigenous costume rather than dressing in the oversize shirts, sequined vests, and jangling jewelry Mami had forced me to model in past years.

So far my mother hadn't given me a second look. Maybe, I thought, Lilly's outfit had satisfied her need for creating fiesta fashion. Perhaps watching TV instead of going to fiestas lay in my future. Or maybe this one time she would let me go to the celebration in regular clothing, jeans and a t-shirt, like a normal kid.

I grabbed a sweat shirt and slipped it over my head, pulled on my striped bell-bottoms, then laced up my high-tops. I was sitting on the sofa with my latest book, *Lord of the Flies*, dressed and ready to go, when Mami found me a few minutes later.

"*Ven*," she commanded, and walked over to her Bernina sewing machine. My feet refused to follow. Instead, I set the book down beside me—hope fading, fear rising. She reached for a cardboard box and flipped open the lid. When she removed the contents, I did not move. I could not move. If I had moved, my legs would have collapsed from under me. My ears caught fire and heat spread across my face. I suspected I was dying of internal combustion. And when I saw what Mami proudly held up between her fingers in all its glory, I welcomed that death.

Looking back at me was a one-of-a-kind garment she and her Bernina had spent many late nights sewing. A dress made from more than a *dozen thrift store neckties*.

"*Póntelo*," she said, looking eager, as if expecting me to share in her excitement.

Put it on? Are you joking? These were the thoughts behind the half smile that crossed my face. Mami wanted me to go to the Santa Barbara Fiestas—the most public place of the year, an event where I would undoubtedly run into my classmates—and she was insisting that I do it wearing a frock made from men's neckties. I would have preferred a flaying, or a second man-o-war sting, or listening to an entire afternoon of mariachi music while drinking a cup of *atole*—the pineapple gruel I was given at Christmas that I always poured down the drain when Mami's back was turned.

My mortification must have been evident, because Mami's smile disappeared and her pride went with it. She pointed toward my bedroom. "*Póntelo*," she insisted in a voice that left no room for questions.

I snatched the despised outfit from her hands and stormed through the dining room.

Once in my bedroom, I yanked off my clothes, threw them across the room, and pulled at the edges of the necktie dress with all my strength, trying to rip it at the seams. But I may as well have tried to tear apart an industrial carpet. The dress was as resilient as a fortress, made to outlast any siege; it wasn't about to give up its shining moment in the sun. I slipped into the dress.

I grabbed my sweatshirt off the floor and put it on. At least it would hide the top half of my outfit.

When I came out of my bedroom, Mami gave my sweatshirt the hairy eyeball.

"I'm cold," I said, crossing my arms against my chest. It was the middle of summer, I was lying, and she knew it.

"*Vámonos*," she said, grabbing her keys and a small cooler of sandwiches.

Unlike Lilly and me, Mami was not sporting an Indian outfit or a tie dress. Instead, she wore brown nylon slacks and a paisley blouse. I looked at Lilly; the once forlorn Indian Princess was now grinning at my necktie couture, informing me that my ensemble was even worse than I imagined.

I took a deep breath and decided it couldn't be that bad. Three, perhaps four hours, and I would bid adios to this ridiculous getup. Next August was a whole twelve months away—more than enough time to devise a plan to avoid another fiesta fiasco.

I trudged down the driveway—past Ray and Art, who were washing their Austin-Healey, a sporty vehicle they pooled their money to buy and painted British racing green. One glimpse at me and my brothers burst out laughing. Ray pressed the handle on the hose nozzle and squirted me with a stream of water.

It won't last forever, I told myself as I wiped my face dry in the back seat of Mami's station wagon and we pulled onto the street. *Just a few hours more and it will all be over*, I convinced myself as we drove toward Santa Barbara. *I won't see anyone I know*, I ventured as we parked in the city lot—right beside a sedan belonging to the parents of a girl in my class. As she stepped out of her car dressed in jeans, a tight blue T-shirt, and matching baseball cap, I ducked down, pretending to smudge out a stain on my shoe.

A crowd already packed the county courthouse where the Mexican singers and flamenco dancers were scheduled to perform. My mother set the cooler down, then took the picnic blanket, which I had been using as a shield to hide the bottom of my dress, away from me. I noticed two boys from school; they noticed me too, and then they noticed my outfit. With his hand covering his mouth, the boy with braces whispered something to his tow-haired friend, eliciting a snicker. I turned away and discovered more scrutiny. A lady in a sequined blouse with puffy sleeves pointed at me, insisting her gum-smacking teenage daughter check out my getup. The girl looked as thrilled to be there as I was. She studied me up and down, then rolled her blacklined eyes before blowing a dismissive bubble in my direction.

I searched for mercy elsewhere and spotted Mami talking to a gentleman in a gray suit. An expensive camera on a leather cord hung from his neck. Mami motioned my sister and me over to them.

"Want to have your picture taken?" the gentleman asked.

Do we have a choice? I wondered as he raised his camera.

"Smile!" he coaxed. We did as we were told. After all, what were we but robots in Mami's factory of wants and desires?

After the flashbulb's glow wore off, and I could see clearly again, I found my way back to our spot, claimed a corner of the picnic blanket, and pulled out my book. I read until night offered little choice than to watch the flamenco dancers sweep across the stage, chestnut castanets rapidly clicking and clacking in their expert hands. Their passionate performance cast a spell over the stupefied audience, their faces suspended with admiration. I, however, was oblivious to its wonder—a child rendered immune to their charm by the curse of a necktie dress.

On Sunday morning, two days after my necktie debut, Orange delivered the newspaper to our doorstep. I swapped him a piece of dog kibble for the paper, searching for the funnies before Art or Ray showed up to steal them. When I saw the entertainment section, though, I lost my desire for comedy. In this newspaper, read by thousands of people, a black-and-white photo of Lilly and me took up a quarter of a page. The caption noted that my mom was the architect of my attire. I shoved my face into the daily news and screamed.

When Mami saw the photograph, her pride resurfaced. Her creative efforts vindicated, she laughed like a child and gave me an *I-told-you-so* look before disappearing into her bedroom to dress for Sunday mass.

I didn't need to go to church to thank God my penance was finally over. That night I thanked him, Our Lady of the Perpetual Green Light, and even the magical creatures in *The Lord of the Rings* that I'd survived the humiliation of fiesta madness. But atonement was far from achieved.

The next day, Mrs. Langley greeted the class, her hair in a new curly bob that made her dour expression seem more cheerful.

"Settle down, children, I have an important announcement to make," she said.

I saw the Sunday entertainment section of the newspaper protruding from her hands and I slunk down into my seat, cursing her bob under my breath. Mrs. Langley held up the paper for the class to see and announced my new fiesta fashionista status. Some kids laughed; others nodded their heads as if impressed. I heard someone whisper that they'd seen me in the dress and that I'd looked weird.

When my head was inches from the floor and my shame could travel no further, I glanced at Sarah, who eyed me with pity and shrugged. What more was there to say? Her best friend was a bona fide necktie superstar.

Once the fiestas faded into memory and Santa Barbara returned to its sleepy beach city routine, I stuffed my necktie dress into a box and shoved it in my closet.

The worst day of my existence was over. I breathed freely, knowing that no matter how many times I'd already said *It cannot get worse than this . . .* now, it *really* could not get worse than this.

But despite the garment's exile, my legacy as the girl in the necktie dress marched on.

Olivia, a distant relative of Mami's, lived on the north end of Carpinteria with her husband, Silvestre. I dreaded our visits to their house. Everything in their home, from the walls to the carpets, smelled like *menudo*, a classic Mexican dish made from tripe. I was not vegan yet, but the overpowering smell and slimy texture of cow intestine chunks sliding down my throat still made me gag.

"*Hola, Corbatas!*"—Hello, Neckties!—Silvestre would say when he found me sitting on their couch with the see-through plastic cover, hiding my head in my current book. "*Quieres menudo?*" he'd ask, rubbing my head and messing up my hair.

I grimaced at the bowl of tripe he offered me and shook my head, hoping my mother didn't see me rejecting his hospitality. I wasn't sure what was worse: the stench of menudo or the strong, sweaty odor coming from the white Stetson that Silvestre always wore.

When Mami announced we were ready to leave, I jumped off the couch and headed for the door. But it wasn't fast enough to avoid the word that would be forever synonymous with my fall from grace.

"*Adios, Corbatas!*" Silvestre said, his beer belly jiggling, as I reached the threshold. The jab to my gut reminded me I would never live down my disgrace, no matter how many gods I prayed to.

When Olivia and Silvestre visited us the following week and my brothers heard him call me *Corbatas*, they could hardly contain themselves.

"*Hola, Corbatas.*"

"What's new, Corbatas?"

"Corbatas, pass me the mustard!"

Their teasing was relentless.

"*Déjenla en paz!*" Seeing tears brimming in my eyes, Mami demanded the boys leave me alone. With just three words and a warning look from the hairy eyeball, my brothers' laughter faded. I blamed my mother for making me wear that dress, but like a space heater protecting me against the cold, I also felt a deep comfort when she came to my defense. I cherished this moment between us, even when it passed as quickly as clouds drifting away after a storm.

CHAPTER SIXTEEN

Operation Christmas Tamale

THERE WERE THINGS MY PARENTS TOLD ME that I never questioned. How to wash my laundry was one of them.

When clean socks were nowhere in sight, I rounded up my sullied garments and put them into a sizable mound over my bed. Since I spent my free time in the company of two dogs, traipsing through the junkyard, and shooting a basketball, sweat, dirt, and stains were as common on my clothing as flowers, stripes, and polka dots.

Despite the bundle of garments blocking my eyesight, I made it to the bathroom without bumping into any objects along the way. Like a bucket on a bulldozer, my arms unhinged, depositing my undergarments on the cracked tiles.

My washbasin was a clawfoot tub Dad had painted lemon yellow. Under the faucet, I placed a scratched plastic pail that had once held five gallons of coleslaw. From under the tub, I pulled out a small washboard stained with mold. The black blemish blotted out the letters that had once spelled *National Washboard Company.*

Clasping the board by its wooden legs, I held it up toward the morning sunlight peeking through the paint stained window and shifted the slat back and forth, releasing the light trapped within its glass ridges, revealing the tool's hidden magic. Pink, green, and violet hues met my eyes and filled me with wonder.

This washboard and I had a love-hate relationship: I loved the escape and the make-believe world the enchanted light inspired but dreaded the torture the board would soon inflict on my knuckles.

I turned on the valve and filled the pail with frigid water, remembering Mami's lecture that heated water sealed stains into clothing. The dampness in the bathroom chilled my bones; the slight sweatshirt I wore for warmth was an exercise in futility. Though Carpinteria was blessed with a temperate climate, 5515 Escondido Road wore the chill like another skin.

When the bucket was half full, I grabbed a pair of socks and dipped the discolored fabric into the water, swirling it around with my fingertips. When they were sufficiently drenched, I dropped them onto the washboard.

I kneeled on the floor ahead of the tub as though genuflecting in front of an altar, draped myself over the edge, and swiped my socks back and forth with the remnants of a bar of soap, then held my breath, as if not breathing would lessen the shock to come. I ran my hands up and down over the board. The sound of cloth sliding across the glass ridges not only competed with my chattering teeth but also the "*ouch!*" when my knuckles met the board's hard vertebrae.

Every few scrubs, I paused and exhaled warm air into my palms before resuming. I rinsed the socks in another bath of chilly water before tossing them into a separate bucket.

After a few minutes of this, my withered fingers no longer felt the chill, or any sensation at all.

As I scrubbed my socks against the washboard, Dad stepped into the bathroom to wash his hands in the sink behind me. While drying them on a threadbare towel, he surveyed my waterboarding project.

"Chiqui," he said, a little confused, "why aren't you using the washing machine?"

I shrugged. Mami had told me to use the washboard, so it had never dawned on me to clean my clothes any other way.

Dad reached into the bucket and plucked out a sock. Its waterlogged body looked as shriveled as my fingers. He dropped it with a thud. "Get your clothes and come with me."

I gathered my unwashed items and followed him.

Just outside the rear door, we stopped in front of our Maytag washer and dryer, survivors of many mechanical surgeries who, thanks to my father, were still going strong.

Turning nobs, adjusting settings, and separating colored garments from the whites, my father tutored me in the secrets of laundering clothes in a machine. When he opened the drum hatch, I tossed my sportswear inside, and after I measured the powdered soap and promised I'd never add too much, Dad pressed the button on the panel that awoke the beast. The machine clunked hard, then released the torrent of water that freed me from my servitude.

I wondered why my mother hadn't allowed me to use this wonderful device before. *Is handwashing my clothes a punishment of some kind? Did I do something wrong?* Apparently, Daddy didn't think I had. I glanced at my wilted fingers, still numb from the ice-cold soak, and wondered if there was a magical machine to wash tamale husks in.

During the holidays, while other kids baked sugar cookies, sipped hot cider, and sang carols, the Montes De Ocas spent two marathon-long days making tamales while listening to mariachi music on the radio. I knew my role in Operation Christmas Tamale, so this year on Christmas Eve Day, I made myself scarce and fled to the dog kennel, hoping everyone would forget about me. But eventually, the gate opened and Lilly discovered me curled inside a doghouse.

"Mami wants you," she said with an authorative voice that came from being nine years older. I didn't have to ask what Mami wanted. I knew it involved tamales, white string, and, like laundry day, cold water.

Mami had learned tamale-making from Abuelita and felt it was her duty to pass on the tradition to her daughters. Like an admiral delegating commands on a sea voyage, she took the helm, issuing orders to my sister, me, and anyone else who stepped into her culinary domain. Lilly, her first officer, handled important duties like pressing the buttons on the food processor, which groaned as it kneaded the thick maize dough, and sauteing the savory fillings on large cast iron pans over the stove. As a low man on the tamale totem pole, I was sentenced to my usual position worshipping the claw-foot tub in the bathroom. This time, however, instead of scrubbing socks on a washboard, I gazed at a sea of dried corn husks soaking in chilly waters.

The first dip into the cold soup was the worst. My hands swam across the tub, submerging any sheaths daring to pop to the surface. When the corn husks were sufficiently drenched, I removed a handful, freed them of any clinging silk strands, and deposited them into a gigantic stainless-steel container. With a thin white towel, I dabbed the moisture off the hulls. Once the basin contained twenty corn husks, give or take, I carried it to the dinner table.

In seconds, the eager hands of my sister, my mother, and sometimes my brothers grabbed a husk and plopped a dollop of *masa* in its center. After smearing the dough across the inside, a tablespoon of filling, either savory or sweet, followed. If the wrap was big enough, it was folded over and tied at one end. If not, a second tamale husk was added over it to keep the filling from oozing out. This is when my next responsibility as apprentice tamale maker came into play.

At the Top Knot, the beauty shop Mom worked in, the towels used for a variety of hairdressing purposes arrived stacked and bound by a white string—and Mami, day after day, took those strings and rolled them one over the other. By year's end, the ball was the size of a grape-fruit. My job was cutting the string into six-inch strands so the tamale makers could secure the ends of their tamales.

It was a tedious job. I never seemed to cut fast enough for those waiting on me. While the others laughed and carried on, I brooded. But my bad temper only encouraged my brothers' teasing, which led them to anoint me *Cinderella*.

When Mami allowed me to make a tamale rather than just cut strands of string, my efforts were never a pretty sight—*too small, too fat, not so much filling, don't do it like that* . . .

I grew tired of the Tamale Approval League, criticizing my best attempts.

"Carlyn must have made this one," Ray said, smirking, and held up a tamale so pudgy that *masa* oozed from its seams. Everyone laughed but me. My face burned. I didn't like to be teased, though I did envy how funny my siblings were. I wished I could be as skilled at the art of the tease as they were.

That night, I prayed to Our Lady of the Perpetual Green Light to grant me the powers of wit.

"Please make me funny. Please let me be as smart as they are. Please . . ."

I didn't give a fig whether I could make the perfect tamale; I just wanted to have funny comebacks at my disposal.

Operation Christmas Tamale was a holiday tradition that continued over the decades even after the cast of characters changed. When I was older and my parents were no longer with us, I helped Lilly make Christmas tamales in her home.

Even after twenty years, I automatically gravitated to the same role I'd had as a kid. As I submerged the parched corn husks in my sister's utility sink, cold water gushing down from the nozzle, Lilly came into the laundry room and peered over my shoulder. Without a word, she leaned in, turned off the cold water, and released the hot, covering my hands in a warmth more soothing than a cup of spicy cider.

I looked at my sister as if awakening from a spell.

"Duh—why didn't I ever think of doing that?" I asked, feeling inept.

Lilly shrugged, knowing full well we came from a family that never questioned my mother or my father's reasoning. What they said, we did. Theirs was the rule of law. Who were we to second-guess them?

According to my parents, obedience brought accord, conformity created peace, and surrender was the only way forward. Living at the junkyard on Escondido Road had its rules, its culture, and its secrets, and no amount of praying to a green virgin, captive in glass, would ever change that.

CHAPTER SEVENTEEN

Sad Happy

MY FATHER WAS AN ENTHUSIASTIC STORYTELLER and could find no better audience than his youngest daughter to listen to his yarns.

Whether he was working under the hood of a car, rifling through baby jars full of screws, or eating dinner, Daddy shared stories about our family's history in vivid detail and surprising length, as though he was reliving each memory in the telling. I was a rapt child with a hungry imagination, pining for adventure. Listening to Dad's tales, I learned more about my father than I did my mother, who kept her own history under lock and key.

My father shared that in the early 1900s my great-grandfather, Vicente, was a landowner and man of means in Mascota, my parents' hometown in Mexico. Daddy was his favorite grandchild. As they walked through the corridors of the family's sprawling hacienda, Vicente, my father's namesake, carried his little grandson on his shoulders, their two bodies melding together as if forming one giant.

For his fifth birthday, Dad's grandfather gave him three unforgettable gifts: a pony with a saddle, a grown man's sombrero, and a set of shiny cowboy spurs. Watching Daddy, in his white T-shirt and grease-stained khaki pants, recount how he'd strutted through his house, parading in front of his younger brothers and sisters, the sombrero drowning his face as his spurs clicked with every step, made me both love my father for the boy he once was and cringe in anticipation of the tragedy to come.

My father was born during the Mexican Revolution—where, as in all wars, it was the innocent who suffered most. Time and again, militias on horseback rode onto the hacienda, threatening Dad's family and demanding money, which my great-grandfather surrendered to keep his loved ones safe. The visitations were frequent and frightening, and came at a great cost. When Vicente's finances dwindled and he had nothing left to give, the revolutionaries tied his ankles to a long rope and, as my father and his family looked on, they lowered the old man head-first into a deep well. Dad's grandfather died a few months later, leaving the family penniless. My father would never mount his pony again, or wear his shiny spurs, or ride on the shoulders of a giant.

After Vicente's death, Dad's father, Raimundo, took out a loan to start a tannery business. But a combination of alcoholism and rheumatoid arthritis soon incapacitated him. His diminished health confined him to the kitchen table, a towel draped over his head to block the light from his hyper-sensitive eyes. With a debt to pay and mouths to feed, the responsibility of caring for the family fell on Dad's young shoulders.

My father was an avid student who absorbed information like a sunflower inhaling the high desert sun. He dreamed of a profession as an engineer, but his family's circumstances forced him to leave school and run the tannery to support his mother and six younger brothers and sisters. Dad was twelve years old.

As his father's health deteriorated, my dad juggled several jobs to feed, clothe, and educate his family. Besides the tannery, he worked in coal mines where conditions were poor and accidents many, on building sites doing menial labor, and later as a projectionist in the local movie house. With a mathematical and methodical mind plus a motivated spirit, my father learned engineering, mechanics, and construction. When he was older, he even brought light to Mascota by building an electrical network at the power plant.

Dad often spoke to my sister and me as though we were precious rosebuds he watered with tender words—but not always. And perhaps because his love felt so much sweeter and the spark in his eyes shined that much brighter than Mami's, his anger hurt me much more. When Dad exploded, I turned into the Vesuvian dog—a petrified relic taken unaware by the fury of a dormant volcano.

One afternoon, after I'd completed all my chores—*more or less*—I sat down to watch cartoons. Lilly, now nineteen, wasn't home often; Ray and Art were away at college; and I was out of books to read. Even Orange and Bandit were not enough to keep me entertained that day.

Dad came in for lunch, which I'd prepared earlier by spreading the contents of a can of tuna fish between two slices of white bread and calling it a sandwich. Lilly's culinary talents weren't contagious, yet Dad never complained about my cooking. In fact, he acted as though everything either of us made was the best meal he'd ever tasted. Even when Lilly forgot the cookies in the oven and they emerged charred, Dad ate the remains, insisting he loved them black and crispy.

"How's your day going?" he asked.

"I am soooo bored," I whined, rolling my eyes.

My father didn't respond, just took a sip of coffee as if nothing was amiss.

When Dad had taught me how to wash my laundry, letting me in on a mystery that until then had belonged to grown-ups, it was as if I'd left a piece of my childhood behind. Now, I felt as though I was climbing another rung toward maturity by confiding in him about my genuine feelings of boredom. Unlike my school friends, who complained, nagged, and talked back to their parents, my siblings and I never did. We were polite and did what we were told. I broke that rule today with my four words, and it was freeing. I felt a closeness was born between Dad and me—that we were growing beyond father and daughter and becoming buddies.

But this was a flight of fancy that would soon crash and leave no survivors.

Dad picked up his plate, took it to the kitchen, and set it in the sink without even a thank you. Then he opened all the cabinets and in a calm voice said, "I want you to wash every single dish in this kitchen." I stared at the open drawers filled to the rim with pots, pans, plastic containers, lids, glassware, CorningWare, and utensils. "That way you won't ever be bored again," he said as he walked out the door, the screen door slamming behind him.

Like Lot's wife, whom I had learned about in a Sunday sermon, I stood paralyzed—not by salt but by dismay—as I gazed around the narrow room at the kitchenware spreading from floor to ceiling. Resigned, I reached for the radio on the shelf and turned the dial on with a click.

As if scoffing at my punishment, mariachi music greeted me. Quickly, I switched the dial to a station playing top-forty hits from the '70s. I sighed, ready to serve my sentence—washing dish after dish like a scullery maid.

The Beatles did their best to keep me company. But after an hour of washing and drying cookware, I felt even more bored than I had when I started. Although it was summer, the kitchen was dark, dank, and chilly, and the sun shining through the paint-stained window above the faucet—warm and inviting—tempted me.

Through the screen door, Orange scrutinized my gestures, his eyes willing me to abandon my servitude and join him for a romp. That's when the obvious hit me.

"How will Daddy ever know whether I washed all the dishes or not?" I asked Orange.

He refused to answer but continued luring me with his sad eyes.

I peeked out the front door and spotted Dad working on his vise— an iron behemoth with steel jaws attached to a metal pole. I calculated that he would be there for a couple of hours before coming inside for a break. That was more than enough time for me to defy him.

I pulled plate after plate from the cabinets—freeing spiders, releasing dust—and loaded them into the dish drain. Then I emptied spoons, forks, and knives onto the counter over a white towel bearing the stains of a chemical hair solution similar to Mrs. Water's blue hue. Then, like a priest blessing his congregation with holy water from an aspergillum, I anointed our tableware with droplets from the tap.

Once every cabinet was clear, I surveyed my work: glass, ceramic, and stainless steel stacked high and wide—evidence of my discipline, diligence, and obedience.

Satisfied, I went outside to play hide-n-seek with my dogs.

Dad found me not long after.

"Did you do what I said?" he asked.

I nodded.

Dad's face didn't flinch. He simply motioned with his forefinger for me to follow him, just like when he'd shared his wisdom about the bees. A pang of excitement shot through me. Perhaps he had another secret to reveal.

I followed my father inside the house and into my bedroom, where his eyes scanned the menagerie of stuffed animals on my bed until he settled on the one I loved most.

When I was born, Lilly had gifted me Happy, her most prized possession: a plump, brown creature with a white chest and tears streaming down his rubber face. Over time, Happy's pilled coat had worn paper thin. The torn stitches on his neck now revealed innards made of cotton clumps. His face was filthy from my unwashed hands and years of kisses. But his head was protected by a small, snow-colored beanie with a multicolored tip that I'd crocheted during two sittings of *The Twilight Zone* under Tia Petra's tutelage.

When a forest fire had erupted in the nearby mountains behind our house not so long before this, Mami had handed me a king-size pillow case and instructed me to pack it with my most valuable things should we have to evacuate at a moment's notice. I'd looked around my room, assessing what I could not live without. Into the tube-like case I'd stuffed a paperback copy of *A Childhood's End*, my worn basketball, a music box that no longer sang, and Happy, the saddest-looking teddy bear ever created, then I'd tossed the sack over my shoulder and sat on my bed like a hobo waiting for a train.

The flames that threatened to consume our home eventually died out, and the sack proved unnecessary.

I adored Happy and wondered why my father was staring at him now.

"Take Happy, wrap him up, and give him to the Gomez girls for Christmas," he said.

I stood my ground, not because of defiance but because the blood had just drained from my body.

"What?" I asked, certain I was in the middle of a bad dream.

"You heard me," he said, and then he left the room, as if he'd just instructed me to do a casual chore, not rip out my heart. My feet, cased in invisible cement, struggled across the linoleum. I took Happy into my arms and clenched him like a mother about to lose her child.

"I won't do it," I said. My bed's forlorn guts creaked as I climbed onto it with Happy crushed in my arms. The fury of my tears mirrored my bear's permanent expression.

I pulled the covers over us, knowing it was a useless shield. In my mind, I conjured ways to thwart my dad. *Can I say I did what he asked but hide Happy in a box in the closet under my necktie dress? Can I call Lilly? She always knows what to say to handle my parents.*

Rage emboldened me—but adrenaline is a false god made of broken promises. The thought of opposing my father was something I was sure I would not survive. I feared the blow of his callused hand, the burn of his belt, and the anger that drove it, which was as painful as any physical hurt.

I carried Happy to our artificial Christmas tree, which stood decorated on top of my mother's sewing machine. Beside it was a box brimming with used wrapping paper and frayed bows. I dug out the most beautiful piece of holiday wrap—gold and dark green spirals with red reindeer—and draped it over Happy's head. To keep it snug, I tied a crimson blue ribbon around his neck. A bow tie for a hostage— yet there would be no ransom for my friend.

Five minutes later, I rang the doorbell at Chez Gomez, a small wooden bungalow next door that was guarded by pink plastic flamingos on either side of the entrance.

As I waited, I thought of the Gomez girls. One was older than me, the other a couple of years younger; both were being raised by a single mother who worked as a checker at the local drugstore. They shouted back, high on spite and proficient in their use of curse words that I sometimes had to look up in the dictionary and usually couldn't find. Even as ten-and-twelve-year-olds, the girls went where they wanted and when they wanted.

I lived in a junkyard with antiquated parents, but I preferred it to the Gomez house, which smelled thick from shuttered windows, floral potpourri, and unabashed belligerence. How could I abandon Happy to this lunacy?

I rang the doorbell again. Mercifully, the Gomez clan was not in.

Back at home, I set Happy under the Christmas tree. I could have watched TV, I could have read the funnies, but instead I stared at my beloved bear—currently being suffocated by a battalion of paper reindeer—not wanting to take my eyes off of him.

When Mami arrived home from work that day, she found me perched on the couch, staring at the wrapped bear under the Christmas tree as though I were in a trance. I figured my mother had probably run into my father as she walked up the driveway and he had filled her in on my sins. I waited for her disapproval like a peasant awaits the guillotine.

"Why does Happy have that paper over his head?" she asked from the dining room as she unloaded cans of green beans, peas, and carrots onto the table.

When I failed to answer, her footsteps drew closer until she stood over me. "What happened?"

The urgency in her voice melted the knot in my throat. "Dishes, punished . . . Happy . . ." I sputtered these words out between sobs.

Mami's jaw clenched as her head slowly turned from side to side. I waited for her venom—the slap of her hand across my upper arm, some disapproving words. None materialized. Instead, she pulled Happy from his seat, knocking strands of tinsel from a tree branch in the process, and—like a queen pardoning her subject—ripped off Happy's paper helmet and handed him to me.

"Go outside and play with your dogs," she said, but all I heard was the blare of trumpets announcing Happy's stay of execution.

I hopped off the couch, but she reached the front door before I did and stormed outside.

I followed, carrying Happy, and hid behind the garage to watch my parents interact. I wasn't close enough to distinguish their words, but Mami's body language was clear. Hands on hips, head held high, she admonished Dad.

Dad's nod signaled his surrender. He shrugged. Mami turned back in a huff and headed for the house.

My mother was fierce when defending her children, even from my father. And today she was my champion.

I lingered in the dog pen with Happy, Orange, and Bandit until dinnertime. Once inside the house, I hid Happy in my closet, lest my father find him and send him to the Gomez clan.

Later that night, I retrieved my teddy bear from his hiding place and wrapped him in my arms, smothering him with the protectiveness my mom had modeled earlier. Mami had saved Happy from a life of debauchery with the Gomez girls. She might have given Melanie away, and broken my heart in the process, but tonight I was grateful to her.

"I'll never let you go," I promised Happy.

To this day, he still sits on my bookshelf.

CHAPTER EIGHTEEN

Trolling for Answers

RAY, ART, AND LILLY were as essential to my being as my four limbs were to my body.

Like teal blue belongs to the ocean, my siblings and I were spun from the same thread. A fabric, invisible to outsiders but woven over time and through mutual experience, bound us together. As a collective, we understood what was expected and accepted of us in our life in the junkyard, and we conformed without question. I admired my older siblings, envied them, and hoped to one day be just like them. I couldn't imagine life without them in it. Yet I also wondered why we were so different.

In July, we celebrated both my brothers' and my sister's birthdays, which all fell within a few weeks of each other. At some point during those celebrations each year, we gathered near the bathroom door with two instruments in hand—a #2 pencil and the Carpinteria phone book—and, starting with Ray and ending with me, we each took turns standing against the long strip of gray plywood at the bathroom doorway.

Since they were taller, my brothers held the phone book above our heads while my mother took a pencil from dad's shirt pocket where he always kept one secured by a clip, and drew a line across the wood with the pencil point. Next, Dad removed a tape measure fastened to his belt and offered me an end. Proud to be selected for such an honor, I held the metal measuring tape taut while Dad pulled the other end up to the marked line and announced our heights for the year. Ray was at the top, followed by Art, then Lilly. As usual, I always came in last.

"Why are you so short?" Art taunted me for the hundredth time while pushing the phone book down on my head, forcing my tiptoes to give way. Unwilling to concede any ground, I imitated a giraffe, stretching my neck high, until the sting of a rubber band against my arm brought my feet back to earth. I glared at Ray, who rolled his eyes towards the ceiling, pretending the elastic he'd just propelled at me had been an accidental misfire.

It's hard to argue when you're a Lilliputian in a junkyard of giants.

Besides my height, I didn't often notice the differences between my siblings and me. But when Lilly came home from college and picked me up from school in her Hornet Sedan, my classmates asked, "Is that your mom?"

When I said, "She's my sister," they glanced at me, then at her, and said, "You don't look like sisters."

What did they know? I shrugged them off as though their thoughts were not important to me—but they were. Ever since Mrs. Marchand's visit, every way that I differed from my peers had become acceptance or shame, inclusion or banishment, life or death.

"How come I don't look like anyone in my family?" I asked my cousin Marti as we lay in bed, side by side, sharing our deepest thoughts, one day.

"You look like Ray," she said quickly, then changed the subject.

Ray may not have looked like my dad or my mom, but his extraordinary height was reminiscent of my Uncle Benjamin, who bent over in most doorways so as to not clunk his head. And in Marti's family every sibling resembled the next, not to mention our grandparents, aunts, uncles, and other cousins; there was no doubt what family they belonged to.

The dissimilarities between my siblings and me went beyond outward appearances. While we all attended the same parochial schools, worshiped in the same church, and had been raised by the same parents, my rhythm diverged from the band. Intoxicated by the dreamscapes of my books and fascinated by invisible worlds, I escaped reality more often than not. In my fantasies, I sky-dived from planes, lived in the jungles of Africa, hobnobbed with celebrities, and ran a ranch where unwanted dogs could live out their lives free from harm. I believed in angels, devils, ghosts, and aliens, and never stopped to consider that many people might not.

One spring afternoon in the sixth grade, while I daydreamed of Shawn Winslow's platinum mop and our religion teacher, Mrs. Diamante, spoke of saints and sinners, a mysterious thought interrupted both. Mrs. Diamante's words became ambience, present but indecipherable, lost to the dictate of a deeper power. And that's when it spoke to me: an unfamiliar voice; the same voice I would hear again later in life when big decisions required the guidance of something greater than myself. As Mrs. Diamante informed us that all good souls go to heaven, the word *reincarnation* popped into my head. I didn't remember having heard the word before, but somehow, I knew immediately what it meant: all good souls may go to heaven, but eventually, they return to earth.

After school, as our bus cruised toward Carpinteria along the coastal freeway, my mind was so engrossed in thoughts about life after death that I hardly noticed we were driving past the beach enclave of Summerland. If I had paid attention, I would have sensed the dead calm spreading over my fellow passengers—an unnatural stillness tinged with the anticipation of an oncoming tsunami.

"Nudies!!!" Johanne, an otherwise well-behaved boy with a European accent, sprang up from his brick red seat and bellowed like a foghorn.

As if summoned by a higher power, thirty kids vaulted from their bus benches, and like a battalion of locusts consuming a wheat field, they torpedoed the right side of the bus with their combined weight. Through open windows, they screamed the word together—"*Nudies!*"— their wails competing with the roar of traffic and the pounding surf as they pretended to spot naked sunbathers on the beach. The unified heft of the pre-teen gaggle rocked the old bus to the right, then to the left when the hoarde dived in the opposite direction.

Panicked by bedlam, our elderly bus driver yelled for order. The kids obliged with maddening screams—a mob lost in the haze of their own insurrection. School papers floated through the air like slow-moving confetti. Younger kids began crying. I just sat in my seat, eyes closed in reflection, my head leaning against the window, basking in the warm sun.

This was not the first time I'd experienced the mayhem that the idea of naked bodies unleashed in the parochial school bus, but it was the first time I had not taken part. Today, I focused instead on a new and more interesting thought: *reincarnation* and the daydream of past lives.

Ten minutes later, the bus pulled into the parking lot of St. Joseph's Church. The first to exit was the driver, who gave us all a departing glance of equal parts rage and fear as he marched toward the priest's rectory—where, we later discovered, he promptly quit.

On my walk home, I pondered what it was like to die and then be reborn. *Who had I been in another lifetime? What had I done to merit being a Junkyard Girl in this life?*

Reaching our gate, I flipped open the latch and crossed my fingers, as I did most days, hoping that while I was at school the junkyard had magically transformed into a grassy lawn lined with yellow daisies and pink plastic flamingos like there were at Chez Gomez. But when I pushed open the barrier, the familiar lake of the bent, the broken, and the disfigured greeted me.

With immortality still present in my mind, I walked into my house. Mami was home early; she was suffering from bursitis, a painful inflammatory condition affecting her shoulder, the result of wear and tear from her job washing hundreds of heads of women's hair over the years.

"Hi, Mami," I said, then blurted out my current belief—that we didn't go to heaven when we died, but rather we got to come back to life.

I didn't know what my mother thought of my discovery because she never said a word.

"Carlyn, can I see you for a minute?" Mrs. Diamante called out as we began to file out of religion class the following day.

I made my way up to her desk, expecting either accusations for yelling at nudists or her praise for my recent essay on St. Francis, the patron saint of animals. It was neither.

"Where did you hear about *reincarnation*?" she asked. "Did you hear me say that in class?"

Her curious eyes probed mine like a detective looking for clues. I shrugged, awed that besides being a teacher, Mrs. Diamante was also a mind reader. How did she know that reincarnation was what I was thinking about?

"Your mother was so upset she called Father Rightman," Mrs. Diamante said.

Uh-oh. Not only was Mrs. Diamante *not* clairvoyant but my mom, who hadn't shown a speck of emotion when I'd shared my belief in reincarnation, was apparently so incensed by my novel idea that she'd called the parish priest and demanded to know why I was being taught blasphemous notions.

"I don't know where I heard it, but it wasn't from you."

My response elicited a relieved sigh from my teacher.

"Maybe God told me about it," I offered, trying to be helpful.

Pathos crossed Mrs. Diamante's light brown gaze, inferring that I had a lot to learn about life. She dismissed me with a wave of her hand.

I grabbed my backpack and fled.

Today—given the recent anarchy on the school bus and the unexpected retirement of its chauffeur—Mami picked me up after school. But instead of driving home, we turned toward Santa Barbara, en route to the day-old bread store, where I was certain a slice of apple pie awaited me.

I sat in the back seat of the station wagon, playing with three Troll Dolls I'd inherited from my sister and that I'd named Ray, Art, and Lilly. If I'd had two more Trolls, I would have named them after Eduardo and Maggie, my much older half-brother and half-sister living in Mexico, whom I barely knew and had only met a handful of times on our annual summer trips.

As I played with Lilly the Troll, smiling at her oversize feet, glass eyeballs, and bright pink hair, a question entered my mind.

"Mami, why doesn't Eduardo call you Mother?"

Eduardo, a doctor and the spitting image of my father, did not call my mom *Mamá* as Maggie did; he referred to her as *Mari*.

Similar to when I'd told Mami about my belief in reincarnation, she remained silent.

"Mami?" I said again, wondering if she heard me.

The car rolled to a stop at the red light.

"I'm going to tell you why he doesn't call me that, then I never want to speak about it again."

I sat the Trolls on my lap and stared at the back of the driver's seat as if it, instead of Mom, was talking.

"Eduardo is your father's son, but I'm not his mother. When your dad was young, he wanted to marry Eduardo's mother, but her family was against it. They rejected him because he was poor. Eduardo's mother lives in Mascota."

The car moved forward, but I did not. I was still at *Eduardo is your father's son, but I'm not his mother*. I contemplated Mami's words as I looked out the window at the passing buildings and people strolling near them.

"What about Maggie?" I asked, knowing I was violating my mother's rules. But despite my question, I knew some of the answer already. Since my bedroom was next to the kitchen, I sometimes overheard conversations my parents held in low whispers long after they thought I was asleep. Maggie had grown up with my father's family. When he and my mother married, they officially adopted her. Life had not been easy for Maggie. In the 1940s, children growing up without parents were shunned by society, and though Maggie had studied hard in school and eventually become a respected teacher, acceptance was a difficult path in small-town Mascota, where gossip was a staple of life.

"I love all my children the same, whether they are adopted or not," Mami said, interrupting my train of thought, as the station wagon pulled into the bakery.

Mami kept her word. We never spoke of Eduardo's or Maggie's origins again. But I am now certain that on that day, when Mami spoke of the love she felt for her adopted children, she was not only talking about Eduardo and Maggie—she was also talking about me.

CHAPTER NINETEEN

Of Pigs and Gods

EVERY SUMMER, scorching temperatures followed us on our daily twelve-hour drives through the Sonora Desert.

The heat was oppressive. But riding in The International was even more taxing once its passengers dwindled to just my parents and me. This year, without Art making me laugh, Ray teasing me, or Lilly teaching me how to make gum wrapper chains, I sat alone in the rear cabin with only my thoughts and the sea of Saguaro cactus outside my window to entertain me. In order to avoid gas station bathrooms, which were seldom clean and often fly ridden, I ate and drank very little. To get through the monotony I forced myself to sleep. My dreams were a welcome relief from the desert's harsh persistence.

Once we reached the outskirts of Mascota, we drove to a spread of tiny concrete houses along the riverside. As we pulled up the muddy embankment, several farmers, their wives balancing baskets on their heads and their children eagerly waving at us, surrounded the truck.

Don Felipe, a distant relation of my mother's, ran up and greeted us through an open window.

"We are preparing a grand feast in your honor," he said as he opened the door for Mami and offered his hand to help her down the step.

After introductions, the community quickly got busy preparing food. The women, whose skin was parched and darkened by years of manual work in the sun, formed maize balls and then flattened them in a tortilla press before tossing them on a griddle. In a tightknit group near a spit, the men chatted, drinking from beer bottles, laughing, and clapping each other's backs in a show of camaraderie. Kids about my age helped their parents. The younger children hid behind their mothers' skirts whenever they caught me smiling at them.

I wandered into a rickety barn, home to several farm animals, and relished the aroma of hay. While stroking a frisky horse's nose, I talked to the donkeys, and made friends with the tiny chicks.

"Oink-oink-oink," grunted a friendly pig penned inside a small corral. He sniffed the wooden bars between us, then nuzzled my hand with his snout. I plopped down in front of his cage and fed him corn kernels scooped from a nearby bucket. He nibbled them from my palm.

Don Felipe entered the barn. "Don't waste that food—we're going to butcher him later," he said, sliding his forefinger across his neck.

I stared at the slender man as he reached for a leather strop hanging on a bent nail hammered into a beam. My hand slackened, releasing the corn kernels onto the dirt before I fled the barn.

Dad sat on a folding chair in the center of a circle of men, telling a story from his youth. His infectious laugh spread among them and lured others on the periphery to step closer.

I ran up to him and whispered the horrible news into his ear: "Daddy, they are going to kill the pig!"

My father sat me on his lap and continued delighting his new friends with his tall tale.

"Daddy, please, the pig!" I persisted, pulling the sleeve of his white guayabera shirt.

Dad took my hand and excused himself from his rapt audience. "Where is he?" he asked.

I led him to the corral, but when we arrived, the pig was gone.

"Stay here, Chiqui," Dad said.

Through the slats in the barn wall, I watched him walk toward my mother, who was slicing *nopales* for a cactus salad. Daddy took her aside and mumbled in her ear.

"Vince, we can't tell them that," Mami said, pushing away and looking at my father as if he'd lost his marbles.

Don Felipe approached them. "Is anything wrong?" he asked.

"Please don't kill that pig," Daddy said, smiling as though speaking to his best friend and not a stranger he met only an hour ago. "My daughter's upset and to be honest, pork doesn't sit well with me." Dad's hand rubbed his stomach as if trying to soothe it.

I knew the latter half of his statement wasn't true. Dad ate ham at Thanksgiving—two servings—with no negative effects.

"But you're our guest of honor. And it's just a pig. You'll see. It'll be very good." Don Felipe clapped my dad's shoulder, then picked up a knife and began sliding it up and down against the worn strop he was holding to sharpen it.

I don't remember leaving the barn. My feet possessed a will of their own. I reached Dad's side, slipped my hand into his, and squeezed. He looked down at me, his forehead wrinkled, the rest of his face attempting to keep up appearances. I was confident that if anyone could save my friend, it would be Dad, whose veins pumped with the determination of Saguaro.

But a force greater than his came between us, sweeping him aside. My mother grabbed my arm and pulled me out of the way so no one could overhear.

"Wipe that look off your face," she said sternly, her lips barely moving. "These people are going to a lot of trouble. They're going to kill that pig, that's all there is to it, and you need to toughen up."

As she finished her sentence, terrorized squeals tore through the camp. Don Felipe's razor-sharp knife may as well have cut out my heart. My lips trembled, tears streamed, and I fell on my knees, covering my ears to keep out the shrieks.

Mom grabbed my arm and forced me to stand. "Stop it!" she insisted and smacked my bottom with the flat of her hand. "Stop crying now!"

I sobbed louder, not because of the strike of her palm but the sting of her anger.

Through the chaos of squeals, shrieks, and sobs, I didn't hear Dad approach or what he whispered to Mom, but she let go of my elbow and marched off, her recently cut shoulder-length hair bobbing as she walked.

Dad kneeled beside me, wiped off the dirt and tiny pebbles stuck to my knees, and handed me the handkerchief he kept in his pant's pocket. I bunched it into my hand but didn't bring it to my eyes.

"Want a 7Up?" he asked as the pig's cries subsided.

I shook my head. A warm soft drink wasn't going to appease the tangled knot in my stomach.

Daddy looked toward the empty corral. "They're poor people. It means a lot to them to do this for us. We can't insult them, Chiqui." He wiped my tears away with his fingers, kissed me on the forehead, then walked back to the circle of admirers waiting for him to finish his story.

Later that afternoon, the entire town feasted on the pig's body. I sat at the end of a table, glaring at anyone who came near. No one bothered me except for the one person who was not afraid of my mood.

Mom set a plate of pork rinds in front of me. "Eat it," she said.

I searched for a hint of kindness in her eyes, but only found glacial waters.

"You heard me," she said, her voice barely audible, the air sharp between us.

My spent body was no match for her strength. I was a child, and she was my mother. I had no say, and she had it all. I brought the crisp to my lips and took a nibble: salty, tasty, and sickening.

Satisfied by my compliance, Mom left me and headed toward the spit, where lively men and cheerful women toasted life with the help of tequila. I spit the rind into my hand and fed it to a skinny dog missing clumps of hair who was begging under the table.

I left the party and wandered down the riverbank, where I watched the current carry soap suds downstream from clothes being laundered upriver. I pined for Orange and Bandit, and thought of life's unfairness.

Especially when you are a pig, living in a corral, born to be eaten.

A woman carrying a hefty laundry basket on her hip passed by, her daughter's hand in hers. When Mom held my hand, she pulled me behind her or told me to hurry. There were occasional moments when she became *Mami* again and the warmth of her coursing blood blended with mine. But today was not that day. Today, I'd discovered that I had two mothers living inside one body and I could never again be certain which one would show up.

At the villagers' urging, Mom sang a song, accompanied by Don Felipe strumming a battered guitar. My mother sang this same song, "La Llorona," at home while cooking in the kitchen. Both haunting and heartfelt, this folk-lament spoke of the trappings of sorrow. Dad watched Mom sing, his concern for me replaced by his pride for her. As I observed my mother's performance, I questioned her love for me. If she cared about me, as mothers are supposed to cherish their daughters, then how on earth could she strike me when I felt so wretched?

That night, whether from hunger or because I was realizing that the fracture between my mother and me teetered upon irreparable, I took my pillow and into its depths I yelled, "*I hate you!*" Tears watered the roots of resentment that years before were seeded in my heart when Melanie was taken from me. My mother's face faded as sleep arrived and gave way to dreams of a heaven where pigs ran free in peaceful pastures under the protection of a more benevolent god.

CHAPTER TWENTY

The Iron Curtain

DESPITE THE WIDENING BREACH between us and the conflicting emotions competing in my heart, I still cherished my mother.

When I brought my lips to her cheek, I'd exaggerate my kiss with a loud smacking sound that made her laugh. When she least expected it, I slipped into her room to tickle her bare toes poking out from under a blanket. Though she didn't approve of card games, she relented when I asked her to *pick a card, any card* from my deck of TV magic cards.

Mami's smile melted my indignation, and her approval validated my worth. But over time, these moments increasingly gave way to resentful grudges and long silences. Like a dandelion caught in a gust, I was being pulled apart, piece by piece, with no possibility of returning to what once had been.

Caprichosa, voluble, terca . . . My mother accused me with words I didn't understand the meaning of. It was clear, however, that they were not complimentary. Only as an adult would I discover that she was describing me as moody, fickle, and stubborn.

I was twelve, craving independence and not getting it. Riding my bike beyond the brick strip at the end of the driveway, calling friends over the phone, or talking to boys were the small tastes of freedom my mother kept from me without explanation. Every morning before I left for school, she insisted on brushing my hair into a tight braid. Her uncompromising strokes bent the strands to her will. I wore a blue

"Why?" I asked, pleading more than asking.

The hairy eyeball informed me this was a command and not a discussion.

"Leave it open," she said and walked out.

"I hate you," I whispered after she left. "I hate you." I turned to the plastic statuette of Our Lady of the Perpetual Green Light. "I wish I were an orphan," I informed her.

She smiled sweetly at my misery from inside her glass cubbyhole.

Days after the door incident, I came home from school and found a sky-blue curtain hanging from a rod over my bedroom doorway. Its chiffon fabric was so sheer anyone walking past could easily see through it. The flimsy cloth would never give me the privacy I longed for. My mother's attempt at compromise allowed her to continue looking into my room and into my private life.

As long as her eyes were on me, Mami thought she could keep me safe from life's perils, prevent my missteps, and protect me from reality's sharp edge. But all I saw was her intrusion.

Transparent as the drapery was, it was a thread of independence and I embraced it wholeheartedly. From then on, I kept the blue veil at the entrance to my bedroom closed at all times.

That May, I suffered from a head cold. The virus turned into bronchitis. Bronchitis became asthma. The vise-like constriction in my chest made every breath a struggle and confined me to bed.

Mami took me to see Dr. Kingman, a robust woman with a gray crew cut whose gruff manner I immediately disliked. After Dr. Kingman checked my lungs with a frosty stethoscope, she informed my mother that I needed to be hospitalized.

I may have been wheezing, coughing up yellow phlegm, and felt as exhausted as a deflated balloon, but spending three nights away from home and Mom's hairy eyeball sounded like a splendid adventure.

At Saint Francis Hospital, I watched TV most of the day while aides brought me vanilla ice cream and strawberry Jell-O. Instead of brushing my hair harshly and securing it in a braid, a young nurse ran a soft hairbrush through it and allowed my long hair to flow. Doctors checked in on me, asking questions in a kindly way, and telling jokes. And my *closed* door gave me privacy and a feeling of maturity. Being so sick had never felt so good.

On my second day, Art stopped in accompanied by a box of Oreo cookies and an *Archie and the Jugheads* comic book. The inside of the cookie carton was half-eaten, but I didn't care about that. What could be more wonderful than lying in my own room, on a mattress that didn't sag, and watching TV with my big brother?

Down the hallway, a little boy cried out for his mother, wailing that he wanted to go home. I wished the opposite; I hoped my stay would be extended ad infinitum.

The one thing Escondido Road had that this hospital did not were my lifelines—Orange and Bandit. I missed my dogs and hoped they weren't bored locked away in their kennel without me, but I trusted that my mom was looking after them.

After taking the requisite drugs, using an inhaler several times a day, and sleeping more than usual, my breathing improved and Dr. Kingman said I was well enough to leave. My hospital vacation came to an end. An aide arrived, wheelchair in one hand and a stick of gum in the other. I thanked him for the treat, popped it into my mouth, then took a seat on my traveling throne. He rolled me out to our Kingswood station wagon, parked alongside the curb. I was going home—or so I thought.

Less than half an hour later, we pulled up to the end of our driveway. I opened the car door.

"Close it," Mom snapped.

Why? I wondered—but even as I did, my thinking surrendered to hardwired obedience and I shut the door.

"Your brother's graduating from law school and we're driving to Arizona to see him," Mom said, grabbing her keys and stepping out of the car. "The doctor says the dry air will be good for you. Stay here."

Mom opened the driveway gate only enough to squeeze her body past it. Usually, the latch's hard click notified my dogs that we were home and sent Orange into a barking frenzy. Today, he was silent. *If the dogs were out, they'd have poked their noses underneath the fence by now*, I thought. But that didn't happen either.

The gate creaked open and my parents emerged carrying two suitcases. Dad loaded them into the back of the wagon as Mom turned the key in the ignition.

"Who's taking care of the dogs while we're gone?" I asked as the car pulled away from the house. My parents' eyes met briefly, but neither answered. I asked again, a little louder, "Who's taking—"

"Just read your book," Mom said, her voice as sharp as a blade.

Even though I'd read *Archie and the Jugheads* twice while I was in the hospital, I opened the paperback and turned to a dog-eared page that smelled like Oreos. As I did, I concluded that our next-door neighbor must be the one feeding our dogs while we were away. My mind accepted the logic but remained uneasy.

The smell of old chocolate, the motion of the car as I read my book, and the antibiotics in my stomach made me queasy. I rolled down my window and breathed in the ocean air as we left Carpinteria behind.

Mom drove in silence, facing forward, her eyes unblinking in the rearview mirror. Dad sat in the passenger side, gazing at the ocean as if contemplating the world's troubles.

Lately, Mom seemed angrier than usual. Sometimes I deserved her ire for misbehaving, like the time I got caught eating a second slice of pie without permission or tried the "F" word out on Lilly. But sometimes I didn't know what I'd done wrong or why it annoyed her. My confusion moved from frustration to capitulation. I gave up figuring out my wrongdoings and concluded that I was damaged, just like the broken gadgets in our yard.

When we stopped to get gas in San Bernardino, I asked about my dogs again. Mom answered by handing me an icy soft drink. Near Palm Springs, I mentioned Orange and Mami made a pit stop for a date shake. As we approached Phoenix, I told a story about Bandit and was silenced with a chocolate-covered cherry from a five-pound box of See's candy.

Something was not right.

That night, we arrived in Phoenix and checked into a motel. My parents took the bedroom and the plaid couch butted against the window became my bed for the night.

Dad came and sat beside me, tucking the surrounding bedsheet into my sides.

"How are you feeling?" he asked.

"Daddy, what about Orange and Bandit?"

Dad's dimples faded and his eyes lost their sparkle. "Go to sleep, Chiqui," he said, leaning over to kiss my forehead. He then went into the bedroom and closed the door behind him.

I heard my parents' hushed voices beyond the wall, their words muffled by the drone of the humming fridge.

Soon, I drifted into a restless dreamscape.

The next morning, Mom woke me, then handed me two capsules and a glass of water.

"Get ready, Ray's graduation starts in a few hours," she told me as I swallowed my medication.

Mami's eyes brightened whenever she spoke of my big brother. When she was seven months pregnant and a passenger in a car driven by Dad's brother, they'd gotten in an accident.

I pictured her that day with the glow of an expectant mom, the wind from her open window brushing back her dark hair as she daydreamed of holding a baby in her arms, never imagining the danger lurking ahead.

Everyone survived the crash, but the trauma forced Mom into early labor. Ray was born shortly after, so premature and tiny that he barely fit into the palm of Dad's hand. *Nothing can be done*, the doctors said, and they told my parents to let their child die at home.

5515 Escondido Road was Buckingham Palace compared to the one-bedroom shanty my parents were living in back then. While my father worked in the strawberry fields during the day, Mami sat holding her child in a rocking chair Dad had built from discarded pine. For a month after his birth, she carried Ray close to her chest, feeding him from a dropper like a hatchling—and my brother not only survived, he excelled. One day, he would make us all proud by becoming a superior court judge.

In years to come, Mami would have more children, but Ray held a special place in her heart. I never felt jealous of my big brother for having my mother's affections in a way I did not. Neither did I envy Lilly for getting the piano lessons I always wanted while I was handed a guitar. And the only rivalry I had with Art was over who was the more clever teaser. In my mind, my siblings walked on water. They were the second coming. They were my superheroes.

But I wasn't thinking about them right now; I was thinking about my dogs. I set my empty water glass on a nightstand as Mom unsnapped the clasps on her suitcase and pulled a green dress, white laced ankle socks, and black patent leather Mary Janes from its mouth.

I ignored the outfit; today, only one detail pressed on my mind. "What about Orange and Bandit?" I asked again, like a broken Victrola.

"You have a one-track mind," Mom replied. I'd heard this phrase from her many times before, though I wasn't sure of its meaning. "Put these on." She handed me the socks.

My fingertips took them from her and then promptly dropped them onto the floor. It was an act of rebellion and we both knew it.

Dad's hand slipped into mine. He kneeled down to my level and looked me in the eye. "The doctor told us the dogs caused your asthma . . . so we gave them away," he said as if this information were simply a fact like *The sky is blue*.

I don't know when the diesel truck struck me, but after it did it lurched to a sudden stop, backed up, and rolled over me again. Quietly, silently, eternally, the earth fell out from under me. I was certain I was dead. But then I realized it was worse than that. I was breathing and alive in a world where my dogs were gone.

That's when I screamed.

"No, no, no!!!" My chest tightened, but asthma was not the cause. Like a tracking device programmed to locate true north, my heart was pounding its way out of its cavity, trying to find Orange and Bandit.

Daddy wrapped me in his arms, holding me against his chest, trying to absorb my pain.

"Stop it—stop crying!" Mom demanded, just as she had done the day they slaughtered the pig.

I cried harder. What could she do to me now? She had stripped me of what I loved most. Beating me to death would be a mercy.

"We're going to be late, Vince," she snapped.

"I'm not going," he replied.

"What do you mean? You have to. It's your son's graduation."

"You go, Mary, I'm staying here."

I stopped crying long enough to realize that my dad was choosing me over my mother, my brother, and everything else. With a shake of her head, Mom grabbed her purse, opened the front door, and slammed it behind her. Her heels clicked across the parking lot pavement and soon faded.

Daddy stroked my hair and explained that Orange and Bandit were at the local dog pound, where they would find a wonderful home with a fine family. If he'd said the Virgin Mary had adopted my dogs, it wouldn't have made a difference. My best friends were gone, erased from my life because of a doctor's theory (which, by the way, would one day be proven untrue: it was the dampness and the mold in *the house that moved*, not my beloved dogs, that was causing my asthma).

We sat together in the motel room, the summer sun beating its way through the dark shades, sadness filling the empty spaces in my body.

When I could no longer cry and my lungs were only faintly wheezing, I fell asleep in my father's arms, hoping I would soon wake up from this nightmare.

After the graduation, we gathered at Ray's house with some of his law school friends. We ate my mom's home-cooked enchiladas, shot hoops in the driveway, and despite my mother's disapproving stare we played cards.

As my mother laughed with my brother over tequila and a joke that afternoon, I splintered like a brittle tree. In my fractured state, I believed that Mami didn't love me, and in turn, I buried my love for her under a veil of rage that would take decades to lift.

When we got back to California, I grabbed my duffel bag out of the car and walked down the driveway towards the dog pen. Like a canine ghost village, it stood vacant, except for the memories refusing eviction. I've heard it said that all sounds since the beginning of time continue to exist, even though human ears can no longer hear them. My dogs were gone. Their cage was empty. But their yips and barks, the sound of their eager clawing against the wooden gate, and their duets of ardent howls still echoed through the air.

That night, I pleaded with Our Lady of the Perpetual Green Light for a miracle. Her peaceful half-smile gave no sign she heard me.

A daring idea came to mind. I got out of bed, grabbed my school backpack, and stuffed it with a change of clothes, my hefty piggy bank (mostly filled with pennies), and Happy. It was well after midnight as I tiptoed through the kitchen, unbolted the door latch, pushed the screen open, and stepped into the spring night air.

It was about ten miles to the dog pound. I calculated that if I start-ed walking now, I would get there by early morning. Once I arrived, I'd find my dogs and set them free, and then we'd run away together. *Where?* I didn't know, but I hoped to figure it out on the long walk ahead.

I slipped past the *other house*—where Dad had been sleeping ever since Mom complained he snored too loudly and usurped his bed with boxes of beauty supplies—and continued to the kennel, where I pressed the flat of my hand against the wire mesh, imagining Orange would meet it with his paw and warm tongue.

The steel barrier stood lifeless.

I climbed inside, scooted onto the large doghouse, and lay on my back looking up at the stars and moon, remembering a day not long before when I'd rested on the same spot, looking toward the clouds, asking when my real parents would come for me.

As I watched the stars, I drifted in and out of dreams, my eyelids heavy from crying, until dawn peeked over the mountain. Instead of walking to the pound to save my dogs, fear had gotten the better of me, robbed me of my resolve, and stripped me of all courage.

Tired and cold, I let myself out of the pen, retraced my steps to the *house that moved*, and climbed into bed.

The following evening, as I slid carrot slices back and forth across my dinner plate, Dad stood abruptly, causing our hefty wooden table to quake.

Startled, I dropped my fork. It clanked against the CorningWare.

"I can't take it another second!" Dad announced. He marched into the kitchen, where Mom was dicing potatoes on a cutting board. "I can't look at her like this anymore," I heard him say. "I'm getting those dogs back."

My mother didn't argue, though her tense grip on the knife suggested the russets were headed for a merciless death.

Dad walked out the front door, his eyes committed to his mission. I thought I was dreaming and put a carrot in my mouth. Its bland taste confirmed that this was real life. My heart raced. Hope surged past the lump in my throat. Orange and Bandit were coming home!

In the morning, the smell of cinnamon pancakes woke me. Pancakes were a Sunday affair. Today was Monday. I glanced at my clock; 6:00 a.m., it read.

Dad sat on the edge of my bed. He rarely entered my room this early except on my birthday, when he and my mother came in singing "Las Mañanitas," the traditional Mexican birthday song. Something felt amiss.

"Did you get them?" I asked with guarded excitement. "Are Orange and Bandit back?"

"I tried, Chiqui, but only Bandit was still there. Someone with a big ranch adopted Orange. Imagine that! Orange has acres of grass to run through."

It was a beautiful story Dad was telling; if only it was the truth. But I knew my father's tell—the slight quiver of his lip—and his lip was trembling now.

I also knew, however, that Dad was telling this lie to spare me, and I appreciated his kindness; it was a stronger healing salve than my mother's indifference offered. So, I listened, nodded, and smiled, though my heart was empty and a chill not originating from the damp living in the walls began to fill it.

"I have to get ready for school," I said, biting down hard on the inside of my cheek to keep from crying. I reached for my uniform skirt at the edge of the bed and noticed where Orange's drool had left a spot in the shape of Texas.

Dad nodded. His lip now steady. He got up and walked out through the blue curtain.

Orange was gone, and he wasn't coming back.

Bandit was a purebred Basenji—information Mom was proud to share with others. Orange had been a black lab mix, unrefined and without pedigree.

Bandit didn't deserve my distance or my anger. Because my mother preferred him, I began to identify Bandit as *her* dog, and my love toward him cooled; a fact I regret to this day.

That morning, I changed quickly—before anyone else came past my bedroom and spied me dressing—and as I buttoned my blouse, I made a vow: My mother dominated every detail of my life, but she'd never control my heart again. The flimsy blue curtain across my doorway might not keep her out physically, but I could wrap a different cloth around my spirit—an iron curtain made from rage and reinforced by my will. Mom might take away my dogs and sentence me to this abysmal life of junk-hell, but my iron shroud would be so steadfast that even she, a force of nature, could never make a dent in its fabric.

Once I built this impenetrable barrier, I tossed its key into oblivion and promptly forgot its whereabouts.

PART THREE

"I thought of complaining to all the angels last night
About your treatment of this 'Homeless child,'
But then I remembered they too
have a long list of love-complaints . . ."
—Hafiz

CHAPTER TWENTY-ONE

From Froggy to Doggy

TWO YEARS PASSED, and the only time we spoke the word "orange" was when referring to the color of pumpkins in the local patch around Halloween.

Bandit died about a year after Orange left us. My mother said it must have been something he ate that ended his life, but I suspected it was his heart, because the pain lingering in mine was killing me. Several times a day, I walked past the barren dog kennel where my dogs had once lived. The emptiness clawed at my gut and stirred up an increasing resentment toward Mom, which I hid under a permanent scowl.

After the Orange affair, my mother and I reached an impasse neither of us would breach. Pride, ego, or resentment—perhaps all three—fed the growing beast. We spoke less and less and shot each other bitter glances more and more. The silence between us was charged and awkward. When I wasn't playing basketball on my own, I spent hours in my bedroom, my face concealed in a book, sparsely shielded behind the translucent blue cloth hanging in my bedroom doorway.

Early one morning, before leaving for school, I stepped inside the bathroom and, as if assessing a stranger, studied myself in the mirror.

Mom no longer insisted on brushing my hair. She'd given up the battle after seeing me yank a rubber band out of my braid as soon as I left the house. Without my mother's attentions, my long hair now hung limp. I brought a strand in front of my eyes and inspected it, noticing that the tips were brittle white from split ends. In the

159

classroom, when my mind drifted from the teacher's words, I often took a shaft of my hair and pulled it apart, watching the fiber shrivel and coil like a curly cue.

My droopy hair made my face look plump. But this wasn't all I found defective. My cheeks were too fat, my nose too round, and my eyebrows were full and bushy. In many parts of the world, a gap between your front teeth is considered the mark of a beautiful woman. But I was a gawky teenager, and in my opinion, the dark slit between my incisors was not an asset.

"You've got something in your teeth!" the boys shouted at lunchtime.

"No, I *don't*," I yelled back, practically spitting at them.

But they didn't wait for an explanation before running off and telling their friends what they'd discovered in my mouth.

The girl in the mirror examined me now—the space between my teeth, the limp hair, the squirrelly eyebrows—she saw me for what I truly was: *ugly*. Like the disemboweled car intestines in our yard, I was a piece of rubble. I was nearly thirteen and lived with parents who didn't understand me. My siblings were gone, Orange was who knew where, and Bandit was in dog heaven. To make matters worse, Sarah had told me she no longer wanted to be my best friend. Then, to cement the deal, she'd become pals with a girl who frequently bullied me (and would continue to do so well into high school).

The further I sank into loneliness, the more I carved out an inner world only I possessed the key for. At night, I entertained darker thoughts, imagining what death was like and when it would come for me. But these notions were short-lived. Even if I escaped to the here-after, I suspected my mother would come after me—her anger severe, her reprisal grim.

"I'll get you another dog—any one you want," Dad had said to me after the Orange and Bandit incident. But I'd barely heard his words. The trauma of losing my dogs had deadened my senses; it was like he was speaking to me from a far off realm.

. . .

I forgot all about his promise until we went shopping at a department store one Sunday morning. As we approached the front entrance, I noticed a tall cardboard box on the pavement with two teenagers monitoring its contents. A cluster of people *oohed* and *aahed* when the carton jiggled.

Once inside the emporium, Dad made his way toward the tool aisle, while my mother headed for the housewares. When they weren't looking, I snuck back out to inspect the mysterious moving box.

Scribbled on the outside of the carton in red marker were two simple characters: $5. When I peeked inside the box, three balls of tan and black fur squirmed into and onto each other, attempting to find the most comfortable spot to nestle against before falling into a snoring stupor. Their masked faces, endearing and hopeful, reminded me of how much I craved a dog in my life.

When a second wave of people gathered, I acted fast: I raced inside the store, searching for Dad.

I found him inspecting a drill.

"Daddy, there are some puppies outside and they're for sale."

"Mm-hmm," he said as he changed the drill bit.

"Daddy." I tugged on the sleeve of his checkered Pendleton shirt and sneezed. Then sneezed again. I kept sneezing until one loud, long sneeze brought my bout to an end. Dr. Kingman had concluded that besides dog dander, I must also be allergic to wool. I wondered if Dad would have to get rid of his shirt as I'd had to get rid of my dogs.

"Are you sure they're still there?" he asked. "Go and see."

I did what he said and ran outside, not realizing his ploy was a distraction to buy time.

Outside, a college-aged couple dressed in matching torn jeans and black peacoats handed the teenagers a five-dollar bill. In return they got a groggy three-month-old shepherd-mix puppy. I watched them walk away with a pudgy ball between them, as elated as if it were their own child.

When I turned back, a little girl about my age was inspecting the carton. Only one dog remained inside: a furry, fat ball with an ear flopping over her eye scanned the skies, searching for her vanishing siblings. I looked at the blue-eyed girl; she glanced at me. Her golden hair was held in place by a rosey-colored headband that matched her puffy jacket. I imagined her riding a pink Schwinn bicycle, a white threaded basket on the handlebars, a silver bell at the beckon of her delicate fingertips. Then I thought of my bicycle: a rusty contraption that had sat in our garage for years before Dad restored it. My father's abilities to rehabilitate unwanted scrap metal would have made Dr. Frankenstein jealous. My new-old bike was an eyesore, but it soared down our driveway like a hawk in flight.

The blue-eyed girl smiled at me, her eyes softening.

We might have been friends someday, this perfect child and me—but today was not that day. I ran inside the store and found my father admiring a set of screwdrivers.

"Daddy, there is only one puppy left!"

"Go tell your mom," he said without looking up.

I refused to budge. I wasn't falling for that ploy twice.

Dad sighed and put down the tool. "Okay, where is it?"

I spun around and raced outside through the automatic doors, toward the squirming box, followed by the man who could alter my world with a five-dollar bill.

When we got there, my hopes sank into my sneakers. The golden girl held *my dog* in *her arms*, whispering her love into fuzzy ears, nuzzling her delicate nose into fur, making her way into *my puppy's* heart. It was over. I looked at Dad and shook my head with resignation, wondering if he'd be upset if I dissolved into the concrete like the dark liquid oozing from a toppled soda can on the sidewalk.

Then a miracle happened. Our Lady of the Perpetual Green Light must have heard my silent pleas, because instead of paying the teenagers and taking the dog, the girl's father pried the puppy from her grasp.

"Let's think about it inside, okay?" he said, giving me a wink.

Reluctantly, the girl followed her father into the store, her blue eyes mushrooming as the squirming ball of fur met my embrace.

Iris, the name I would one day call this dog, burrowed her tiny, wet snout into my armpit—and straight into my soul. I looked up at Daddy, he looked down at me, then we both stared at the glass doors that held my unsuspecting mother behind them. Dad sighed, reached into his pocket, and pulled a five-dollar bill from his wallet—the price of my eternal happiness.

Mom and Dad didn't speak the entire drive home. I didn't care. I had a puppy in my lap, and she was all mine. My dog didn't care whether I had split ends in my hair, overgrown eyebrows, or a gap between my teeth. The heat of her wet tongue on my face, the innocence in her eyes, and her sweet, musty breath filled my heart with a love that I was as desperate for as air. Although we lived in one of the most pleasant climates in the country, a polar ice cap had grown within me in the time since I'd lost Orange—one that refused to melt. But now Iris had let the sunshine in.

At least for a while.

CHAPTER TWENTY-TWO

Riding in Cars with Rosaries

MY HUNGER TO PLAY SPORTS rivaled my desire to read, eat, or even watch television.

During recess, I ate my lunch like a starving wood chipper, gobbling down my sandwich in record time so I could join my friends for a quick basketball game before class. After school, as a new member of the Mount Carmel girls team, I rushed outside the moment the school bell rang, excited to dribble a ball down the court, strike the heart of a softball, or launch a volleyball over the net.

Not only did I revel in the comradery of my teammates, I also thrived on learning the mysteries of these games that Coach Melissa, a grad student at a local private college, revealed to us at every practice.

My involvement with sports was something my mother encouraged, so a ball in hand became a pass out of my isolation. Athletics gave me a sense of purpose and distracted me from my ever-darkening moods.

When the hour arrived to face one of our softball rivals, a game we needed to win to reach the playoffs, Coach Mel came up with a novel idea—and a bribe. To inspire victory in our thirteen-year-old hearts she told us that for every home run we hit, she would buy the batter an ice cream sundae from a local shop.

That afternoon, I hit three homers. We won our game by a land-slide, but it was the last time Coach offered that incentive. At the end of eighth grade, I attended the annual Mount Carmel Sports Banquet with my parents. After several speeches, the top female and male athletes in softball, volleyball, and basketball received trophies. One after another, the best players in the school approached the stage and took their honors. I clapped politely for each of them, my feet tapping with exuberance, hoping my turn would come.

When the trophy for *excellence in basketball* went to another teammate, my spirits capsized. I glanced at the counter, where the handsome silver and gold trophies stood. The space was now empty. I'd believed I was one of the better players on our team. My vacant hands clarified that I was not. I felt my teammates' eyes on me as my face burned hot. Humiliated, I looked down at my shoes, hoping my friends couldn't read my disappointment, but I knew their sharp eyes already had.

"We have one last trophy to give—for best all-around player," Coach Mel announced to a surprised audience. Like a jack-in-the-box, I sprang up in my chair. In Mel's grip was the statue of a tall angel standing on a wooden spiral post, her wings outspread, a golden ball the size of a walnut resting in her upturned palms.

I don't remember Coach Mel's exact words in the seconds that followed. I recall something about *persistence, sweat,* and *effort,* and then . . . "Carlyn Montes De Oca!" Her Nordic blue eyes looked into mine as she called out my name.

It was nearly summer, but I sat frozen in place, listening to the enthusiastic clapping and cheering ringing throughout the auditorium. Mami nudged my ribs with her elbow. She and my father were clapping louder than anyone else. Her beaming smile made her look younger than thirty-nine, the age she still claimed.

Mom had told me repeatedly that I could do or be anyone I wished to be. I believed her. Yet how often had I darned my socks, washed my clothes, or cleaned my room only to be criticized for doing it all wrong? If I couldn't manage these ordinary tasks, how could I aspire to an extraordinary life? Mom claimed I could have the world, but her judgment didn't make it easy. Today, though, as she applauded with the other spectators, I relished her pride in me. A resurgence of love, something my anger had been chipping away at, made an appearance. Her smiling eyes motioned me forward. I took her cue and headed toward the stage.

Moments later I held the celestial statue in my hands, astounded that an object so exquisite was mine. My teammates surrounded and congratulated me, Dad hugged me hard, and strangers patted my head. Over and over, I read the inscription on the shiny brass plate— *Most Valuable Player—Carlyn Montes De Oca.* I was certain life would get no better than this.

Joy became euphoria when the school principal, Sister Diane, flagged down our station wagon as we were leaving the school parking lot. Mom slowed to a stop as Dad rolled his window down.

Out of breath, Sister Diane leaned over and looked inside. "I have great news—great news!" she gushed. "Carlyn is being offered an athletic scholarship for high school."

Dad let out an enthusiastic guffaw, his face a beacon of pride. He turned to the back seat and slapped my thigh.

His joy matched my own. Like a rookie on the side of a cereal box who gets a contract to play on their favorite team, jubilation flung me toward the stars. But in the next breath, my spirits crashed to the ground.

Mom glanced at Sister Diane and shook her head. As if reprimanded by the pope, the nun stopped her chatter and her attractive Greek features turned from saintly to perplexed.

"It's a great honor," Sister Diane added, not sure what else to offer.

My mother turned, blankly staring at the road ahead, and placed her hands on the steering wheel. Mom had two primary expressions: aloof and unreadable. She was wearing both right now, and the duo was draining Sister Diane's olive skin of its rich color.

Mom's rejection confounded me. From a young age, my siblings and I understood that my parents wanted us to excel in school. How often had Dad stressed that each upcoming generation must be and do better than the one that came before? Why had they even come to this country except to give their children the life they could not have for themselves? For this reason, attending our local public school, which Mom and Dad deemed academically challenged, would not do. In a few months, once summer vacation passed, I'd attend Bishop Garcia Diego High in Santa Barbara.

Mom and Dad worked long hours but we were not wealthy people. Not once had I seen them go out for dinner, take a vacation without us or exchange gifts. Perhaps the junkyard held a fortune in scrap metal, but we were decidedly lower-middle class and Bishop, the only Catholic high school in the area, was not cheap. How could Mom turn away from the offer of free tuition?

Sister Diane studied my mother's profile before straightening up, adjusting her veil, and glancing beyond the baseball field to the mountains, as if searching for inspiration. "Think about it, all right?" she said to my parents.

Dad took the nun's hand and shook it profusely. Mom nodded, but it meant nothing. I knew her well enough to know her mind would not change. A sports scholarship was not my destiny.

Transitions have always been difficult for me. When I'd left Saint Joseph's School to attend Mount Carmel, I swam against choppy waters that only eased once I had made friends with Sarah Marchand. Leaving a classroom of twenty classmates to attend a high school of over two hundred felt overwhelming.

During my first week at Bishop, tryouts began for the various sports teams. I was both nervous and elated to get onto the courts. First was tennis, which I wasn't very good at but did love to play. With the right coaching, I hoped to improve.

The following day, a list appeared in the outdoor hallway beside the administrative offices, revealing who had made the team. My heart surged when I spotted my name on it.

Mom had been so proud when I was the best all-around player at the sports banquet, and it had delighted her when I'd hit those three home runs and gotten those ice cream sundaes from my coach as my reward. She also consistently encouraged me to practice hitting tennis balls against our fence, even though they sailed into the neighbor's yard more often than not. One of her salon clients, a writer on a television show, had even gifted me fifty dollars to buy a tennis racquet of my own. So I knew Mom would be proud of me for making the team, and I couldn't wait to give her the good news.

But when I got home and told her I'd made the tennis team, Mom was as excited to hear about my success as she was about the sports scholarship.

"You won't be playing sports anymore," she responded matter-of-factly.

"What do you mean?" I asked, chuckling, certain she must be joking.

"I'm not driving all the way out there to pick you up every day after school."

"That's okay," I said, "I can get a ride home from someone else on the team."

My mother shook her head, picked up a T-shirt from the laundry basket, and snapped it in the air before folding it.

"No more sports." Her tone signaled a familiar finality.

I stood dumbstruck, devoid of words, swallowing my dismay—and then, like a sack of cement, it hit me: she'd said the word *sports*, not *tennis*.

"What about basketball?" I demanded, a desperate note lacing my voice as my heart sank. "The tryouts are tomorrow!"

Tennis was one thing, but she couldn't mean basketball. She knew what the game meant to me. Mom averted my gaze, folding towels as if I wasn't there. I willed her to meet my eyes. Instead, she picked up the laundry basket, indicating our conversation was over, and headed into the dining room. The gavel struck. There would be no appeal.

Mom's decision dazed me. For years I'd been practicing free throws in our driveway, perfecting layups, and climbing over rusted furniture to retrieve my basketball in order to avoid the potato bugs who lived under it, until darkness forced me indoors. Tearing me from my favorite sport was not as heartbreaking as my dogs being sent away, but it wasn't far from it. This news exposed my old wound to a fresh wave of hurt. How could she keep taking away things that gave me joy and purpose and claim to love me at the same time? And without my dogs or a basketball, the pillars of my identity, who was I?

My relationship with Mom, a skiff that had once glided across the sea, was slipping farther and farther into murky waters, and its hopes of staying afloat were diminishing daily.

Unlike grammar school, there was no bus to drive us the fifteen miles between my house and my new high school, so our parents took turns carpooling every day. I didn't mind when it was another mother driving. When it was Mom's turn at the wheel, I would have preferred being run over with her station wagon instead.

The first time my friends hopped into the rear seat of our car, Mom showed her proficiency at multitasking: she pushed down the gas pedal, pulled a rosary from her purse, and made the sign of the cross as she drove toward the freeway entrance.

Praying the rosary in Spanish was something Lilly and I had learned as young girls. Not only were we expected to memorize Hail Marys, Our Fathers, and Glory Bes, we were also forced to master the Litany of the Blessed Virgin Mary. For every bead crossing our thumb on the second lap of the rosary circuit, we beseeched the CEOs of our faith with brief requests to help us atone for our sins. *Lord have mercy on us . . . Holy Mary, pray for us . . . Holy virgin of virgins . . .* My sister and I prayed while kneeling across from each other in my mother's bedroom. Lilly's rosary was composed of tiny polished wooden pellets held together by a delicate silver chain. My beads, purchased at a local carnival, were the size of overfed garbanzo beans, with the added feature of a fluorescent green glow similar to the statuette of Our Lady of the Perpetual Green Light.

Mami kneeled in front of us, leading the prayers, her eyes glued to the picture of St. Anne and the Virgin Mary hanging on the wall over her bed. "Hail Mary, full of Grace, the Lord is with thee . . ." The words poured from her in a steady stream of devotion. Like runners on a relay team, when my sister and I heard the words and *blessed is the fruit of thy womb, Jesus,* we took the baton handoff and sprinted as fast as possible spouting the second half of the prayer.

"Holy Mary Mother of God, pray for us sinners now and at . . ." we chanted in a rhythmic monotone like fast-talking auctioneers. I never paid close attention to the words we spoke; I didn't stop to think about what they actually meant; I just said what I was told. Soon I grew bored and yawned, glancing at the clock with the cracked face on the nightstand, hoping our communications with the divine would not force me to miss *The Twilight Zone.*

Impatience was not my only sin. During our worship I once made the fatal mistake of peeking at my sister, who looked a vision of piety—eyes gazing toward heaven, dressed in white, her long, jet black hair braided in two. Like a lizard she waited, nimble, deadpan, and adroit; when our mother turned away, she stuck her tongue out in my direction, then flicked it back without missing a beat of the "Lord's Prayer."

An avalanche of laughter poured from me—unstoppable and ill-timed.

"*Cá-lla-te!*"—Quiet!—my mother said, her head spinning toward me, enunciating all three syllables as if I was deaf rather than impertinent.

I tried defending myself, but my cackles rendered my speech into stutters. As words escaped me, all I managed to do was point weakly at Lilly. But when Mami turned to look at her, my sister pointed back to herself, her innocent expression that of a martyr unjustly accused of wrongdoing.

With a choice between her obedient oldest daughter or her scrappy younger child, our mama bear always believed the former.

Mom's hairy eyeball tempered my outburst. I got back on track with my Hail Marys and did my best to behave. But Pandora and I shared something in common: a curious nature. My gaze veered toward Lilly, a Venus flytrap waiting for me to fall into her snare. When her tongue moved underneath her upper lip and her eyes widened, my sister transformed into a chimpanzee.

It was more than I could stand. I dropped my head into a pillow, hoping to stifle my uncontrollable cackling, but when I surfaced from under the cushion, and took another look at my sister's face, my convulsive laughing fit resumed.

Today, as my high school friends sat in the back seat of our station wagon listening to Mom communicate with the Virgin Mary via her rosary, shame torched my ears. *It'll be over soon,* I told myself. *It's only a twenty-minute drive.* As Mom prayed to her unseen gods, I prayed to mine for a quick end to my disgrace.

I was sorely disappointed. My mother's next statement nearly compelled me to open the car door and fling myself into oncoming traffic.

"*Resa,*" she said.

I stared at her, incredulity stealing my words. Not only was she praying out loud in Spanish in front of my high school friends, she was now insisting that I pray with her. I mumbled something in response.

She slapped my thigh with the back of her hand, her message clear. "*Resa,*" she said again, louder this time.

I didn't have to be a mind reader to know I had better get praying or face her wrath at home.

"*Ave Maria, Madre de Dios…*" I recited the words like a puppet, stealing glances at my watch and hoping my prayers would create a miracle to speed up time.

Mom's eyes glanced in the rearview mirror and inspected her passengers in the rear seat, as if expecting them to take part in the prayerfest. I peeked over my shoulder at a cute blond-haired boy, an atheist whose father drove a Beamer. He grinned back, amused.

The after-school carpool ride was just as wretched as the morning drive. While the other parents let us listen to Led Zeppelin, Stevie Wonder, or Earth, Wind & Fire on their car radios, my mom did not. When it was her turn to drive we listened to the Mexican radio station. For half an hour, twangy five-string guitars, lively violins, blaring trumpets, and a plucky guitarrón accompanied the *ay-ay-ay-ays!* of the mariachi musicians.

This humiliation, as an insecure thirteen-year-old, in front of my peers was something I could only combat by slinking down into my seat.

"Don't slouch," Mom said.

I studied her for sometime and wondered what I had done to deserve this life.

Perhaps it was guilt that made Mom want to make things right, because a few days later I found her sitting on my bed with a book on her lap.

"It's a journal," she said, handing me the red hard cover. "You can write down all your thoughts here."

Mami knew I wanted to be a writer. When my seventh-grade English teacher, Mr. Wormel, had given me a D+ on a writing assignment and then informed me I would never be a writer, Mom made a special trip to school and confronted him, insisting he was wrong.

"You can be anything you want to be," she told me later.

Motivated by her belief in me, I worked harder on my next assignment. When I got it back from the teacher, it boasted an *A*, with the word *Excellent* beside it. When Mr. Wormel asked me how I'd made so much progress in such a short amount of time, I told him what Mom had said about being anything I wanted to be—and that what I wanted to be was an author like those whose names lived on the dusty bookcovers inside *the other house*.

When my mother handed me the journal, I thought she was supporting my dreams and acknowledging my passage into maturity. I opened the book and gently ran my finger down a cream-colored page. The journal's clasp had a keyhole, but Mami never gave me the key. *An oversight*, I decided. Or she'd found my gift in a thrift store, where so many items were missing their essential parts.

That night I wrote in the journal, sharing my most intimate thoughts with my new confidant, then slid it under my mattress to protect its secrets.

The following day Mom sat in my room again, my journal resting on her lap.

"How could you write all those things?" she asked, fury simmering underneath her detachment. I was taller than my mother by almost an inch by this point, but when she stood, her ire made her formidable.

She had read my private writings—burrowed into my most intimate reflections. It was a betrayal that was hard to swallow. For the next thirty years I would censor anything I put down on paper, always second-guessing my thoughts, even when it was simply a grocery list.

Mom tossed the journal onto my bed before marching out. I watched her go; the curtain clung to the back of her dress like a blue wedding train as she pushed through the fabric. Behind the voile, I watched her sit at the dining room table, her fingers separating whole pinto beans from the damaged ones before sliding them into a cooking pot.

I never wrote another word in that journal again.

That night, I sat with Iris in the dog pen, watching the moonlight through the leaves of the fig tree. During the day, I took her out of her kennel whenever I could. Occasionally, Daddy even allowed me to walk her around the block. But it was my mother who insisted that I put her back into her cell every night, and despite my protests she would never explain why.

Perhaps Mami lived in a cage of her own brought on by a past I was unfamiliar with. I could not say. But like a tiger I once saw pacing restlessly in his enclosure at the zoo, I struggled with the enigmatic confines of my life. No matter how many rosaries I prayed or how much I pleaded with Our Lady of the Perpetual Green Light, I did not expect to be set free—*ever*.

CHAPTER TWENTY-THREE

Rebel Yell

TO SURVIVE HIGH SCHOOL, I learned to be a chameleon and kept my true self hidden.

Whether I was with popular kids, book nerds, stoners, or regular Joes and Josies, I maneuvered through each clique by flashing a smile or mouthing off a sassy barb—anything to throw them off the scent of my freak flag. While some of my classmates enjoyed coming-of-age activities such as school dances, worshipping the sun at the local beach, and attending ball games, I went home as soon as the bell rang where I hung out with Iris, timed myself to see how long I could spin my basketball on my forefinger, and was in bed by 8:30 p.m. At school, I listened to girlfriends gossip about kisses from handsome football lettermen and who they planned on inviting to the upcoming Sadie Hawkins Dance.

"Who are you bringing?" Millie asked.

Thinking fast, I came up with, "I don't think I'm going. I have a boyfriend at another school and he's busy that weekend."

Necessity made me adept at creating many alibis to excuse my absence from school functions—*I have to babysit, we have guests that weekend, we're traveling out of town.* As my classmates rode into their futures on magic carpets, I watched enviously from the sidelines with no clue as to where my life was headed.

Now that athletics were off the table, I needed something else to ease my boredom. My only recourse was to study more and fill my head with new ideas. I enjoyed earning As on assignments, getting accolades from my teachers, and feeling the admiration of my classmates. Other than playing with Iris and the occasional visits from my siblings, attending school was the only time I felt stimulated, happy, and free of my parents' constraints.

"Why aren't you smiling in any of these pictures?" my cousin Marti asked as she turned the pages of a family photo album during one of her visits. I looked over her shoulder at the faded snapshot: At four years old, I stood in a cherry red dress beside my sister's life-size doll. The doll, wearing a similar red dress and matching black shoes, smiled sweetly; I looked sullen.

"What is there to smile about?" I snapped at Marti.

Mom was in the kitchen stirring a pot of beans on the stove, appearing indifferent to our conversation, but I knew she was listening. Without glancing up, she said, "*No hagas mala cara,*" referring to my grumpy face.

My scowl only deepened.

Ray, Art, and Lilly were well aware of how unhappy I was. With every visit home, they witnessed the ongoing war between my mother and me. Our battles lasted days, sometimes weeks. We seldom used words. Silence was our ammunition, stubbornness forged our shields, and bloodshed came from the wounds of our unraveling connection.

My *grumpy face* had its perks. When Art was studying at one of the most prestigious photography schools in the country, he sometimes paid me twenty-five cents to model for his assignments.

"Ready?" he'd say before pressing the camera's shutter. I nodded, grinning, large and toothy.

"Don't smile," he directed from behind the lens. "Look the way you usually do. Just pretend you're looking at Mami."

His direction worked. My somber expression peering through our front door window, a silhouette of me jumping rope against a stormy sky, and my frown while wearing a straw hat during a parade were some of the images my brother captured. My grim look, caught on celluloid, made it evident that a dark cloud brewed within.

On the morning of my first day of sophomore year in high school, I was brushing my hair in front of the mirror in the girl's bathroom before class, when Patsy, who I had gone to school with since first grade, walked in.

Patsy had smacked my back and congratulated me in front of our other friends for wearing my first bra after noticing the strap under my white blouse. In eighth grade, she'd told the entire class how grown up I was because I plucked my eyebrows—an act I'd done without Mom's blessing and one that had left my bushy arches looking like a field plowed by crazed orangutans.

Today, she opened her eyes freakishly wide and applied a coat of black mascara, then glanced away from her saturated lashes and looked me over. "Wow, you got pretty," she said. Her voluptuous figure, pencil-thin eyebrows, and expertise with a mascara wand made her an authority on teen beauty.

"You think so?" I asked, analyzing the mirror, hoping to steal a glimpse of what she saw.

Patsy nodded, then smacked her metallic red lips twice, as though she were kissing her own reflection. Satisfied by her appearance, she dropped her maquillage into her jeweled purse and left me alone to assess my transformation.

The morning bell, a three-minute alarm announcing the next period, instigated a frenzied rush of bodies racing across the schoolyard. The blare could have been a warning for a nuclear attack, for all it mattered to me. I stared into the looking glass, wondering when Froggy had left the building, because gazing back at me wasn't the gawky, bushy-eyebrowed, gap-toothed kid I was used to. Instead, my brown hair was shoulder-length and wavy, thanks to the perm I'd begged Mom to give me after witnessing Dorothy Hamill's sweeping hair wings on TV; my figure, though not as enticing as Patsy's, was proportional—my breasts and hips about the same size, my waist was slim—and thanks to Mom, the gap between my front teeth had been reduced to the size of a black sesame seed.

A year earlier, she'd offered me a surprising choice.

"For your birthday you can either get the space between your teeth fixed or you can have a *quinceañera*," she said.

Quinceañeras were the Mexican version of white America's sweet-sixteen parties, given on a girl's fifteenth birthday to commemorate her journey from child to womanhood. These coming-of-age celebrations were often as extravagant as weddings. I had been to several—including Lilly's, which was held in Mascota. The girls wore frilly cotton candy-like gowns of pastel pink and sky blue along with big hairdos. Often, mariachi music was involved. Based on this intelligence, it took me a heartbeat to make my decision.

"I'll take the teeth," I said.

Mami nodded, nonplussed. She knew I'd been dreading my fifteenth birthday, and that I wished for a *quinceañera* about as much as I hoped for food poisoning.

After three months of wearing a retainer, the space between my teeth had shrunk into a tiny gap. Before this, I didn't think of myself as pretty, but in that moment, smiling at the girl in the bathroom mirror, I glimpsed what Patsy was talking about.

And soon, boys started seeing it too.

Mike O'Malley found his way into my teenage heart by teasing me whenever he passed my locker. When he asked me to go out to the movies on Friday night, I didn't have to ask my parents for permission to know they would never give it.

Late at night as I lay basking in the glow of green fluorescence, I pictured Mike's chestnut-colored eyes, freckled nose, and nearly perfect lay-up, which he practiced on the basketball court at lunchtime. He'd grin when he spotted me watching, then dribbled the ball behind his back and between his legs before shooting again. But if I couldn't spend time with him other than during school hours, how would I ever keep his affections?

I remembered a conversation I'd overheard at my locker. A football player chock full of beans had bragged to a cheerleader that the night before, he'd sneaked out of his house to go to a party. I looked at my bedroom window, which did not require curtains since a hill of dented metal furniture blocked the view from the outside. *Would I dare?*

The following morning, I assessed the mishmash outside of my window, then got to work. Over the next few minutes, I stacked Pepe's empty birdcage, a chair missing its seat, and the scrap timber to one side, clearing a path just wide enough for me to fit through.

That night, I set the alarm clock for 10:30, then stuffed it under my pillow. Two hours later, I woke to my alarm's muffled cymbals. I checked in with myself and was relieved that my nerve had not abandoned me while I slept. I slipped out of bed.

My bare feet met the chilly linoleum, and I tiptoed to the window. When I unlatched the screen, its liberation was more than the decayed frame could handle: the rusty screen tumbled out, the metal edge banging onto the pointed legs of an inverted chair. With the speed of a fox caught in a chicken coop, I leaped into bed and feigned sleep, waiting for my mother to barrel through the blue curtain.

She never did.

Minutes later, I slipped silently over my desk and into the night air, pregnant with the sweet scent of freedom.

Under the night sky, Mike O'Malley and I sat arm in arm on the dewy grass beside the basketball courts of the now defunct St. Joseph's School, talking, joking, and necking—the perfect first date. I was a neophyte at making out, so I wasn't sure what Mike's lips were doing to my neck. His affectionate nibbles were not comfortable or romantic, but I allowed him to continue impersonating a famished octopus until he'd had his fill.

The following morning, my alarm clock's clanking pierced my brain. I slapped it silent, then opened my eyes.

"Uhhhhh," I uttered, drained of life—the result of sleeping only two hours.

I stumbled into the bathroom and looked in the mirror. A ghoul stared back—bleary-eyed, disheveled, and . . .

"What the!?" One look at my neck told me that Mike the Octopus had not been *kissing* my neck.

"Hickeys," I whispered into the mirror, aghast, certain the glass would keep my secret, but wondering how I would hide my activities from my all-knowing mother.

Although the weather announcer reported that the high in Santa Barbara would be 89 degrees that day, I wore a turtleneck sweater under my blouse to hide my neck from curious eyes. By fourth period, the humidity and tedium, combined with my exhaustion, were making me so drowsy that my forehead landed on my desk during algebra class.

"Feeling all right?" Sister Agnes asked, inspecting me through her bottle lenses.

"Yes, Sister," I lied, forcing my pencil to draw a hypotenuse triangle in my notebook.

On the ride home from school, I shared my late-night escapade with my fellow carpoolers. For dramatic effect, I pulled down my turtleneck's collar, revealing my suitor's affections.

You did not! Whoa! I would never do that! were some of the reactions from impressed classmates. Their admiration brought me a welcome shot of self-confidence. I no longer felt like some Mexican kid who lived in a ramshackle house surrounded by junk. In their eyes, I was a genuine rebel.

During religion class the next afternoon, a wrinkled note appeared on my desk. *Want to hang out tomorrow?* read Mike O'Malley's scribble. When the teacher turned to write on the chalkboard, I looked back. Mike sat low in his seat two rows behind me with his long legs outstretched, the brim of a baseball cap pulled down over his eyes.

The pencil he gripped between his pressed lips reminded me of Iris carrying a bone.

Tomorrow was Wednesday, which meant Mike was asking me to ditch school. It was a risky proposition. What if we got caught? The idea filled me with excitement, terror, and everything in between.

The wise answer would have been, *No,* but wisdom was not my guide; hormones were. We agreed to meet at ten the following morning at the bowling alley up the road from our high school.

When our carpool driver dropped us off the next day, instead of going to my first class, I hightailed in the opposite direction. At the bowling alley, Mike met me with a long kiss. Hand in hand, we walked together for about a mile until we reached his house, which was empty of the most important element—*adults.*

That afternoon we watched TV, talked about basketball, and made out, though I insisted hickeys were now off the table. Mike and I had ditched school together and I wore his teeth marks on my neck; these acts, I was certain, officially made him my boyfriend.

Before class the following morning, I dropped off a note at the dean's office excusing my absence the previous day. I wasn't afraid of getting caught, because I'd mastered forging Mom's signature. Side by side, the two autographs looked identical. No one would be the wiser.

During history class, while I was daydreaming about Mike's lips instead of the American Revolution, a senior student popped his head through the doorway. "Carlyn Montes De Oca is wanted in the dean's office," he announced like a military cadet at attention.

All eyes drifted from the teacher and fell on me. I closed my book and followed after the boy.

From behind an enormous desk in a spacious office, Mrs. Beal, an attractive, thickset blonde, held up my note as I walked in. "Did your mother really sign this note?" she asked.

I stared at my mother's forged signature and slowly shook my head, my life force ebbing.

The dean set the paper down in front of her and, with a quick movement of her nose, her glasses slid up, closer to her arctic blue eyes. "Mike O'Malley's mom called the office yesterday looking for him. But he wasn't in school. She asked if you were in school, and you weren't. I take it you ditched together?"

It was the end. By tomorrow, my parents would realize my sins.

Their judgment would be swift—their retribution, fierce.

"My mom is going to kill me," I whispered, more to myself than to Mrs. Beal. As time froze, I imagined the many ways I might die: beating, starving, death by mariachi music.

The dean gave her oversized glasses another nudge with her nose, just enough for me to notice mercy crossing her face. "Look, you're a good student. You're always on the honor roll and you've never been in trouble before. I'm not going to call your mom. But Mrs. O'Malley is. I'm telling you this now so you can tell your mother what you did before she calls."

The consensus among my classmates was that Mrs. Beal was a ball-buster. But the dean gave me a stay of execution, albeit a brief one. In my eyes, from that moment forward, Mrs. Beal was nothing short of an archangel.

At lunchtime, I found Mike hiding behind his locker door, looking sheepish.

"My mom doesn't want me to see you anymore," he said. "She thinks you're a bad influence." His eyes refused to meet mine. Instead, he grabbed his basketball and bounced it on the walkway.

As the ball's echo spread down the corridor I blinked repeatedly, trying to grasp what he was saying. Two years from now, Mrs. O'Malley would give our class a sex-education lecture that boiled down to *Say no to sex*. But for now, she just wanted her son to say no to *me*.

"She's planning on calling your mom on Saturday," Mike said, closing his locker door.

I thought he'd offer to carry my books as we walked to history class together, or whisper something funny to make me forget my impending death. Instead, he lifted his backpack onto his shoulder and wandered toward class alone, taking his affections—and mine—with him.

By the following week, Mike O'Malley's devotion would belong to another girl: Cindy Small, one of my best and prettiest friends. But I didn't know that yet—and besides, I had bigger worries to deal with.

That night and every night until Saturday, I fervently prayed to Our Lady of the Perpetual Green Light to get me out of the mess I was in. *Please, please, please help me.* I repeated those words so many times they echoed all night in my dreams.

The following Saturday morning, a blast of mariachi music woke me. At some point that day, Mrs. O'Malley would call and ask to speak to my mother. I was fifteen years old, and certain I would never reach sixteen.

I hadn't a clue when Mike's mom would call or what to say to her when she did. I focused on doing my Saturday chores near the telephone. Since our house could never be tidy enough or sufficiently organized, I was replete with tasks. Luckily, Mom worked a full day at the beauty salon and Dad spent the entire afternoon absorbed in projects throughout the yard.

When the lunch hour arrived and went and the phone remained silent, I dared to hope that Mrs. O'Malley had changed her mind. After all, there were five O'Malley children besides Mike to distract her.

As the minutes ticked, I forgot about the O'Malley threat and the heartbreak of being dumped by her freckle-faced son. I turned on my favorite weekend show. Unlike Lilly, who preferred *American Bandstand*, I was more of a *Soul Train* kind of gal. While the Spinners, Marvin Gaye, and Gladys Knight belted out their tunes and the audience members danced a Soul Train Line, I boogied across my living room, unaware the phone was ringing. When I finally registered the sound, I decreased the TV's volume, ran into the dining area, and yanked the receiver off its cradle.

Breathless, I brought the mouthpiece to my lips. "Hello," I said, clearing my throat and hoping I sounded older than fifteen.

"Mrs. Montes De Oca?" asked a woman's voice. Her tone was serious, like that of a doctor calling to say the person on the other end of the line has developed an incurable disease and only has three weeks left to live.

I considered taking a message or pretending I was Lilly. But my death wish brought me to new heights. "Yes?" I replied with a confidence that surprised me.

The woman said nothing. I'd blown my cover. It was over. I was dead. But then . . .

"This is Mrs. O'Malley, Mike's mom," the voice on the other end replied.

"Yes," I answered, throwing in a touch of impatience that I thought made me sound more mature.

"Well . . . I'm calling to apologize . . . for any influence my son may have had on your daughter . . . for ditching school, I mean."

"Yes," I said again, adding an air of aloofness. Just as with her signature, I imitated my mother's voice perfectly. "Thank you so very much for calling."

"But . . . I just wanted to say . . ."

I set the phone down on the cradle and cut Mrs. O'Malley off mid-sentence. I waited, expecting her to ring back, but she never called again.

On Monday, I shared my Saturday drama with my best friend, Lindy, near the bulletin board where the Honor Role was being posted by the cadet boy.

The list contained the grade point averages of the highest-ranking students during the last quarter. A rebel in her own right, soft-spoken Lindy listened to my animated play-by-play of Mrs. O'Malley's phone call. She offered me a piece of her chocolate bar while shaking her head in disbelief.

Between the two of us, I was not the troublemaker. Lindy didn't bother looking at the list for her name; she was failing religion class and would soon transfer to a public high school where she could dress how she wanted, smoke pot, and not have to answer to Mrs. Beal's lectures.

Carol, another friend, approached the board, scanned the list, and found her name near the top. Then she spotted mine—so close to the bottom it nearly didn't fit on the page.

"Hey Carlyn, what are you doing way down there?" she asked.

Since the previous quarter, my name had plunged from a 3.8 grade point average to a 3.0.

"What's the matter with you?" She looked me up and down as if stupid was my new school uniform.

I thought about wowing her with my story of sneaking out of my house in the middle of the night to meet Mike, or of forging my mother's signature or impersonating her on the telephone, but I knew delinquency would not impress Carol.

"You're smart," she chided. "You can do better than that."

Carol was five feet tall and as sharp as a ninja's blade. Her opinion as my peer carried a significant punch. I might be a rebel in certain people's eyes, including my own, but to Carol, my dismal grades were nothing to write home about—and that stung.

Even after my narrow escape from Mrs. O'Malley's censure, I continued sneaking out of my bedroom window. I met up with friends at the local Fosters Freeze stand or simply wandered barefoot in the grassy field next door. This was my only way to escape the stranglehold of Mom's rules—even if only for a short while. But motivated by Carol's judgment and an actual love for learning, I studied hard that quarter, and soon my grade point average leaped to a 4.0.

I didn't consider then that my grades would one day be my golden ticket out of Escondido Road—toward a future I'd never even imagined, and far away from my mother's rule.

CHAPTER TWENTY-FOUR

Post-Traumatic Daughter Disorder

"THERE'S A SCHOOL DANCE on Friday night. Can I go?"

"No."

"Can I go to Lindy's next Saturday?"

"No."

"Will you sign this so I can get my driving permit?"

"No."

"But I'm seventeen and all the other kids got their licenses last year!"

"No, no, no, and NO!" Mom's steely finality left little doubt she was fed up with my begging.

"But why?" I asked her.

Her stony silence answered me.

The word *no* appeared in my life so often that I began reacting to it in a peculiar way. It started with a few tears, then graduated to uncontrollable weeping; it was as if my nervous system had reached its capacity of *nos* for a lifetime.

"I don't know what's wrong with me," I stuttered between sobs, my body shaking. *Why was this upsetting me so much?*

Mami took my hands in hers and looked into my eyes. The hairy eyeball bored its way inward, hoping to find a hint of what was causing my strange malady. I didn't feel Mom's criticism; I felt her worry.

"Can I get a job?" I asked a few days later. "There's an opening on Saturday afternoons at the health food store in town."

Of course, I expected Mom to dismiss my request with her usual *no*, so when she nodded *yes*, I was astonished.

I thought I was hallucinating, so I kept rambling. "Lilly's friend Tom owns the shop. You remember Tom, right?"

"Te dije que sí"—*I said yes.* Mami's response was gruff but to me it sounded like a choir of angels singing "Hallelujah."

Three hours a week working at Carpinteria Health Foods inspired my lifelong love for healthy living. I learned the art of making avocado sandwiches and whipping up strawberry-coconut smoothies, and the ding of the cash register after each sale felt like I had hit a home run. Every Saturday, I left the store with fifteen dollars in my pocket and a dose of self-confidence in my being.

Working had another unexpected effect on me: my cryptic crying stopped. Now, whenever my mother said *no*, having a job of my own was the cushion that softened the bite.

One day after work a faded red GMC Travelall pulled up in front of the store. The car's coat was oxidized, but its engine purred—restored by my father and brothers' meticulous industry.

"Wanna ride?" Art asked from the driver's side as I walked out the shop's door.

The distance between my house and Carpinteria Health Foods was only half a mile. Walking at a snail's pace gave me an extra fifteen minutes of freedom to myself, but hanging out with my cool older brother was something I eagerly looked forward to.

"Do you think you'll go away to college?" Art asked while we idled in front of the red light at the intersection of the two main streets in town.

"Go away? What do you mean, go away?"

Art gave me a sideways glance as if to say, *What do you mean what do I mean?*

"Well, yeah," he said. "Haven't you thought about it? What do you want to do with the rest of your life?"

Until this point, I was convinced that Ray, Art, and Lilly knew every-thing there was to know. But as I looked at him now, I was sure my brother didn't know a darn thing.

"What are you talking about?" I said, watching the streetlight change from red to green. "I'm never getting out of that house."

"Carlyn, in a year you'll be gone," Art said as he shifted the grinding gears.

I had a job now, and I was allowed to walk home by myself from time to time, but when it came to leaving the homestead, I was certain of my fate.

"They're never going to let me go anywhere," I insisted. "I'm never getting out of here." Feeling stifled, I rolled down the window to get some air. My mother had always told me what to do; why would things change now? I would live out the rest of my years on Escondido Road and continue to sneak out my bedroom window just to get a whiff of freedom every now and again. Sure, I'd go to college—the local city college or UCSB, like Art had done—but I'd never leave home like my friends were preparing to do. This was my life, and I was resigned to it.

The following morning, as I ate breakfast and read the back of a cereal box, Mom dropped a stack of envelopes beside me.

"They're for you," she said in a curt tone as she hurried about the kitchen, running late for work.

I rarely got mail so I excitedly ripped the packets open. Inside, I found colorful brochures advertising trips to Africa.

When Mom had torn my Jimi Hendrix poster off my bedroom wall, I'd retaliated by plastering pictures of gorillas, chimpanzees, and Jane Goodall over my bed that I'd cut from fossilized *National Geographic* magazines that sat in boxes on our couch. Inside these publications, I'd also found mailers for free travel information. I must have mailed fifty of these cards, and now the responses were filtering in. Pictures of elephants crossing wide savannas, hippos with mouths agape, and the amber stare of a gorilla made me long for a country I had only seen on television and read about in books. I might never travel to Africa, but that morning, Africa visited me.

As I rifled through the brochures, lost in a fantasy of befriending Jane Goodall and meeting great apes, my mother asked me a question. I mumbled back something unintelligible. Lately, she and I communicated mostly by mumbles, grumbles, or silence.

I don't remember what I said or how I said it that morning, but whatever it was, she was not happy about it. When I got up from the table, Mom blocked my way. Like a wasp ready to sting, her hand swung toward my face—and without thinking, my arm swept upward. I caught her wrist with the side of my forearm and held it there—*easily.*

Though I no longer played organized sports in school, my love for basketball was alive and well. After dinner, and into the night, I shot basket after basket until dark. While watching TV, I often did twenty pushups and a hundred sit-ups to impress my parents. A fan of Dad's well-defined biceps, I never complained when I carried the trashcans out on garbage day, since that was how he told me he'd developed those powerful arms. I may have been shorter than everyone else in our family, but I was tougher than I looked.

Shock was not an expression Mom ever showed—and at this crossroad in our uncivil war, she was not about to surrender any ground. She swung at me a second time with her free hand; like before, I blocked her, this time with my left arm.

A slight smile—unexpected, unplanned, and uncontrolled—slowly spread across my lips. My mother was not stronger than me. With that realization, the lifelong trance I'd been in, the one where I'd been convinced this was true, vanished.

It had not always been this way. In kindergarten, a teacher once asked me how I'd gotten the raised marks on my right arm.

"I don't know," I lied, remembering that earlier that morning my mother had struck me across the arm with my father's weathered leather belt.

Slaps, spankings, and the strap were not uncommon forms of

punishment from both my parents. I was used to it. I was afraid of it. And I provoked their anger more than any of my siblings did.

But at the breakfast table that morning, supported by images of Africa, a belly full of Corn Flakes, and my new superpower, Mami and I both knew she could never physically hurt me again. She dropped her arm, along with her anger. We exchanged no words. As she turned away, I noticed her weariness; it was as if the pillars of control supporting her reign of authority had just cracked.

A few minutes later, I joined my mother in the Kingswood.

Our carpooling days were dwindling; most of my friends had their driver's licenses and had been gifted cars that they now proudly drove to school. I longed for both, and had neither. Still, I'd rather suffer without a license or a car than endure the humiliation of praying Hail Marys in front of my peers.

As Mom pulled out her rosary beads today, however, she didn't demand I pray with her. We had arrived at a new and unknown reality— one where I recognized her as fallible, vulnerable, and all too human. Today, instead of our voices supplicating The Almighty in unison, my mother prayed to her own god in silence.

CHAPTER TWENTY-FIVE

The Golden Ticket

DURING MY SENIOR YEAR IN HIGH SCHOOL, I contracted a severe malady common in irritable teenagers approaching graduation: *senioritis.*

Studying had once liberated me. Now, learning lulled me into a stupor. A growing ennui and lack of motivation fed into a melancholy, which spread beyond the borders of Escondido Road. I was sullen with my friends and temperamental with my siblings, and the guilt from my wretched behavior fed into self-loathing.

Perhaps my misery affected my parents, because they loosened their reins—*slightly.* Dad taught me to drive, I got my license, my bedtime changed from 8:30 to 9:30 p.m., and I was even allowed to attend my senior prom.

Despite these adjustments, my itch for freedom worsened. I longed to soar. But as long as I was a parrot trapped in a cage, I wasn't going to fly anywhere.

I sat at my desk during Spanish class, my head resting on one fist while my other hand doodled Snoopy the dog wearing a fez. As Señora Reinhardt conjugated verbs, I lip-synced my responses with the rest of my classmates: "*Yo voy, tu vas, ellas van, nostros vamos . . .*"

I yawned loudly, inciting giggles from my chums. I wanted to study French as Lilly had, but Mom had decided my penance for refusing to talk Spanish at home was to take it at school. Here, in Spanish 101, I had no choice but to speak the language of my ancestors.

It wasn't the first time Mom had thwarted me in this way. Many a Saturday as a little girl, I'd sat on the world's stiffest sofa, listening to my sister play "Fur Elise" on her piano and dreaming that one day I too would move my hands with grace across the spinet's keys. When I begged for lessons, however, Mom insisted I learn guitar instead. When I argued, she laid down the law: it would be guitar strings or nothing.

I took lessons after school with my cousin Katrina, who sang at our local church with her sisters on Sunday morning. Under her tutelage I discovered the poetry of Bob Dylan, learned Joni Mitchell's opinion about clouds, and absorbed the protest melodies of Crosby, Stills, Nash & Young. I played these tunes on a large sunburst beauty with two F-holes that I begged Mami to buy at a swap meet because it reminded me of my heartthrob David Cassidy's guitar on *The Partridge Family*.

I liked practicing my music in private. Whenever I spotted Mom standing behind the blue curtain in my doorway, listening to me play, my hand stopped mid-strum and only returned to the strings when I was sure she was no longer there.

Mom wouldn't force me to play for her when she was alone with me in the house, but when visitors came by, she frequently invited them into my room and insisted I sing and play for them. When she did, I glared at her and crossed my arms in front of my chest. But you didn't say *no* to my mother. Her flinty expression conveyed a simple message: *If you don't do what I want, there will be a price to pay.* So, like a trio of misfits, awkwardness, anger, and I banded together and played "Leaving on a Jet Plane"—which, in that moment, I was desperate to do.

My musical abilities bordered on the mediocre as it was, and during these forced performances humiliation fogged my memory, causing my fingers to forget the location of chords that I'd known only a minute before. The expressions on my relatives' faces as I sang offkey made my shame that much worse.

When my recital ended and the audience abandoned my room, I'd toss my guitar into the corner, as though it was the instrument's fault that my life was crap. Not long after, I gave up practicing altogether, and Mom canceled my lessons.

In Spanish class, Señora Reinhardt interrupted my musings, calling on me to answer a question she'd just asked the class. With little thought, I rattled off a response in Spanish.

"How did you know that?" she asked. Her pale blue eyes opened wide like a meerkat.

"I don't know." I shrugged. "It just sounded right when I said it."

Señora Reinhardt turned to my classmates and announced, "When you get to a point where you can say that to me, you will have mastered the language."

Carol, my moral compass since the day she reproached me for my poor showing on the dean's list, gave me a thumbs-up from across the room.

A knock shifted our attention to the open doorway where Sister Madeline, a tall redhead, waited patiently. The sisters had ditched their traditional attire years before. Today, Sister Madeline wore a plain, buttoned-at-the-shoulders dress that was the color of a paper sack.

"I'm sorry to disturb. But if you don't mind, I'd like a word with Carlyn."

All eyes turned to me as if I was in trouble. I hadn't ditched school since the Mike O'Malley incident sophomore year, so I couldn't figure out what I'd done wrong.

Señora Reinhardt waved me toward Sister Madeline. I grabbed my backpack and followed her to her office.

"How come you haven't been in to see me?" Sister Madeline inquired once we sat in her cubicle.

"About what?"

"College."

"College?" I repeated, as if it were a foreign word.

"Yes, what do you want to study? Where do you want to go? What do you want to be?" Her sincere attention on my wants and desires felt unfamiliar. It warmed me to the bone like soothing hot broth on a wintry day.

I blurted out the first thought that came to mind: "A journalist." For a moment I allowed myself to imagine a reporter's life working for *National Geographic*—on assignment in Africa, interviewing Jane Goodall.

"With your grades, you can go to some good colleges."

I shook my head. "I don't think so."

"And why not?" Sister Madeline studied me through copper-colored glasses that complemented her cinnamon spice mane.

Even with my closest friends, I kept the details of my home life to myself. No one knew my parents were hoarders, or the extent of their overprotective natures, or the depths of my shame. But looking into Sister Madeline's concerned gaze persuaded me to trust her with my thoughts.

"My parents will never let me go," I admitted.

"Why do you say that?"

"I just know it," I said.

Sister Madeline blinked three times, as if sending Morse code to the angels. "Well, we'll see about that."

Leaning back in her chair, she motioned me toward the door with a tilt of her head.

As I dozed in Spanish class a few weeks later, listening to Señora Reinhardt read a conversation between Pedro the Cat and Coco the Clown, Sister Madeline appeared in the doorway.

"May I make an announcement?" she asked, her sack dress replaced by a floral print. Señora Reinhardt nodded, her meerkat figure tightening as if danger lurked.

Sister Madeline stepped inside the classroom holding a manila envelope in her freckled hands. "I'm pleased to announce that Carlyn Montes De Oca was just accepted to three prestigious universities for the upcoming year: UCSB, USC, and Loyola Marymount University. She has received scholarships to all of them."

Clapping and cheers filled the room. Stunned by the news, I stared at Sister Madeline, unwilling to let her out of my eyesight lest I wake up and discover I'd fallen asleep in class and was still dreaming.

When she passed me the pouch, the weight of it in my hands convinced me I was awake.

"Give these papers to your parents, choose a college, and return the documents to me signed," she said crisply.

"Thank you," I whispered reverently as if I'd just been presented with the Dead Sea Scrolls.

Then I glimpsed Señora Reinhardt's wastepaper bin in the corner and imagined my mother tossing the paperwork into our trash—just before I carted the can outside in order to firm up my biceps.

When I walked through the front door of our house after school that day I immediately spilled the beans, telling Mom all about Sister Madeline's visit.

"You'll go to UCSB," she said, shattering any hope of my escape.

UCSB, though a perfectly respectable school, was located in Santa Barbara, which meant that I'd be living at home. I remembered my conversation with Art in the Travelall when I told him my parents would never let me leave Escondido Road. I was sure of it now.

"Tsks!" I hissed my disapproval without caring about the consequences of my disrespect, then stormed past my mother and fled to my room, where I flung myself onto my bed.

From her glass nook, Our Lady of the Perpetual Green Light smiled down as if all was perfect in her world—but only a miracle would make things right in mine.

When Dad arrived from work, he found Mom in the kitchen, preparing our evening meal. Their words turned into whispers. I tiptoed to my bedroom doorway and stood behind the blue curtain, straining to overhear their conversation. When the word *colegio* reached my ears, I picked up Sister Madeline's envelope, kissed it for luck, then joined them.

"My teacher asked me to give you this," I said, putting the envelope into Dad's hands—thick, callused, and blemished from years of manual work in the sun.

"Tell me what the sister said, Chiqui," Dad said, his voice calm.

I reiterated the nun's announcement word for word while Mom tackled the lid on a tin of green beans with a can opener.

"You'll go to UCSB like your brother," Mom said after my explanation, flipping the can's contents into a stainless-steel pot.

"Where do you want to go?" Dad asked.

I didn't expect this question from him, neither did my mother, who darted a sharp glance in his direction.

Although I'd convinced myself my chances of going to Loyola were zero, I daydreamed of attending this university in Los Angeles, two and a half hours from Carp. My classmates who planned to attend there had told me that not only was the campus close to the beach, but *Playboy* magazine had also rated Loyola the third biggest party school in California. Loyola did not boast a journalism department, but there was a communication arts branch where I could study film and television production. Movies? TV? I could study my favorite pastimes? Loyola sounded like heaven on earth.

"Loyola!" The word burst out as I dared to dream big.

Dad looked at the envelope, as if staring at it would reveal something more. Mom ignored us, stirring the contents of the pot on the stove forcefully as if trying to quell a vegetable mutiny.

"Then that's where you'll go," Dad said.

"*Que?!*" Mom glanced up, clearly surprised and ready to argue, but a firm glance from my father stopped her mid-sentence.

"*Todo hombre muere, no todo hombre vive, Mary,*" Mom heard his words, as did I… *Every man dies, but not every man lives.* Dad's decision deflated my mother and sent my dreams soaring. "I'll sign these tonight. Take them to the sister in the morning," he said, then left the kitchen without another word.

The winds of change struck me like a long-awaited thunderbolt from heaven. After seventeen years of strict house rule, my freedom was within reach.

That night, I lay in bed under the glow of our Lady of the Perpetual Green Light, unable to sleep, waves of excitement flooding every molecule in my body. In three months, Desmond Hall at Loyola Marymount University would be my new home. A place where I would make my own decisions and come and go as I pleased.

I remembered the last time Dad had defied Mom and tried to get my dogs back after she sent them to the pound. Why would he let me go to Loyola when she was determined to keep me here?

The answer, I would later realize, lived in the regrets of his youth.

My father loved to learn. But he never made it past the sixth grade. His father's death and the ensuing responsibilities of caring for his mother and siblings forced him to leave school. In *the other house*, among the mildewing paperbacks of *And Then There Were None* and *Charlotte's Web*, I'd discovered radio repair mail order manuals that my father had sent away for so he could study them at night after work. In this way, he'd advanced his knowledge enough to repair shortwave radios, record players, and TV sets.

My mother also never stopped learning. Before she became a beautician, she'd taught English to Spanish speakers, taken sign language classes, and enrolled in a typing course. Countless times she encouraged relatives to better themselves, whether it was by losing weight to get healthier, leaving unhealthy relationships, or going to night school. Because of her, several people in my extended family ultimately found their careers as hairstylists.

The education Dad never had for himself, he wanted for his children. Mom desired the same thing, but preferred I remain at home where she could protect me. From what? I did not know.

. . .

Fearing my parents might rescind my upcoming release, I decided to toe the line and become the best-behaved daughter imaginable during my last days at 5515 Escondido Road. If I adhered to absolute obedience, I reasoned, they'd have no excuse to withhold my future.

Acquiescence didn't come easily, and the closer I drew to freedom, the more I resented living among the disordered overflow inside and outside of our home. But three months was a blink of an eye compared to the seventeen-year sentence I'd already served. Nothing would impede my golden ticket out of Escondido Road. Not my mother's anger. Not her intimidation. Not even her love.

"You'll need new clothes for college," Mom said as I rifled through the sales rack at Sears.

I picked out a cotton sundress, a handful of blouses, and two pairs of jeans—all clothing *I* chose, not garments she dictated I wear.

There were other changes too. My father put me in charge of paying the household utility bills, I learned to use a checkbook, and my bedtime fell by the wayside altogether. With my new driver's license in hand, I even drove to Santa Barbara on an errand for Mom one afternoon. Every second of that journey—from the wind blowing my hair wildly to the radio blasting top ten hits—I savored like a chocolate mint melting on my tongue.

As things got better, they also turned worse. Despite my efforts to be the perfect daughter, my mother and I continued our silent tug-of-war between her need to control and my eagerness to escape. My girlfriends confided in their moms as if they were buddies. That kind of closeness seemed unimaginable between Mom and me.

Does she even care about me? I wondered, as I had so many times before.

Days before my departure to Loyola, I was standing in the living room, ironing my new sundress, when Mom came up beside me.

I expected her criticism. From washing the dishes to making my bed, nothing I did ever seemed good enough. Her way was always better.

Mom stared at the iron gliding back and forth over the yellow daisies on the fabric. *Don't do it that way, do it like this*; I imagined her rebuke and entertained sassy comebacks in my mind—but of course never said them out loud. I bit my cheek, determined not to let my emotions get the better of me. Come heaven or hell, Loyola was a port I would fight any storm to reach.

I drew a deep breath, bracing for the sting of her judgment.

"Everything I've done is because I love you," she said so softly that I thought I imagined her words.

Like a rogue wave, Mom's vulnerability knocked my ship off course.

When I replay this moment in my mind, as I have thousands of times since, I think of what I could have done differently, instead of what I did. I could have turned and hugged my aging mother and forgiven her. I could have said, *I love you and always will.* But even though Mami had just exposed her soft underbelly to me, I could not bring myself to show mine. The iron curtain remained steadfast, uncompromising, and unyielding. The barrier I'd forged held strong, fortified by my resentment. To surrender my position and throw my arms around her now would destabilize me. Tears filled my eyes, but I refused to let them spill. I forced myself to swallow them instead, adding to the enormous lump stuck in my throat. I said nothing and continued ironing the same spot I had been for the last five minutes.

Mom didn't tell me I'd punished the dress long enough. She did not get angry at me because I refused her tenderness. Instead, she walked into the kitchen and finished making the sandwiches we'd eat on our journey south. Our moment for connection evaporated, and we never spoke of it again. The key to the iron curtain remained lost, and not even a mother's love could find it.

CHAPTER TWENTY-SIX

Junkyard Girl
Goes to College

THE DAY OF MY LIBERATION, in August 1979, looked much like any other.

Outside, the summer sun melted a thick layer of early-morning fog, but inside our house, the chill between Mom and me showed no signs of lifting.

A month earlier, I'd packed my belongings into two cardboard boxes and a suitcase with a duct-taped handle. Eager to embrace adulthood but not yet willing to relinquish every vestige of childhood—Happy, my teddy bear, and Bernie Bernard, a talking dog—took up an entire box. My favorite books occupied the second carton. My new clothes filled the case. At night, before I drifted off, my eyes rested on these three symbols of my deliverance. In the morning, as soon as I woke up, I searched them out. My baggage reminded me that college wasn't a fantasy.

On this my last morning at home, I gave my bedroom a final scan, making sure nothing critical was left behind. Our Lady of The Perpetual Green Light, with whom I'd shared my bedroom with for so many years and whom I begged for so many favors in silent conversations, stood as she always did—immobile, pleasantly smiling, arms outstretched. *Thank you*, I mouthed, and I meant it a hundred times over.

Dad poked his head inside the blue curtain. "Be ready to leave by eleven," he said, tapping his wristwatch like a train conductor on a tight schedule.

I spent the next hour sitting beside Iris in her pen, wishing I owned an enchanted chest to bring her with me. My father liked my dog but Mom complained that she was too much work. Her words brought back memories of the day in Arizona when I discovered that she'd surrendered my dogs to the pound. A surge of powerlessness moved through me now, just as it had when I'd tried to run away but couldn't muster the courage. I was abandoning my best friend.

Iris' whimpers confirmed that she knew this. *I have to save myself,* I rationalized, fighting the guilt that warned me this was a myth. I stroked her fur and fed her kitchen scraps. "I'll be back, girl," I promised, uncertain when that would be.

"Time to leave," Dad said when he found us together. I kissed Iris' soft head, long and hard, breathing in her fur as if forcing her memory into my fabric, then reluctantly dragged myself away.

When I stepped out of the pen, Dad handed me the keys to the car. "You drive," he said.

I glanced at my mother, an automatic gesture on my part from years of asking for permission. She didn't give it; her face remained a neutral slate as she stepped into the back of the station wagon.

I'd never driven longer than thirty minutes at a stretch. A two-and-a-half-hour trip lay ahead. Times had changed.

As my feet crossed the threshold and into my dorm room on the second floor of Desmond Hall at Loyola Marymount University, the gods smiled. Enormous, immaculate windows covered its south side, inviting in the brilliant California sunshine. Room 221 was double the size of my bedroom at home and contained matching single beds, two cavernous desks, a sink, and a tiny fridge.

When we arrived, the roommate I was assigned wasn't there. But three matching tan suitcases, a far cry from my cardboard boxes, rested on one bed. Over the headboard was a black poster with a red tongue between ruby-colored lips and the words *Rolling Stones*. Another poster with a second set of lips hung on the closet door. In dripping blood, it was captioned *Rocky Horror Picture Show*.

Mom regarded the images, her grip tightening on her vinyl handbag. She had ripped my Jimi Hendrix poster, a lot less provocative than this, off my wall because she thought Jimi and his guitar resembled Satan and his pitchfork. Lucifer or not, I hoped she wouldn't tear off my room-mate's posters and embarrass me in the first minutes of my new life.

The din in the hallway went from buzzing to raucous as parents dropped off their excited teenagers. Dona from Long Beach, my new roommate, sauntered through the doorway wearing peach-colored terrycloth short shorts and a strapless shirt. The aroma of cigarette smoke lingered behind her.

I held my breath, certain that Cool Dona was more than my parents had bargained for. Their next words would certainly be *vámonos—let's go.*

But they remained silent.

Two exuberant fraternity brothers wearing matching yellow shorts and navy T-shirts bounded into our room. Dona's cat-shaped eyes, reminiscent of Marlene Dietrich's, gave the fellows a once-over, deemed them beneath her, and returned to unpacking tank tops from her suitcase.

I was not as picky. "Hi!" I said, forcing my dimples into a perky smile.

"Hey, there's a party tonight in our dorm—you comin'?" College Boy Number One asked, tossing his sun-kissed hair to one side with a flick of his head.

I glanced at my roommate for guidance. Too cool to commit, Dona shrugged a shoulder as if saying, *Maybe, if you're lucky.* I peered at my parents, who shot a quick look at each other. I expected them to forbid it, but again, they said nothing.

"I'll be there!" I proclaimed—my first adult decision in eighteen years.

"Great, see you then!" The brothers from another mother darted out and stuck their heads into the room next door. "Hey, we're having a party—you comin'?"

"It's time to go." Dad's powerful arms wrapped around me, as if infusing me with his strength. He kissed the top of my head lightly. "Be a good girl, Chiqui," he whispered before stepping through the open door.

The door. It was the first time I was aware of the thick wooden structure. Gone was the thin blue drape. The key for unlocking—and locking!—this door was safe in my pocket. I reached for it. The sturdy metal reassured me my new life was happening.

Instead of a hug goodbye, Mom's fingertips made the sign of the cross from my forehead to my chest, then touched each of my shoulder blades as she murmured a blessing in Spanish to protect me from unknown danger. My cheeks fired red, my typical shame face, as I wondered what Cool Dona thought about this open display of religiosity. Her sultry green eyes caught mine placidly, as though she had seen it all.

"Bye, Mami," I whispered. I leaned in for a brief hug but her arms pulled me in closer and held me longer than she had in a very long time. Her embrace enveloped me like the warm waters of a mineral bath—nourishing, comforting, and eternal. For those few seconds I forgot all about our contentious past, and my shame dissipated into memory. I was a child once again, feeling the love in my mother's arms. Then, abruptly, she pulled away and followed in my father's footsteps.

I raced to the window and looked down at my parents' figures. Slowed by time, age, and life, they walked together across the grassy courtyard. Mom was sixty-two years old, Dad sixty-five. But today, as they left their youngest daughter behind with a cat-eyed roommate, eager college boys, and a frat party that would last into the early hours, they seemed older.

My parents turned the corner and disappeared from sight. I held my breath, waiting for them to come back. But they never did.

Finally, my breath released loud and long. *This is what freedom tastes like*, I thought to myself.

I didn't know it then, but that day marked the final time my parents would ever tell me what to do. Until now, they'd protected me by tethering me on a short leash. There would be no transition to a long line; in fact, there would be no leash at all. In my new home, in the presence of Cool Dona and the *Rocky Horror Picture Show* poster, I was baptized into adulthood, set free to determine my life's path and stand or fall by my choices.

But self-determination is not always easy, and the future is never as luminous as it seems.

PART FOUR

"Your heart and my heart
are very, very, old friends."
—Hafiz

CHAPTER TWENTY-SEVEN

The Nature of Love & Hate

WHAT HAPPENS WHEN, overnight, you step out from underneath an umbrella of control and into a downpour of freedom?

Like a kid with a sweet tooth left unattended in a candy shop, I tried everything university life offered: alcohol, sex, weed— rinse and repeat. I was so busy rabble-rousing during Frosh Week that I didn't even know classes had started until Cool Dona shook me awake one morning.

"Are you ever going to go class, or are you just partying your way through college?" she inquired before stripping me of the comforter I lay tangled in. My hands clamped onto my forehead as if they possessed the power to heal my pounding hangover. I pulled the comforter back over my head and groaned, then shoved it away again and forced myself onto my feet.

While my college friends earned degrees in biology, economics, and English, I learned the language of movie-making. As a film major, I met students from all walks of life who opined like seasoned experts over the movies of Francis Ford Coppola, Steven Spielberg, and George Lucas. Growing up on Escondido Road, my opinion had not been encouraged, and now I didn't have one to share. I felt unprepared for this life and hoped my savvy new friends would not discover I was a fraud.

Over the next four years I relished life at Loyola as one might take pleasure in a cold pool in the middle of a sunbaked desert. I came and went as I pleased, explored club life on the Sunset Strip with friends, worked on student films on weekends, and took a year to study abroad in Madrid, Spain. I even curbed my social schedule long enough to graduate with a bachelor's degree in Communication Arts.

Soon after graduation, I landed a film editing job at Lucasfilm, the home of the original *Star Wars* movies, located in the San Francisco Bay area.

To outside eyes, my world seemed enviable. With Loyola in the rear-view mirror, I moved to one of the most affluent areas in the country, lived in a cool country cottage with my dog, Iris, (whom I'd rescued from Escondido Road after Mom threatened to take her to the pound), and made enough money to work only seven months out of the year. When I wasn't film editing, I traveled and attempted my hand at writing screenplays. More importantly, Marin County, where I now lived, was six hours away from my parents' rule and the junkyard on Escondido Road. My future was a snowball of momentum, picking up speed as I sailed through life.

The only problem was the ball repeatedly crashed at the same junction. When it came to the complexities of love, I was a mess.

As a teenager, my parents had forbidden me dating and Mom had discouraged friendships with members of the opposite sex. Because of this, the rules of courtship had never been clear to me. To add to my confusion, the men I met in the film industry differed from the boys I dated in college. For approximately two months, the Toms, Joes, and Jims seemed smitten; then, without explanation, their affections switched to Ellens, Janes, and Lisas. Their sophistication enticed me as much as it perplexed me. Love, it seemed, was a mystery I was incapable of solving.

My peers navigated romance as easily as they did their grocery shopping. By contrast, my heartbreaks gutted me, exposing my entrails for vultures to feast on. Each failed relationship chipped at my self-worth, leaving me increasingly vulnerable as time went on. I wondered if there might be something wrong with me.

It didn't help matters that I tended to choose older men—often divorced and emotionally unavailable. (If they spoke with a British accent, all the better!)

One night, after being dumped by someone who fit this description, I lay down on my futon bed beside Iris. Her soulful eyes looked up into mine with concern as the tears from my break-up moistened her fur.

Why do I feel such intense abandonment? I wondered. *Where is this coming from?* Certainly not from my parents, who'd married in their early twenties and, I was certain, would remain together the rest of their lives. As distant as Mom was, and as much as I questioned her love, no doubt existed in my mind that she would be there for me if ever I needed her; all I had to do was pick up the phone and ask for her help. Which, of course, because of our strained history, I would never do.

A therapist had told me that my mother's emotional distance was a type of abandonment. I'd witnessed her remoteness growing up and become accustomed to it, and now I was replaying that dynamic in my relationships with men.

Her theory made sense, but not completely. Something lay deeper in my psyche—a primal wound I couldn't identify.

Early the following morning, I took Iris for a walk. She dragged behind me panting. I cupped her face in my hands, studying her expression; her eyes looked tired and her body quivered.

Later that afternoon, a local vet took a blood sample from her and ran tests. I didn't worry about what he would find. Iris was twelve years old, but I was a child in Neverland, expecting her to live forever.

"Cancer," the vet's voice said into the phone forty-eight hours later. The word pounded me like a two-by-four whacking my gut. "She has six months," he said before hanging up.

I looked down at Iris. She stared up at me, her forehead wrinkled as if wondering why I was worried, her bent ear falling over her eye like it had the first time I met her, a fat ball of fluff in a cardboard box.

Six weeks later, my dog was gone.

The dismay I felt over the end of my last relationship was harsh, but losing Iris was like being skinned alive. For days I cried, hunger eluded me, and sleep was my only salvation from the loneliness now sharing my bed.

A week later I drove toward the Marin Headlands, absorbed in a haze.

Usually, Iris copiloted my drives. But her nose sticking out the window, her mouth open as if laughing, her barks when we neared our destination—these were the domain of memory now. My dog's ashes rested beside me in a cheap plastic box on the passenger's seat of my pickup truck.

Most weekends, Iris and I hiked together on the open space of the breathtaking peninsula at the northern edge of the Golden Gate Bridge. Afterward we'd sit on a cliff, side by side, taking in the stunning views of San Francisco as twilight descended.

Today, I stood in the same spot. The container holding her ashes shook in my hands as waves of grief swept through me, their exhausting riptide keeping me from the safety of shore. I opened the box and peered at Iris' remains for seconds, or an eternity, until the gods sent a gust of wind, urging me to say goodbye.

I tipped out the sandy residue and let my dog's ashes soar over the vast waters of the Pacific Ocean. From my backpack I removed a purple iris, picked from my garden earlier that morning. My lips met the petals as though kissing my dog for the last time, then I released it over the edge. It tumbled against jagged rock and over mossy stones until the sea caught it and consumed it in its wake.

"I'm afraid if I hug you, you'll break," my friend Dara said, noticing my ten-pound weight loss in two weeks.

"I'm fine," I lied.

"How's it going, Susie Vega?" Ray asked over the phone, referring to the skinny folk singer whose dark melodies reminded him of the only two colors I wore these days: goth black and charcoal gray.

"Fine," I said between my teeth, annoyed by his needling.

"You sound awful," Lilly told me. "Did you and your boyfriend break up?"

"Yes, and I'm fine," I said, fed up with everyone's concern.

"Yeah? Well, you don't sound it. Here, talk to Mami."

"No, wait, Lilly!"—but before I could stop her, the phone passed to a familiar voice.

"I'm coming to see you," Mom said.

"Now isn't a good time for me. I'm busy with work . . ." I tried dissuading her, though I hadn't set foot inside an editing room in months.

"I'll be there as soon as I can," my mother replied, seeing right through me. For over a decade, I'd fought Mom's dominion, determined to win out. But today, I didn't have it in me to go the distance. I threw in the towel before the twelfth round.

From curbside at San Francisco Airport, I waited in my idling pickup truck and watched Mom walk toward me, pushing my niece Tracy's stroller ahead of her. Lilly worked long hours as a physical therapist, so she left Tracy at Escondido Road under Mom's care during the day. Mom had brought her along on this trip.

My niece's adoration for my mother, now seventy-one years old, was as palpable as Mom's unwavering devotion to her. This little girl showered her with hugs and kisses, and my mom returned her affections as though she were her own child. Seeing their tenderness for one another, I winced, wishing it had been this way for Mom and me.

"Hi, Mami." I gave her a hug before loading her luggage into the cabin.

Tracy reached up for me, her arms wide, face beaming. Like a proper aunt, I bent down and gave her a squeeze, but not even her unconditional love could pull me out of the dumps.

"Say cheese!" Mom said, snapping a picture of Tracy and me, as we strolled along Fisherman's Wharf the following day. My niece's baby teeth sparkled as her tiny hands clapped with excitement. I forced a smile.

Later, when I saw the photos, the joyful look across my face didn't match the gloom I felt inside. I stuck the Polaroid on my fridge as a reminder that although we might smile like angels, it doesn't mean we're not wrestling with our demons.

We spent five days together, Mom, Tracy, and I—and each hour was more awkward than the previous one. Losing my dog and boyfriend in such a short time weighed on me like a boulder, making it hard to hold a conversation. I needed to cry, but privacy in my six-hundred-square-foot cottage was in short supply. The iron curtain I'd forged in my childhood to keep Mom out had been rendered impenetrable by time. No matter how much her touch might bring me comfort now, breaking down in front of her would leave me defenseless, and that was a position I'd sworn I'd never be in again.

It wasn't easy for Mom to see me distressed. Her relationship with her own mother had also been one of control versus rebellion and now the film was playing back, with me replacing Mom as the main character in the drama. We clung to what we created: long-held patterns cemented by ego and disagreements that time was slow to mend.

To bridge our inelegance, Mom and I avoided painful subjects. During her visit, we never spoke of why she'd flown 350 miles to visit, or why I looked rail thin and refused to eat. We processed sorrow in different ways. After Abuelita died, I watched Mom deal with painful emotions while standing over a pot of beans, her hand gripping a ladle as if stirring her grief into the meal. My remedy for heartache was to climb into bed and allow sleep to usher me from reality, hoping that hours later, when my eyes opened again, the pain would be gone.

How one becomes a demonstrative mother and a loving daughter after years of conflict were rules of engagement neither of us understood. So Mom spent the hours playing games with Tracy, crocheting a blanket, and making enchiladas in the hope that my favorite childhood meal would cheer me up.

But not even the aroma of cumin, oregano, and cinnamon simmering in red sauce wafting through the cottage could snap me out of my hopeless funk.

· · ·

As challenging as my mother's visit felt, solitude proved a daunting roommate for me to face alone. Not long after she left, I agreed to spend ten days with my parents at a house they owned in Guadalajara, Mexico.

The house, with its black wrought iron front door and matching window grilles, was at the intersection of two bustling streets in a congested part of town. In the middle of the night, I woke to wailing police sirens, music blaring from radios, and people's conversations as they hurried to the local bar. During the day, the unrelenting traffic and food vendors shouting from behind adobe walls settled into a background din.

After breakfast, I read a book. After lunch, I took a two-hour nap. After dinner, I read some more. When I finished my novel, I turned to page one and plowed through it again.

Aware of my tedium, my mother invited me to watch Mexican soap operas with her. I declined. Time trickled at a sloth's pace.

Early one morning, I sat at the kitchen table eating homemade corn tortillas, steaming fresh, from the local tortilleria. The sun's rays peered over the roof tiles, hinting at the rising temperatures to come. Despite all the window screens Daddy built to keep them at bay, a family of flies joined me at breakfast, picking at the tiny crumbs of *pan dulce* that lingered on the tablecloth. I stared at the plastic wall clock, willing time to move faster between mouthfuls of thick, warm dough.

"When your father and I first got married, we lived in this house."

I started; lost in my thoughts, I'd forgotten I wasn't alone in the room. I glanced at the kitchen sink, where Mom stood washing dishes. She looked out the window through a glass pane protected by iron bars, head tilted to one side.

"We had a baby here. His name was Joel." Mom spoke out loud, but her far-off gaze informed me that the spirits of the past were gathering around us now.

"He had blue eyes and everyone said he looked like an angel." I sensed her smile, though I couldn't see her face. "I needed to go on an errand. I didn't want to leave him but I had to. I asked a neighbor to watch him while I was gone. I told her not to feed him peanuts, that they weren't good for a baby . . ." Mom's voice faltered. She set the sparkling glass down on the stainless-steel basin, as if it was too heavy to hold. "She gave him some peanuts anyway. He choked on them. He was only eighteen months old when he died."

Like a film strip caught in the teeth of a movie projector, life stood still, burning a hole in this frame of time. I stopped chewing. The street, usually teeming with cars, fell strangely quiet. Even the flies quit buzzing, waiting for the projectionist to fix the damage, eager to see the ending.

"After he was gone, I would look out this window at the neighbor boy across the street," Mom continued. "He was five or six and every day he sat in an old chair on the sidewalk, sunning himself. He was slow." Mom pointed to her temple as if this were the place *slow* lived. "He talked nonsense and drooled when he ate. Sometimes he shouted out loud for no reason. I was angry at God and said to him, *Why, why did you take my beautiful child?! Why didn't you just take that boy instead?*"

I imagined Mom's harsh conversations with the almighty—fire from earth launched toward the silence of heaven.

She turned off the faucet and dried her hands with a colorful hand towel.

Sitting there, the iron curtain living inside me—the barrier I'd solidified with my bitterness and will—cracked as Mami opened her heart to me. I stood up, walked over to the sink, put my arms around her waist, and rested my chin on her shoulder.

"I'm so sorry, Mami," I said, feeling my tenderness toward her awakening.

I had heard the story of the baby blue-eyed infant named Joel over the years. The death of her firstborn child had sent my mother into a five-year depression. Dad had feared she would go mad from anguish. In the wake of their loss, my parents had tried to get pregnant again, but to no avail. To make matters worse, a doctor had informed Mami she could never bear children again. *I'll give birth to a baby before you ever do*, he'd told her without empathy or hope.

For Mom, who longed for a family above all else, the doctor's diagnosis was a death sentence. *There are better doctors across the border*, Dad told her. And with that, my father put his affairs in order, they said goodbye to their families, and they left Mascota, searching for the promise that lay in America. And in the US, Mom indeed became pregnant again, just not four times, as I'd always believed—only three.

Still, Joel's death was a blow my mom had never fully overcome. There was a missing member in our home, a baby who'd died on her watch and had taken with him her belief that the world was a safe place.

We stood over the kitchen sink in the Guadalajara house—Mami, the past, and me. My arms held her longer than they had in years. I breathed in her scent—the mixture of an English garden and Mexican earth. I wanted to stay like this forever, but her subsequent words jarred me.

"Learn to hate," she said, her tone as matter of fact as if she was telling me to finish my tortilla.

The iron curtain, sensing a breach, slammed shut. I took a step away from her.

"What?" I asked, uncertain I heard her correctly.

"Hate can make you strong," she replied, punching her fist into the open palm of her other hand. "That's how you survive this life."

No, no, no! my mind shouted, conjuring every ounce of strength, stamina, and sanity it could to keep this disquieting advice from taking hold. My recent losses had created a sinkhole around my heart— an area vulnerable to suggestion.

Mami loved me and didn't want me to suffer. She'd endured the unimaginable, and discovered, in the process, a weapon to subjugate her pain: hate. She'd wielded it when her mother left her as a child to search for and bring back the father who had abandoned them; it had kept her strong when, as newly arrived immigrants to America, World War II separated her and my father; and it had been the lifeline Mami reached for to pull her out of the all-consuming grief surrounding the loss of her firstborn son.

Hate brought my mother a sense of control in a turbulent world. Perhaps this is why she insisted on keeping so much *stuff* around her. The accumulation of junk on Escondido Road may have filled me with shame, but my mother's things offered her a sense of security, safety, and refuge. You never knew when it might all be taken away, so everything must be kept in excess, just in case.

Loneliness was a difficult bedfellow for me to live with. But the thought of harboring an emotion as explosive as hate sent an icy touch up my spine. My mother's manner of handling life's trials would never be mine. I had to find my own way.

CHAPTER TWENTY-EIGHT

The Fall of the Iron Curtain

STEVEN AND I were forged from opposing elements.

My new surfer boyfriend was quite different from the men I'd dated in the film industry. Steven had minimal ambitions and was content to live a simpler life. I moved through my days like wildfire, enthusiastic about my burgeoning film career and thirsty for life experience. Steven's lack of drive, my long work hours and our conflicting moral compass where I faced east, and he firmly faced west— incited fiery arguments between us. We fought as often as we laughed and were miserably in love. To keep the peace, I tiptoed around him and played small so as not to upset his moods that ebbed and receded like the tides. Clearly our temperaments were as compatible as fire and ice. I considered leaving more often than not. But Steven's crystal blue eyes, sparkling with angst, reeled me in time and again, like a kid hooked on sugar.

Tired of failing at love, I decided that this time defeat wasn't in the cards—that I could fix Steven. This savior mentality, of course, was a surefire recipe for disaster. It's easier to keep a soufflé from collapsing than to save someone who doesn't want saving.

We tried all the usual stopgaps to repair our relationship: taking breaks, signing up for therapy, and mending our hurts by saying, "I love you." None worked for very long. Finally, we devised a foolproof plan to fix our problems: we got married.

The charged silences, growing resentments, and makeup sex continued for three and a half more years.

. . .

On an immaculate Southern California day, while sun worshipers romped on a nearby beach, Steven and I argued inside our apartment— *for hours.*

"Why do you have to be so judgmental?" He yelled.

"Why do you have to be so controlling?" I shouted back.

Finally, we hit an impasse. Steven demanded that I accept him just as he was or the marriage was over. There was one word that could save our union. It rested on the tip of my tongue.

Okay.

The word *okay* would do it all; signal my surrender to Steven and at the same time, summon my spirit's executioner.

Exhausted from arguing and afraid loneliness would again demand to share my bed, I decided *okay* was the way out of our stalemate. But when my mouth opened, a clear, firm, and assured voice demanded, *Don't say it!*

Steven didn't hear the voice. No one did. It only existed in my head. It was the same voice I'd heard whisper *reincarnation* in fifth grade religion class.

The future of my marriage teetered on one simple word, so I tried ungluing my lips. But the unspoken voice controlled my facial muscles and refused them permission to move.

Steven leaned against his surfboard, his expectant eyes awaiting my answer. I'd miss swimming in the ocean of those aqua pools, but instead of saying *okay* to his demand, I kept my mouth closed and said nothing.

Two weeks later, Steven moved out.

After my wedding, Mom wasn't shy; she asked me often about grand-children, hoping her dream of having babies would become mine.

I knew it never would now, but I hated disappointing her. Family meant the world to my parents, who traveled thousands of miles to a new country to create one. So, I waited as long as possible to break the news that all my marriage would produce . . . *was a divorce.*

When Thanksgiving arrived, it was time to face the mariachi music.

A few years before, 5515 Escondido Road had undergone a facelift. Not just a little Botox—a full nip and tuck. As I pulled into the driveway, a tan two-story stucco house with multiple balconies and four bedrooms greeted me.

I was thrilled when Ray first proposed constructing this residence on the front third of the property. Instead of sliding across decaying linoleum, my bare feet now sank into plush new rugs. Hot, steamy showers replaced baths in the clawfoot tub. And best of all, standing in front of a furnace to warm the chill was a memory. Now, forced air blew through vents, creating a toasty decadence in all the bedrooms.

To make room for this new home, a caravan of dumpsters driven by multiple men over several weeks had hauled away sheets of scrap metal, rusted car engines, dozens of toilet bowls, and plastic tubes and steel cylinders in all sizes—and those were just the tip of the iceberg. Among the exodus were countless items that we scratched our heads over, trying to figure out what they might be.

Mom and Dad had encouraged the building of the new house, but taking a hoarder's possessions is like stealing treasure from a king. So, despite this impressive cull, piles of junk stayed behind. My parents remedied this by moving the cache to the back of the property, filling the already inundated space with familiar friends.

My parents could not let go of the past. Neither could I. I'd hoped that clearing the front section of the yard would also sweep away the dark moods that had pursued me into adulthood. But shame defined my childhood. No matter how far I moved away, no matter how many interesting new friends I made, no matter the distant countries I traveled to—whenever I came home, the junk surrounding the old house resurrected my powerlessness again. Like an obese person who loses weight yet continues to see themselves as fat when they look in the mirror, I still saw myself as a Junkyard Girl.

I left my car and found Dad working near the boysenberry bushes, trapping an unsuspecting metal pipe in the jaws of his industrial vise.

My father, now in his mid-eighties, might be all gray hair these days but his biceps still impressed, as did his energy: He continued to work manually from sunup to sunset.

After a quick hug, I tried explaining, in awkward fits and bursts, the collapse of my marriage.

Dad put the vise aside and looked into my eyes. "Just tell me what's wrong, Chiqui." He sat down on the cement wall that bordered the boysenberry bushes.

I sat next to him, my eyes on the spot of concrete where the names of my dogs—*Bandit, Orange, Iris*—were etched.

"St . . . Ste . . . Steven . . . and I . . . are . . . are . . . are . . . br . . . br . . . breaking up," I stammered. Like a ripe peach hitting the pavement, I burst into tears—then immediately stopped, clenching my jaw to stifle my weakness, so hard that it clicked.

"Shhhh, it's okay, it's okay, Chiqui," my father whispered, patting my back.

I embraced his permission and the dam collapsed, releasing the flood.

Less than a minute later, my chest stopped heaving and my eyes braved his. I expected disappointment in his green gaze. What I got instead was understanding.

"Are you sure? Your decision . . . is it final?" Dad hated uncertainty as much as he despised fools.

I loved Steven and wasn't 100 percent sold on divorce, but I knew he would never change enough for our relationship to work and neither would I. *Yes*, I nodded.

"*El hombre pone, y Dios dispone*"—What man proposes, God disposes —Daddy stated matter-of-factly, summing up the end of my marriage in one fell swoop. "Let's have lunch," he said. And with a final pat on my back, Dad ended my pity party.

With my father's support, I felt greater confidence sharing the bad news with Mom.

When I entered the house, I found her in a familiar position: standing in front of the stove, stirring a pot, her face giving nothing away of how she felt.

Mom had always been impossible to read. She'd seemed to like Steven. After all, he was her best hope for grandchildren—something she wanted so badly that even before I dated him, she'd offered to raise my child should I decide to get pregnant. Her statement had astounded me then, much as her response to the news of my impending divorce surprised me now.

"Why should you be unhappy?" she said, flipping a tortilla on the burner.

I leaned against the kitchen wall. The cool surface against my back assured me I wasn't dreaming her acceptance. Next to *I love you so much,* or *This is your new dog,* or *Jane Goodall's your biggest fan,* I couldn't imagine five better words.

I might have disenchanted my parents by not living happily ever after with Steven, or at least producing the grandchild my mother longed for with him, but they didn't let on. Mom and Dad backed my decision without question, judgment, or vexation.

That day, my heart surged with appreciation and love for both of them. Their support stoked a fire so fierce that the iron curtain, the invisible divide that had stood for decades between Mami and me, began to melt.

I thought life would fall apart after my separation, but soon after my luck turned. Not only did my parents support my eventual divorce— lock, stock, and barrel—but I also found a lovely new apartment a block away from the sand in Redondo Beach. Sun-kissed marigolds and violet pansies bloomed from flowerbeds in the windows of the country cottage. *The rent is tight,* I confessed to my older landlady— who then reduced my payments by $200 a month. And despite her solid rule, *No Pets Allowed,* Vera both welcomed my cat Cody and let me have another four-legged roommate, a hefty tuxedo cat rescued from the streets of Hollywood whom I named Jester.

"You won't be here for long," Vera said as I signed the lease documents. "You'll meet someone new in no time."

I smiled, pretending to agree with her assessment, but I knew it was untrue. This kind lady wasn't aware of my abysmal track record with love. *There is something wrong with me!* I wanted to shout at her. *No one will ever love me enough to stick around.*

Instead, I handed her the rental agreement in exchange for the front door key.

But Vera was right. Two months later, a man like no other entered my life.

CHAPTER TWENTY-NINE

A Sock and a Shoe

MY RINGING PHONE jarred me awake. I sat straight up, confused, searching around me, trying to figure out where I was, then realized I had been laying on my office couch taking a nap in the middle of the afternoon.

Working as an executive director of a film production company by day while earning my master's degree in Chinese medicine at night, I was burning both ends of a short candle. What little free time I had was spent inhabiting a depressive fog brought on by the end of my marriage.

I grabbed the receiver when the call refused to go to voice mail.

"Hello—this is Carlyn," I said, forcing myself to sound professional rather than discombobulated.

"Did I wake you?" a man's voice asked pleasantly.

"No, no, of course not," I said as if what he suggested was ludicrous. "Uh, who am I speaking with?"

"Ken Fischer," he said.

Ken Fischer. I hadn't seen or spoken to Ken in twenty years—not since we'd worked together at Lucasfilm in Northern California.

"Wow," was all I managed to say as I struggled waking up.

Ken told me he was calling on a whim, looking for a Spanish translator for a media project he was working on. For the next hour, we reminisced about our days in the cutting rooms. I was surprised by our effortless repartee and the generous laughter between us.

I didn't get the job, but I got the guy.

223

After our phone call ended, Ken and I began an email correspondence. Every night after work, I raced home to my computer. *You've got mail*, AOL's robotic voice announced. At first our communications were playful, but as the weeks passed, we exchanged deeper sentiments. Ken listened thoughtfully as I shared my journey mending from the shards of my broken marriage. My heart ached for Ken when he shared that his wife, Lucy, had died of breast cancer two years earlier, leaving him and their young children, seven-year-old Gina and ten-year-old Greg, behind.

I hadn't known men like Ken existed—at least, not for me. Kind, honest, responsible, and a one-woman man who could make me laugh like no one else . . . these were qualities I expected to evaporate once the real Ken materialized. They never did. Night after night, month after month, we connected through pixels on a white screen. In this way, a single girl in Southern California and a father of two in Northern California fell in love over the immortal words *You've got mail.*

Three months and dozens of emails later, a message arrived from Ken: *Why don't we meet?*

Heavy traffic delayed my arrival to Los Angeles International Airport.

Mortified by my lateness, I ran toward the arrivals gate. Blisters formed on my ankles from sandals made for style, not running track. I was out of shape and a little heavier than I would have liked. The pint of coffee ice cream that had kept me company the night before had left me with shot nerves and puffy eyes.

I reached the arrivals gate sweating and breathless, but it was too late. Not a soul remained in the area from the incoming flight.

"Carlyn," a man's voice said.

I glanced over my shoulder. The guy I'd known twenty years before was not the man standing behind me. A slimmer version in a blue polo shirt and khaki pants with salt-and-pepper-speckled hair stood in his place. In his hands was a bouquet of jet-lagged purple irises, their stems wrapped in tinfoil.

"Irises are out of season," he apologized, then explained that this was something he'd discovered after stopping at three florists and almost missing his flight. Limp violet petals, tired of clinging to their stalk, floated onto the carpet. Ken fumbled, his forehead sweating, as he tried to put them back.

I blamed myself for his nervousness. I wasn't the slim, long-haired twenty-four-year-old girl he remembered. He'd just flown 337 miles to find shorter hair, a wider waistline, and bloodshot eyes.

My worry was needless. Ken's brown-eyed gaze came alive when it met mine, and his radiant smile told me he was far from disappointed.

A month later, I flew to San Francisco and met Ken's children. Our bonding began over a game of HORSE on the basketball court, then grew stronger over vegetarian pizza and Scrabble. If I had any doubts that I was falling in love with this man, hearing him sing an out-of-tune lullaby to Gina at bedtime about oats, peas, and barley cinched the deal.

That night, I lay with Ken where red rose petals had sprinkled the covers only a few minutes earlier. Listening to him breathe, I remembered a recent conversation with my gods: *Don't bother sending anyone else into my life unless he's The One*, I'd demanded, sitting on my apartment floor with Jester and Cody both purring in my lap. Perhaps Our Lady of The Perpetual Green Light had heard me from her niche in my childhood bedroom on Escondido Road, because the gods had done what I asked: They'd sent Ken. And he was *The One*.

Trust was not a trait my parents easily embraced. While my father's big smile and hearty laughter made strangers feel welcome, my mother's unflappable gaze, curt conversation, and intimidating hairy eyeball put many visitors on edge. I expected this behavior from her as Ken and I drove toward Escondido Road and warned him about it, but he shrugged me off. His excitement to meet my family was palpable. I wondered what was wrong with him.

When Ken stepped over the threshold and into our home, my brothers, weary of my bitter mood since my divorce, greeted him with open arms and christened him in the waters of relentless teasing.

"Hey, veggie boy!" Art roared at my vegetarian boyfriend while handing him a beer before he could even say hello.

"*Run mijo, run!*"—*Run, my boy, run!*—Ray added, bringing the house down.

Wrapped in a shawl and sitting alone on a piano bench, Mami watched Ken interact with her *familia*. Months before, she'd begun showing signs of dementia—struggling to remember things that had occurred only a few minutes before and leaving the burners on the stove lit so many times that Lilly, afraid the house would burn down while she was at work, had removed the knobs.

As her dementia worsened, Mami had grown irritable, confused, and withdrawn. Her indifferent demeanor didn't bother Ken. He sat beside her, offering her a slice of cake. I cringed watching them; his eagerness, her dismissiveness.

"Your mom was perfectly nice," Ken told me as we walked hand in hand toward my Volvo Sedan. It was parked in the same spot where thirty years before Mrs. Marchand had hurried her daughters into a similar vehicle, eager to leave the junkyard and me behind. "I don't know what you mean about the hairy eyeball. I like her," Ken said.

Hearing Ken's take on Mom left me bewildered. I had spent so many years thinking that she was old-fashioned, intimidating, and unfriendly. I couldn't understand how anyone might feel otherwise.

During our drive back to Los Angeles, I tried visualizing my mother through Ken's unspoiled eyes. It was refreshing to imagine my relationship with Mami as a *tabula rasa*—an empty slate devoid of our tense history. But the two-hour ride could not erase our past.

A few weeks later, Lilly shared with me a recent war of words she'd had with our mother.

"You're so bitter," Mom said.

"Yes, Mother." Lilly sighed, having heard this line of criticism many times before.

"How will you ever find a husband?"

"I don't know, Mother," Lilly responded, ladling soup into a bowl while searching for patience.

"What ever happened to that nice boy from San Francisco?" Mami asked.

Lilly set the dish in front of her, wondering what *nice boy in San Francisco* Mom was talking about. Then she realized.

"Do you mean Ken? Carlyn's boyfriend?" Lilly asked.

Dementia or not, my mother knew a good man when she saw one.

CHAPTER THIRTY

A Wedding and a Funeral

KEN AND I scheduled our wedding for May 2002. But everything changed when my mother's health took a turn for the worse.

Besides her failing memory, Mami suffered from liver cirrhosis—a disease common in people with a history of alcoholism but surprising in my mother, an infrequent drinker.

Her physician concluded that a bout of scarlet fever during childhood must have damaged her liver.

"He suggested we get tested in case it was passed down to us," Lilly informed me over the phone.

"Okay, well, where should I get tested then?" I asked.

"I don't think you have to," Lilly said after a brief pause.

"Why not? You guys did it."

"Yeah, it was negative for us, so there's really no reason for you to do it. When are you coming home next?"

My mouth twisted against the receiver. The doctor wanted us examined to see if we might be susceptible to the same condition Mom had. My other siblings had done it; why shouldn't I?

Lilly continued talking about everyday things—her dog Luna's allergy to grass, Tracy's new school, and the bumper crop of avocados filling her tree. I listened, but I couldn't shake off what she said about getting tested. I felt dismissed, as if my health didn't matter. There was no reason to doubt Lilly. Still, the thought nagged at me.

. . .

When my Uncle Reuben passed away, I drove home for his funeral. Mom was sitting in the living room, staring out a window, when I arrived.

"Hi, Mami," I whispered before kissing her cheek.

"*Mija, como estás?*" she asked, surprised to find me standing there.

"I'm fine," I answered. I didn't need to ask her the same question to know the answer. A walker stood beside her. Propped against the wall was a sturdy cane. Mami's feet, snug in a pair of plush scarlet booties I'd given her for Christmas, were on the footrest of a wheelchair.

"It looks like the wind is moving through those leaves," she said. I followed her gaze outside the screen door to the avocado tree, a prolific giant Lilly had planted from a pit; its deep green foliage rustled in the breeze.

"Look at the wind moving through the leaves."

"Yeah, I see it, Mami."

"Look at the wind moving through the leaves," she said again.

"Mami, you said that three times already," I answered—an impatient response that was immediately followed by a jab of guilt and then regret.

She remained quiet after that.

Later that morning, I pushed Mom's wheelchair toward St. Joseph's Catholic Church, where Uncle Reuben's mass would take place. I smiled while remembering the many times I'd walked, skipped, or run down this same sidewalk to catch the school bus.

The church, modern for its time when constructed in the early 1970s, overflowed with the Montes De Oca and Curiel clan. Many of our relatives had traveled from distant parts of the state to say their goodbyes to Mom's brother, who had died from leukemia.

During the service, I stood behind Mom's wheelchair. My focus was less on the priest's words than on her regal composure as she stared at the shiny casket in front of the altar. Like the queen mum on a mobile throne, Mami shone in her black dress. A gold medallion of Our Lady of Guadalupe hung over the ruby colored wool scarf wrapped around her neck. Mom's lips—a bold vermilion red, a favorite among actresses of a bygone era—added a glint to her glamor. Her short, wavy hair, lined by a streak of gray across the top, informed the world that she wasn't hiding from her age.

"I think someone died," Mom said, loudly enough for my cousins sitting two pews behind us to hear.

I placed my hands on her shoulders and leaned in. "Uncle Reuben, Mami, that's who died," I whispered, hoping that in the future she would keep her thoughts to a whisper.

"Did someone die?" she asked, louder than before.

It was a repeat of the earlier *wind through the avocado tree* conversation. I turned to Lilly for guidance, as I always did when I wasn't sure what to do. My sister shrugged and lip-synced The Lord's Prayer with the rest of the congregation. My mother's last act was a new chapter for her, too.

Back at home, Ken and I talked over our spring wedding plans with Lilly.

"If you want Mami to be there, you need to move that date up," Lilly said as she sorted Mom's meds into a plastic pillbox.

"May's only five months away," I said.

"She might not be here in five months."

The laundry dryer buzzed as if agreeing.

Mami had never been a sun worshiper. Often she walked down a street in July with an umbrella—the only person in sight doing such a thing. As her body grew frail, however, she'd increasingly felt the bite of the cold, even when the sun burned hot outside. These days the Travelall, marooned in the driveway by flat tires and an exhausted engine, was her personal solar oven.

When my cousins Francisco and Rick had recently visited and no one had answered the front door, they'd noticed Mami lying motionless inside the car. Inching closer to the glass they tapped on the window to get her attention. Mami hadn't moved. So my cousins had concluded Aunt Mary was dead. Then, as they'd anxiously discussed what to do next, Mom sat up straight like a mummy in a coffin—a resurrection that gave both of them a fright they would never forget.

She might not be here in five months. Lilly's words echoed in my thoughts.

We moved our wedding date up to early March and hoped for the best.

I called my mother every few days to check on her health. The voice on the other end grew weaker. "*Hi, Mija,*" she'd say in a strained whisper.

Weeks later, she no longer had the strength to say even that.

A couple of days before our wedding, I arrived home and found a chilling site. Mami lay in bed in the new house, eyes closed. Her face was a curious shade, darker than usual. The bones in her cheeks protruded from her skin as though trying to escape. Not long before, Mom's lips shone a vibrant, vermilion red. Today they were pallid and O-shaped. Her breath, uneven and labored, whistled like a mournful ocean breeze. My father sat in a chair next to her. Death sat even closer. A spasm jerked my gut, reminding me that despite our battles, I had often been sensitive to my mother's pain.

When I was six years old, Dad pulled up to the curb of the family home in Mascota. As Mom got out of The International, she seized the doorjamb for support—a second before Art accidentally slammed the door shut on her fingers. When I heard her cry out, my stomach heaved the contents of my lunch onto the cobblestone sidewalk.

Years later, Mom tripped while watering her gardenias. When I heard her yelling my name, I presumed I was in trouble for something I had done wrong, so I didn't hurry to find out what she wanted. If I had, I would have found her lying on the dirt, her face contorted with pain. When Ray carried her into the house and I saw her ankle—blue, black, and swelling to the size of a tennis ball—I bolted into the bathroom and emptied my guts into the toilet bowl.

Now, as I watched Mami on her bed, battling for breath, I forced my nausea into submission.

"How did she get sick so fast?" I asked Lilly.

My sister studied me with tired eyes.

We hired a caregiver to help care for Mom during the day, but at night my sister changed her soiled clothes and turned her over every few hours to prevent sores from developing. Caring for Mom during her last days was something Lilly insisted she wanted to do, but this was her mother, her blood, and easing her transition into the next world was physically, emotionally, and spiritually taxing.

"We should postpone our wedding," I said, tightening my fists to stay composed.

"No," Lilly said. "She wouldn't want that. Neither would Dad. Our family needs this."

My sister's arms reached for me, pulling me in, wrapping her tenderness around me like a warm sourdough bun fresh from the oven.

March 9, our wedding day arrived, bringing with it the chaos of last-minute arrangements.

During the pre-ceremony scramble, I sat alone at the dining room table, staring into a tabletop mirror assessing the circles under my eyes, a gift from a restless night's sleep. My lips were pale and downturned. "You look prettier with a little lipstick," Mami had said to me so many times in the past as I started my car to drive back home. I'd shrug her off as if appearances meant nothing to me. But halfway down the block I'd glance in my rearview mirror and when I was certain she was out of eyesight, I'd apply a quick coat of crimson red to my lips.

My three makeup essentials—mascara, foundation, and lipstick—sat organized in front of me, waiting to do their job. I reached for a hairbrush instead. In my haste, I'd left mine behind in Los Angeles, so Lilly had given me my mother's to use. *Mason Pearson*, read the gold letters on the handle. Expensive and London-made, Mason Pearson was the only brand Mom, an expert in all things hair, had ever used. When I was a child, she'd detangled my lengthy tresses with a similar brush—perhaps the very same one.

I stared at the hairbrush as if waiting for it to tell me what to do next. "I can't do this," I whispered to my reflection as though she were my confidant. Down the hallway, Mami lay dying. *Dying*—a voice insisted inside my head, as if echoing from the bottom of a well. *How can I entertain bright lipstick or slip into an elegant white dress or host a celebration? How can I enjoy the happiest day of my life when my mom is fighting for hers?* Celebrating a wedding felt selfish, insensitive, and indulgent. *Our family needs this,* Lilly had said, but the perplexed face staring from the mirror was not so sure.

I slipped out of my chair and walked toward my mother's bedroom. From the doorway, I took in her emaciated figure, lying still under the covers.

My father sat beside the bed; he only left her side when Lilly forced him to eat. Otherwise, he kept a hawk-like eye on Mami's shallow breathing as if willing her back to wellness. The oddly shaped O rattled with every exhale as Mami shifted in and out of consciousness. In the rare instance her eyes parted, she'd wearily look up at my father and ask, "Are they married?" in a voice not much more than a wispy breath.

"No, Mary, not yet," Dad would whisper back.

A sigh, both fatigued and disappointed, would escape the O as she slipped back to the fragile boundary between life and death—a border she tiptoed across on borrowed time.

"'Are they married yet?' is all she says now," Dad said, his eyes scanning her face. "It's as if she needs to know that you're going to be okay."

My father stepped out of the room and I took his place beside her. I slipped my hand into Mom's—a sheath of silky skin over delicate bones and distended veins. The same hand that had held mine on my first day of school, a time when I'd gazed up at the noble beauty walking beside me and beamed proudly with the knowledge that this was my mother, a time when my love for her still poured from a never-ending stream.

I wished things had been different between us. I wished she and I had known each other better and forgiven each other more. For years, it was anger, not love, I'd offered her in exchange for my pain. As a kid, I'd hidden in my room to escape her. As an adult, I'd moved away to keep her at bay. Despite our long-running war, there had also been moments of deep connection and unspoken understanding, fruits of a shared life between mother and daughter. Yes, I'd fought against her control and felt suffocated by her overprotection—but in that moment, as I watched my mother struggle for her life, I realized my love for her was greater than my resentment. Like a priceless gem, unearthed from a long sleep, my tenderness for mom emerged. And only now was I discovering its true value.

I bent over her body and kissed her forehead. Her skin was warm and smooth; the faint scent of Oil of Olay lingered in the air. I studied the hard-won lines across her face, taking her features in one last time, committing them to memory, then swallowed hard—but the grief stranded in my throat remained.

When I left Mom's bedroom and returned to the mirror, the glass alerted me that my puffy eyes and dry lips weren't going to magically disappear if I didn't get to it. Our wedding ceremony was in two hours.

I applied a streak of mauve across my lips, then sat back and looked in the mirror. My reflection agreed that Mom had been right all those years ago. I did look better with a touch of lipstick.

Ken, my husband-to-be, had worked as a sound editor on countless blockbuster movies, but today he demonstrated a surprising talent as a wedding planner.

The venue he'd secured—Stella Mare's, a French bistro beside the Bird Sanctuary in Santa Barbara—was ideal. The room where the ceremony and dinner would take place resembled a glass palace. During the day it welcomed in the sunshine, and at night the transparent ceiling gave way to a star-studded sky. Inside the restored greenhouse, thirty-five of our closest family members and dearest friends waited, each soul aware of the delicate balance between our new beginnings as a married couple and the end of my mother's life.

In a changing room, I slipped into my wedding dress. Tension clenched my chest like the jaws of Dad's vise. I needed to cry and release my pent-up emotions, but the thought of black mascara streaking down my cheeks kept the floodgates securely in place. For once, my vanity served a good purpose.

When I heard Israel Kamakawiwo'ole's haunting voice singing "Somewhere Over the Rainbow" from Greg's boombox, I took a deep breath and followed Gina, my twelve-year-old maid of honor, down a stone pathway that my seven-year-old niece and flower girl, Gabi, was sprinkling with red rose petals.

The song's message offered hope and the possibility of a wonderful world. Lost in the lyrics, I didn't realize when my feet arrived at the bistro's entrance. Through a giant window, nearly three dozen eager faces met my gaze, their excited smiles dooming my resolve to stay poised.

Then I spotted a familiar face that gave me all the strength I needed.

From the back of the room, Ken's eyes met mine. His incandescent grin, so wide it nearly connected ear to ear, was for me.

My smile came alive and matched his. I stepped inside the glass palace, my sadness washed away by the rush of promise.

During the brief ceremony, Ken and I exchanged platinum wedding bands inscribed with the words *Para siempre*—"*Forever.*" It was the name of the song my father had serenaded my mother with outside her balcony in Mascota when they first met. Leaving the past behind and embracing love—the rudder that had steered my parents' lives together for six decades—was the song's message. I hoped the reminder on our rings would anchor Ken and me through choppy waters, shelter us during unexpected storms, and inspire us to always move toward the horizon.

The moment we said our *I do*s, Lilly and our family friend Alice hopped into my sister's Honda and sped back to Carpinteria.

"They're married," my sister told Dad as she and Alice rushed into my mother's bedroom.

Mom was too ill to be at our wedding, and Dad had refused to leave her side. So I'd figured out another way to keep us connected while we were apart by purchasing two glass lanterns and matching crimson pillar candles, one for me and Ken at Stella Mare, and the other for my parent's bedroom.

Mami often lit a votive to commemorate significant events—birthdays, the anniversary of a grandparent's death. On December 12, there was always a burning candle on the edge of the dining room table devoted to Our Lady of Guadalupe. When I traveled to Europe, my mom lit a candle. When I traipsed through South America, she lit an entire box until I returned safely. Tonight, a lantern holding a flickering flame stood on the night table beside Mami's bed. Its twin flame sat on the mantel of Stella Mare's fireplace; a photograph of my parents, enclosed in a gold-plated frame, stood next to it.

"They're married, Mary," Daddy whispered into my mother's ear after hearing the news from Lilly.

Days later, my father told me that he knew Mami heard him because she exhaled deeply and her breath weakened. She had done her part as my mother, protected me in the only way she knew how up to this point. Though she never said it, I suspect she believed Ken to be the kind of man who would do whatever was required to keep me safe from now on. Mami was unwilling to trust that role to just anyone, including me. What I needed protection from was never clear.

Mami never opened her eyes again. Moments later, in the lantern at the side of her bed, the candle's wick flickered out.

After dinner, Ken and I danced to a compilation of our favorite tunes. My head rested against his chest, feeling his heartbeat rise and fall. A peculiar synchronicity had formed between us. He often voiced thoughts I had just been thinking, and more and more we finished each other's sentences. So, it didn't surprise me when we both turned toward the fireplace at the same moment to look at the framed photograph of my parents as Percy Sledge serenaded us with "When a Man Loves a Woman."

In the photo, Mom sat in a chair gazing up at my father, his adoring smile beaming down at her. Emotion surged through me remembering how Mami had once walked through the world—proud, strong, and timeless. I closed my eyes. *I love you*, I said silently, three times. Like Dorothy in *The Wizard of Oz*, I realized the home my parents had given me wasn't such an awful place after all. Yes, there had been junk everywhere, and I felt smothered by its reach, but what I had not seen was that there was a powerful love living in the spaces in between.

A server balancing a silver dessert tray passed by us. I wondered if she carried a lighter in her pocket, because the lantern next to the picture of my parents, just like its twin beside my mother's bed, had just flickered out.

Early the following morning, the phone in our hotel room woke us.

"Hello," I answered with slight annoyance, the usual way I greeted the day.

"Mami died a few minutes ago," Ray's somber voice announced.

Like a slow-moving poison, numbness spread through my body. The mattress caught me as my legs betrayed me.

Throughout the day, relatives came in and out of 5515 Escondido Road, sharing their condolences, telling stories, and offering casseroles. The numb feeling that had come over me earlier turned into a terrible head cold. Huddled on the couch, I lay under one of Mami's thick blankets, wiping my eyes, blowing my nose, and filling a grocery bag with used tissue paper. I tried to maintain a dignified composure, but all I wanted was for everyone to leave so I could go to sleep and not wake up until the world was painless again.

Art rifled through his old closet and found a super-eight movie I had never seen before. That afternoon, the living room wall came alive with one of our annual trips to Mexico. On the film strip, Mami, just a few years older than I was now, prepared sandwiches on a picnic table. Lilly assisted her, hobbling back and forth on crutches, her leg in a cast from a recent fall. I—an infant in my mother's arms—sucked on a pacifier and frowned as I watched my brothers chase each other. Mami laughed down at me with carefree abandon, her face beaming with belief, hope, and love—the same way Ken had smiled at me the previous day during our wedding.

"She looks like she loves me," I said out loud, dazed by a cloud of antihistamines as I remembered how I questioned Mami's love for me.

My brothers and sister didn't answer. Their own grief held them captive.

"She looks like she loves me," I repeated more softly, then drifted to sleep, where I dreamed of red enchiladas, necktie dresses, and a mother's love.

CHAPTER THIRTY-ONE

Big D, Little D

WHEN MAMI PASSED AWAY, I discovered that the dead leave gifts behind—at least, my mother did. Her gift to me was something I never would have expected. She gave me *my father*.

After Mom's death, my relationship with Dad changed. Instead of superficial conversations, we engaged in more thoughtful talks— about career, marriage, what animals feel but don't say, if aliens exist—spending hours on each subject. When I suffered a miscarriage, we cried together. When I argued with my stepchildren and judged myself a crappy parent, he listened and offered advice. We became what I wished my mother and I had been: good friends.

Despite our deepening rapport however, we never broached the subject that must have weighed on his mind the older he got. He never confessed the secret living under the surface of our lives. I continued to think that he and my mother were my biological parents.

In the spring of 2009, my sister threw a big party. Relatives feasted on Lilly's scrumptious Mexican food, drank copious amounts of lime margaritas, and busted a rib listening to my brothers' irreverent barbs.

Dad now suffered from severe arthritis, and the worn-down cartilage in both his knees created intense pain as bone rubbed on bone. At ninety-five years old, he found it easier to stay in bed on overcast days than tackle the myriad of unfinished projects in the yard. He also missed my mother deeply and spoke more and more about joining her.

Since my father couldn't partake in the celebration outside, the party-goers wandered into his bedroom for a visit. The ticket for this intimate gathering was a glass of alcohol and a witty sense of humor.

"*To El Jefe!*" My brothers lifted their tequila shots in Dad's direction.

"*Tío Vicente!*" my cousins countered with glasses of vino.

Ken and I, the only non-drinkers in the room, celebrated Dad in our own way—me with a bottle of root beer and Ken pretending to sip a shot of special tequila that my brothers insisted he drink.

Lori, one of my San Diego cousins, sauntered into Dad's room, fresh-faced and bubbly. "*Tío, Tío!*" she said, sipping wine from a giant goblet. "Why do you spell *Montes De Oca* with a capital D?"

I winced. Lilly bit her lip. Ray and Art eyed each other and grinned as though saying, *This should be good.* It was clear to my siblings and me which questions went down well with my father and which ones would likely receive the sharp whip of his legendary sarcasm. Lori's question was plainly the latter.

Throughout my entire life, Dad had insisted we spell the second word of our last name with a capital *D*. Yet all other Montes De Ocas, including my father's own brothers and sisters, spelled it with a small *d*. The logic behind the big *D* was one I knew well. Lori was about to get an earful.

Dad explained to Lori that using a small *d* in your last name signified that you were born out of wedlock. The capital *D* meant you were legitimate.

Lori, tipsy from rosé, decided my father was not just old, but also deaf; she leaned close to him and articulated her words in long, drawn-out syllables like a movie playing half speed. "Doooo youuuu meeeean toooo saaaaay thaaaat . . ." she said as though speaking to an infant.

"Baaaa-starrrr-doooooooo," Dad interrupted, matching her exaggeration.

Lori blessed the congregation with a spray of rosé as the room erupted in laughter.

I smiled, used to Daddy's witty one-liners, but I also wondered why, after all Dad had witnessed in his nine-plus decades of life—wars, poverty, the death of a child, my mother's passing—something as insignificant as a capital D was important to him.

Bastards, illegitimate children, babies born out of wedlock—no one cares about such things as they once did, I wanted to tell him. Instead, I watched Lilly dab the wine stain out of Lori's white blouse, not realizing that one day I would discover that *I was the child born out of wedlock.*

Three months later, my father, the mighty saguaro, suffered a fall.

Ray, Art, Lilly, and I stayed with Dad for two weeks before death claimed him. I left an hour before he died. Anguish misled my brain into thinking I had something more important to do rather than be with my father during his last moments on earth.

On my six-hour drive toward the new home Ken and I shared in Northern California, my cell phone rang.

"Dad just died," Ray said.

Tears exploded, hindering my eyesight, blurring the broken white lines in the road.

Whatever my brother said next, I cannot recall. I tossed my phone onto the dashboard and gripped the steering wheel to steady myself.

When Mami died, she left me a gift: she allowed me the space, opportunity, and time to know my dad as I never had before. Our conversations had not only helped me to understand him in a more genuine way; they had also allowed me to see Mami through his eyes. His memories of her—romantic, poignant, and adoring—had softened my own.

Dad, too, left an unexpected gift when he passed: As his spirit gave up his body, his inheritance surged through mine, quelling my tears and replacing them with something much more valuable—*courage.*

My parents came to this country to pursue their dream of having children who would live a better life than they did. It took grit, tenacity, sacrifice, and valor to follow their vision. Just like the day Dad taught me to walk through the swarm of bees and overcome my fear, on the day he died, he gifted me the courage I needed to cope with his death—and to anchor me when, ten years later, the long-kept secret of my adoption swept through my life, fracturing my identity.

PART FIVE

"Anyone pulled from a source
longs to go back."
—Rumi

CHAPTER THIRTY-TWO

The Windy City

FLIGHT 4619, eastbound for Chicago, traveled at 575 miles an hour, but my brain, brimming with restless thoughts, raced at the speed of light.

For three hours I scribbled nonstop in my notebook. The voices of my past echoed around me as if Flight 4619 was carrying a cargo of spirits instead of human passengers. Finally, I closed the pad of paper and rested my head against an icy window as I watched cloud cities pass under me, knowing that with each advancing minute, I grew closer to the fire. *It could be a mistake; maybe I'm not adopte*d, said a hopeful voice in my head, clinging to denial. A second voice, scolding and pragmatic, argued with the first. Like a sergeant addressing his troops, his voice read a detailed checklist that showed that any error was wishful thinking on my part.

Lilly told me I was adopted—*check.*

Sixty-three first cousins confirmed it—*check.*

Ancestry.com scientifically proved it—*check.*

And Martha remembered it—*check, check, and check.*

Martha . . .

I'd grown up with a sister named Lilly. We laughed together, understood each other, and, like a duet performing as one unit, refused to be parted or added to. Yet now I had another sister, a stranger named Martha. By blood, we were more physically connected than my beloved Lilly and I were. *But who was she? What was she like?*

I didn't know the answer to these questions, but I knew she was *familia*.

My parents taught us *familia* was the sky, the sea, and everything in between. Because it was so all-encompassing, I felt an obligation to my new half-sister, though my mind argued against it: *You don't know her. You might not even like her. Lilly's your family. Ray and Art are your family.*

As the plane neared O'Hare Airport, I set my head back against the neck rest, closed my eyes, and took several deep breaths. Instead of calming my nerves, my brow furrowed deeper into my skull as my brain wrangled conflicting thoughts.

When I arrived at the hotel, I rushed to my room on the third floor, unlocked the door as quickly as possible, then stepped inside, relishing the protection of its four walls. Martha and I had agreed to meet in the restaurant downstairs later that night. I only had an hour to compose myself before meeting my sister. *Sister*; the word hijacked all other thoughts. I felt I was betraying Lilly by just thinking it.

I lay down on the queen-size bed, turned on the television, and cuddled a fluffy pillow as though it were a life preserver. After several rounds of mindless channel surfing, I decided on a rerun of *Star Trek*, hoping the Starship Enterprise might distract me.

It didn't.

I arrived at the restaurant a few minutes early and stood in the middle of the room unmoving, staring blankly, trying to determine which empty table to take. The jumble of thoughts racing through my mind made it impossible to think clearly. I settled on a spot near the rear.

As I waited, I explored the menu for vegan options, ordered a green tea from a friendly server, then chewed the inside of my cheek—an unconscious habit I always resort to when on edge.

A minute later, a woman strolled in. Our eyes met. In the few seconds it took for her to reach my table, I studied her in full.

Martha wore black leggings and a flowing blue shirt—an ensemble that, curiously, resembled my outfit for the following day. Like me, she had fine hair, but it was longer than it was in the photograph her husband, Adam, had sent on Facebook two months before. I laughed to myself, remembering that I told him the only similarity between his wife and me was that we shopped for glasses at the same store. Indeed, we both sported dark rectangular eyeglasses—but other than that, I didn't see a resemblance between us.

Or is it that I don't want to? My mind reverted to my state of denial: *Maybe this is all a mistake, maybe I'm not adopted, maybe . . .*

Like clockwork, the sergeant assured me I was wrong—*Lilly, sixty-three first cousins, Ancestry,* they all confirmed the same origin story. Christ, there was even a photo of me with Martha and Robert as children. It was all true, whether I wanted to believe it or not.

"How was your flight?" Martha asked as she sat down across the table from me.

"Good, thanks," I said, straining to sound more assured than I felt.

"Your room . . . it's okay?"

"Yes, fine. Yours?"

"Just fine." Martha's eyes held mine a little longer than was comfortable. My toes flexed back and forth under the table, as if priming my feet to bolt. I reached for my glass, took a sip of ice water, and noticed the deep blue gems sparkling against Martha's dark shirt. Three sapphires set in sterling and held by a silver chain hung from her neck.

"I like your necklace," I said.

Martha took a gift bag off the chair beside her and handed it to me.

Inside the sack was a small turquoise gift box. Within that was a sapphire necklace that matched her own. The word *Sister* was engraved on the back. The pendant was gorgeous, Martha's thoughtfulness touching. I thanked her, but in accepting it I felt a little like Judas betraying my real sister, Lilly.

Time passed in a blur of conversation. I learned that Martha loved fashion, enjoyed decorating her house, and was a devoted mom and grandma. I talked about Ken, the kids, and my animal advocacy work.

After two hours, my yawning signaled me to call it a night.

"If you have any other questions for me, I'm happy to answer them," Martha offered.

Questions? I had a million, but only one came to mind.

"Are you a Republican?" I quipped trying to inject a dash of levity into the conversation. I knew that if Ken was here he would roll his eyes and call my attempt at humor *a Joka de Oca*.

Martha chuckled. Her quizzical eyes looked at me as though I was the quirkiest being she ever encountered. She shook her head.

"No," she said. "Never been."

I smiled. We were off to a good start.

Early the next morning, Martha and I climbed into an Uber and headed for Berwyn, the suburb of Chicago where Lena, my birth mother's sister, lived.

It was my first time in Chicago. The metropolis was how I'd always imagined it—sprawling, inner-city tough, and gloomy.

Thirty minutes later, the car pulled up in front of a small brick house indistinct from the line of brick houses on either side of it.

A portly woman in her mid-eighties wearing a tan ankle-length skirt, bright red vest, and white kerchief over wispy gray hair greeted us at the door. Lena hugged Martha, but over her shoulder, her eyes studied me.

"Maria never told us about you" were Lena's first words once we moved inside. "Never said a word."

We walked toward her kitchen, passing framed pictures of Jesus and statues of the Virgin Mary along the way. 5515 Escondido Road had housed its share of religious paraphernalia—Our Lady of The Perpetual Green Light had illuminated my nights, and St. Anne and her daughter had hung in my parents' bedroom—but Lena's house was its own version of Eden.

"Did those people raise you Catholic?" she asked as we passed an altar holding a vase of fresh daisies and an image of the Madonna and Child.

"Yes, but I'm not anymore," I said, well aware that this was a controversial admission to confess to someone so devout. Lena might judge me for my lack of faith, but my days of hiding who I was had come to a definitive end with, *You are adopted.*

When Lilly visited me in Santa Fe, I'd told her, "This isn't a secret I'm going to keep. I can't hide who I am, no matter how that makes anyone else feel."

"This is your story—do what you need to do," my sister had replied.

Over breakfast, Lena shared what it was like growing up with my birth mother. From a young age, she said, Maria was sullen, kept to herself, and carried a melancholy she couldn't shake. The love of her life was Martha's father—an older man, already married with children. This hopeless situation deepened Maria's depression, and she withdrew from her family even more.

"Do you know who my birth father is?" I asked Lena. My origin story had so many elements to keep me occupied that the question of his identity had not come up before, other than Lilly telling me she'd never known who he was.

"No. We didn't even know Maria was pregnant," Lena said, looking pleased as I put several of the fried potato wedges she'd prepared onto my plate.

I knew the identity of my birth father was a lost cause, but that didn't bother me. Vincent, the man who'd shown me how to navigate through a swarm of bees, who'd comforted me after I lost Orange and Bandit, and who'd opened the doors for me to attend Loyola, was the only man I could ever call *Father.*

"Maria was cursed," Lena said.

I remembered what Martha told me about Maria taking her and Robert with her to visit a *curandero* whom she'd hoped would heal her emotional distress. I wondered if Lena knew what it meant to suffer from bipolar disease.

When she picked up a plastic mustard jar and pretended it was a statue of Jesus, then showed me how to ward off tornados by twirling it in the supine position, I decided to savor my tasty potato fries and keep this information to myself.

CHAPTER THIRTY-THREE

Dos Marias

FINDING MARTHA WAS SURREAL. Meeting my Aunt Lena intrigued me. But coming face to face with my birth mother at the state hospital where she was committed felt like an out-of-body experience.

Martha, Aunt Lena, and I stepped off the elevator and into a bustling ward. Patients suffering from advanced dementia and Alzheimer's disease shuffled about—many talking to themselves, others confusing us for their loved ones.

A lady with a serene smile and gentle eyes followed me as we walked toward the cafeteria.

"You are so pretty. I'm glad you came to visit me. Will you come tomorrow?" she asked, stroking my arm.

I patted her hand and assured her I would, knowing she would ask me the same thing again in a moment. Her distant look reminded me of Mami watching the leaves on the avocado tree rustling in the wind, repeating the same phrase like a circling ship lost in the fog.

"Help me, help me!"

The cry for help caught me off guard. I spun around and spotted a bald gentleman at a round table, sitting as rigid as a plank. A plate of mashed potatoes doused with gravy, a vegetable medley, and a slice of turkey sat uneaten in front of him. He saw me staring and rotated his head left, then right. His blinking eyes, magnified through coke-bottle lenses, reminded me of a mechanical owl I had once seen perched on an office desk.

"Help me, help me!" he said again in a flat monotone that did not match the urgency of his words. No one came to his assistance, and his fellow patients ignored him. Amid the scurry of bodies and clamoring voices, his pleas blended in to the background noise, like a car alarm everyone hears but does nothing about.

A cheerful orderly dressed in sky blue scrubs, her voice loud and commanding, pushed a wheelchair in our direction. As she paused to greet a patient, I saw my birth mother for the first time.

Pale, frail, and petite, Maria sat in the giant chair, her body swimming in an oversized T-shirt. Moon and star patterns covered the tights clinging to her stick legs.

The orderly waved when she spotted us. Maria did not.

Again, denial reared its head. *This must be a mistake. This woman could not be my biological mother.* Ready to contradict me with facts and figures, the sergeant and his automatic checklist appeared: *Lilly said you were adopted . . . sixty-three first cousins confirmed it . . . Ancestry proved it . . .*

SHUT UP! my mind screamed back. I pictured grabbing the checklist from the sergeant's hands, ripping it to shreds, then snapping his pencil in half so he could never write another word.

I stared at my biological mother and concluded that we looked as alike as a penguin might resemble a porcupine. Maria was elf-like. Her features were angular. Her skin, seemingly unfamiliar to the sun, was almost translucent.

I don't scare easily, but when our eyes met, I shivered, just as I had when I'd first lain eyes on her photograph. Her jet-black pools didn't look at me; they looked through me. Instead of feeling a connection to her, I felt miles of distance lay between us. Instead of wanting to stay and understand my kin, I wanted to run to the airport and catch the first flight home. Instead of wishing for other parents and a different life than the one I'd rebelled against as a teenager, I felt awash with gratitude for the parents who'd raised me, loved me, and gave me a chance at life.

"*Hola, Mamá,*" Martha said. She reached to hug her mother, but Maria wouldn't allow it. Speaking gibberish, she waved her hands wildly, pushing Martha away.

"She doesn't like no one touchin' her," said the orderly; attached to her scrubs, a tag read *Shirley*. Maria's chatter settled into a whisper as she brought her long, thin fingers over her mouth.

"She does that all the time, speakin' in whispers like that. Like she's got secrets she don't want no one to know." Shirley had been Maria's orderly for the last year and knew my birth mother better than anyone.

We sat down at a round and spacious luncheon table. Shirley parked Maria's wheelchair between Martha and me. "Just try talkin' to her," she told us. "Maybe she'll settle down."

"Help me, help me!"

"Okay, Phil, I hear ya, Mister. I'm comin'." Shirley left us and made her way toward the owl man.

Despite Martha's repeated attempts to hug and touch her mother, Maria rejected her affection. I realized that if she didn't recognize the daughter that she raised for eighteen years, she'd never comprehend that sitting beside her was the daughter she gave away at birth. I was both disappointed *and* relieved.

Martha left us and joined Aunt Lena on the far side of the table, huddling together in deep discussion. I couldn't speak to Maria, so I observed her instead, memorizing the details of her elfin figure, wondering if there was something wrong with me because I felt nothing for the woman I'd shared a body with for nine months.

An idea popped into my head. *What if I reach over and touched her? Would I feel the missing spark?*

During the fifteen years, I worked as an acupuncturist in private practice, touch was an important part of my skill set; it allowed me to feel the nuance of a patient's qi—the life force of all living beings—and in this way achieve a better understanding of their health.

When Maria looked away, I leaned in and, as delicately as possible, touched the back of her hand with the tip of my index finger. I waited for the charge of electricity to ignite our long-lost umbilical connection, but touching my birth mother was like making contact with a plastic water bottle. I felt nothing.

Despite her dementia, Maria soon realized what I was doing. With a flick of her hand, she brushed me aside as if I was a bothersome bug.

Later, when I recounted the story to my friend Ashleigh, her radiant eyes, the size of topaz saucers, winked at me. "Well, I guess she flicked you twice, darlin'," she said, flashing a friendly Texan grin.

An hour later, Shirley returned, a half-eaten glazed donut in hand.

"Maria, it's time for your meds, babe," the stout woman said, releasing the lock of the wheelchair with her foot.

Maria covered her mouth and whispered something inaudible.

"What's that?" Shirley leaned over, careful not to touch her.

"*Muchas Marias alla abajo*," Maria whispered a second time glancing under the table.

"She's saying something about there being *a lot of Marias* under there." I said.

Shirley peeked under the lunch table then shook her head and chuckled.

"That Maria, she never makes no sense."

Maria's words may not have made any sense to Shirley, but they made some sense to me.

Maria was not only the birth mother sitting beside me now; *Maria* was also the name of the mother who'd raised me, the woman who family and friends called *Mary*. In my childhood bedroom, shining brightly over my bed, was Our Lady of the Perpetual Green Light, more commonly known as the Virgin Mary. When I was a baby, my mother asked her cousin Maria to come and live with us, and it was she who helped care for me during my first year. Even my middle name, *Marie*, honored the lineage of Marias in my life. I wondered if, even in her advanced state of dementia, a small part of Maria's psyche registered who I was.

"Can you ever forgive her?" Lena asked, interrupting my thoughts. I hadn't noticed her standing beside me.

My new aunt was as tough as a tank, her callused hands a reminder of how hard she'd worked throughout her life. Now tears brimmed in her eyes.

"Can you ever forgive her for what she did to you?" she asked again.

I looked at Maria, sitting in her cavernous wheelchair, and thought of Martha's accounts of her childhood—the lack of affection, the physical abuse, and Maria's advanced mental illness. If my adoptive mother hadn't knocked on her friend Molly's door at the exact moment when my birth mother was crying, if compassion hadn't touched my mother's heart when she heard the woman's story, if Mami had been a different kind of woman, I might never have been born.

Mary and Vincent wanted the world for us and worked their fingers to the bone to get it. They clothed, fed, educated, and loved us. I earned a bachelor's degree in communications, then a master's in traditional Chinese medicine. I'd traveled the globe and experienced new and exciting cultures. And ultimately, I had become what I always dreamed of: a writer. But most important, I loved deeply and was loved greatly by many people—family and friends.

When I was a child, I lay on a doghouse looking up into the clouds and wishing my true parents would come for me. I imagined they were royalty, spies, or aliens from a distant land. The mother I found in Chicago was none of these. She was fallible, not magical. My birth mother was not a star traveler but an earth walker struggling to find her way. The parents who had adopted me, in contrast, had turned out to be so much more than I'd ever dreamed. These two people did not have much money or possessions of great value, yet they'd given me everything.

"There's nothing to forgive," I assured Lena.

Her eyes widened; it was not the answer she expected.

"Nothing to forgive," I said again, and meant every word.

. . .

A few hours later, I stood in a sprawling cemetery under a light drizzle, looking down at my half-brother Robert's grassy grave. The weathered plaque where his remains lay was as modest as his life had been.

"Robert was the smartest guy I've ever met," said his boss over the phone. "He was a data whiz at the bank and could handle any problem we gave him. He never talked about his family, though. He was a very private guy."

I looked over the pamphlet Robert's workmates had compiled to celebrate his life. A slim man in a blue button-down dress shirt and slacks, holding his hands on his hips, smiled back at me. *Forever in our hearts*, read the words above the picture. "The Dash," a poem memorializing the way we spend the moments in our life, filled the space beside his image. Inside the pages were recollections his friends shared of what they remembered best about him: his fondness for carrot cake, a unique sense of humor, and his love for epic TV shows like *Game of Thrones*. These were similar joys I could add to the dashes of my life.

As I learned more about Robert, I wished I had acted sooner and taken the DNA test when I'd first entertained the idea years earlier. If I had, I might have had a chance to know my brother before his fatal heart attack.

But just like the uncanny occurrences already surrounding my adoption, such as Martha discovering we were sisters on her birthday, or my birthdate being stamped on Robert's death certificate, or discovering the numbers *4619* on my boarding pass to Chicago, Robert's death was significant in this story. If he hadn't died, the attorney for his estate would not have sought Martha out and informed her that my birth mother was still alive. I would not be in Chicago right now, standing at Robert's grave and saying goodbye to a metal plaque under the falling rain.

An hour later, I reached my hotel room and crawled into bed.

Five weeks earlier, at age fifty-seven, I'd discovered the unfathomable: *I was adopted*. From this epiphany, a sister, a brother, and my birth mother had emerged and become part of my origin story. Now, I was near the finish line.

The following day I'd be back in Santa Fe, safe at home with Ken, but here in Chicago, the revelations were happening so quickly there wasn't enough time to adapt to the unfamiliar air at this new altitude. My situation reminded me of a game I played as a kid where players remove blocks, one at a time, from a tower made of dozens of pieces. Whenever you remove a block, the structure teeters. If the tower falls, you lose. The most foundational block of my identity had been yanked from its base. I'd teetered, but hadn't crashed. Yet it seemed that every day, I came closer. It was all too much, too fast; I felt destabilized.

"I can only handle meeting one new relative a year," I texted Lilly from my bed, where I lay stretched in four directions as though waiting to be quartered.

"I love you more than you know," she texted back.

Early the following morning, Martha and I waited in the lobby until my Uber arrived to drive me to the airport.

"You're not wearing your necklace," she said, disappointed, looking at my chest.

The day before, I'd worn the pendant she'd given me, but that morning I'd buried the jewels deep inside my suitcase.

"I don't want it to break while I travel," I said, knowing my excuse was only partially true. Despite a good night's sleep, I needed a rest from anything to do with the word *adoption*. The necklace was a firm reminder of that.

When my ride pulled up at the hotel's entrance, I hugged Martha goodbye.

"No matter what happens, I'm glad we met," she said.

"Yeah, me too. Have a safe trip, okay?" I put my suitcase in the open trunk, stepped inside the car, and closed the door behind me. Through the backseat window, I waved to Martha, who was standing at the curb and watching us pull away.

As we drove through morning gridlock, I made small talk with the driver, relieved to be heading home and to my everyday life.

I'd come to Chicago seeking the truth and found so much more than I expected. Two Marias would forever be a part of me. One day soon, I hoped they would come into balance. But for now, these women, physical, emotional, and spiritual opposites, lived within me like clashing factions. And the intensity of their polarity was about to take its toll.

CHAPTER THIRTY-FOUR

Boundaries

WHEN I REACHED SANTA FE, I sank into Ken's all-encompassing hug. Over his shoulder, I regarded his welcome gift: a clean house he'd spent all afternoon tidying up. After growing up in a house where junk had ruled, there was nothing I appreciated more.

"I missed you, Socky," he whispered, using the nickname he gave me when we were first dating after I mailed him a tiny metal shoe from a Monopoly game. *Well, if I'm a shoe, that must make you a sock*, he said at the time before putting the minuscule boot on his nightstand.

Like a choice pair of socks set inside a favorite pair of shoes, we've matched each other well over the years.

I craved sleep that night, but my overstimulated mind—thinking, rethinking, and overthinking the previous days' events—kept me wide-eyed into the early morning.

When I finally drifted off, I dreamed of the Amazon River, where I had been years before. This time I sat in the back of a canoe at sunrise, watching a man dressed head to toe in black, digging deep into the current with a long pole.

"Where are we going?"

He didn't answer.

I stood up, trying to maneuver toward the bow, but an invisible quicksand hampered my feet, keeping me from moving forward.

258

"Mister, where are we going!?" I demanded, my voice competing with the river's roar.

The man ignored me and kept rowing in silence, like Charon heading in one direction, without a return voyage in mind.

I woke up trying to make sense of the patterns in the wooden beams on the ceiling above me. My eyes blinked repeatedly until my senses returned.

This dream and its haunting image remained with me for some time.

Over subsequent days, I submerged myself in activity: talking at bookstores, engaging in animal advocacy projects, and spending time with friends. Regardless of how busy I forced myself to be, however, a simmering disquiet lived under the surface of my skin. My birth mother's lack of affection toward Martha and Robert was difficult to swallow knowing that scenario could have easily been the course of my life. My negative feelings toward Maria weren't the only cause of my distress. The pressure to be part of a family related by blood but not yet by heart fueled my unease.

Since my return from Chicago, Martha had texted me every few days with a cheerful meme, a photo of her garden, or a tidbit from her life. It was a lovely gesture—but when she referred to me as *sister*, agitation swept through me.

The more I chided myself that semantics were unimportant, the bigger the wave swelled. I didn't want to be unkind; Martha's past with my birth mother had been tumultuous enough, but forcing myself through the proverbial round hole, into a role I was not ready to take on, fueled my pique.

I decided candor was the best approach. I wrote Martha a letter explaining my situation and asked her for space while I processed my emotions and made my way toward a new normal.

Assuming she'd be upset with me, I braced myself for her reaction. A few days later, I received this email from her in my inbox.

Hi Carlyn, thank you for your honesty! Believe me, I understand, and it pains me to see the turmoil you're going through. As for expectations you're right, we should not presume and fall right into a family type of relationship even though we are related. These things need to be taken one day at time in order for us to have any sort of relationship in the future. Don't worry, things will fall into place on their own. Like you say, stay pawsitive!

After reading Martha's email the weight of obligation lifted from my shoulders. For now, I was a square peg. Perhaps I would one day fit into that round hole; perhaps I would not. Time would tell where my story with my new half-sister would land. But for now, I could allow our relationship to grow organically, like a tree that thrives in an unpredictable climate—one day at a time.

CHAPTER THIRTY-FIVE

The Final Puzzle Pieces

NO MATTER HOW MUCH I learned about my identity or how fast the information arrived, I grasped for more, impatient to reconstruct my new foundation, eager to reestablish order, whatever the cost.

In June I hopped onto an Amtrak train headed for California, in search of more answers. In Los Angeles I met up with college friends I hadn't seen in three decades, and in Santa Barbara I attended my forty-year high school reunion. Like a salamander shedding its skin, I introduced the new me. After sharing my story, most of my friends reacted the same way: either by saying they needed to sit down or by ordering a drink.

During my three-week exploration, I became a sleuth, interviewing relatives for any pieces of information they possessed about my adoption that I did not. As I heard their stories, I borrowed their memories and made them my own.

Some of their recollections were hard to face.

Giselle, one of my San Diego cousins, and I paid a visit to her mother. Eighty-three-year-old Aunt Cara flitted about her kitchen, chatting nonstop with her enviable energy. She set a plastic plate filled with melon balls in front of us while I scribbled her thoughts in my notebook.

With an uncanny memory for detail, Aunt Cara recounted how she and my uncle were visiting my parents around the time Maria gave birth to me.

"You were just a day old and Mary was holding you in a blanket,"

Aunt Cara said, putting her arms together in front of her chest as if cuddling a baby. "When your mother leaned over Maria's bed and showed you to her for the first time, Maria gave you a look like this . . ." Aunt Cara scrunched her face with disgust. "'What an ugly baby,' she said."

Ouch, I thought. *Ouch!!!* Maria's words cut to the quick.

"Mom! Why did you tell her that?!" Giselle's horrified eyes darted from her mother to me, then down to her melon ball, which fainted from her fork and landed on the plastic tablecloth.

"No, no, it's okay," I assured Giselle once the sting passed. "I need to know all of it, even if it hurts."

For decades, a fundamental piece of my identity had lain hidden. I craved the truth. And the truth was that if my birth mother had wanted me, even just a little bit, if she had looked at me with a glimmer of longing, or even found me remotely adorable, I wouldn't be sitting across from a cousin named Giselle or have grown up with a sister I kiddingly called Looscious, or have two brothers who towered over me and showered me with affectionate teasing. My heart took a hit, hearing my birth mother's first thought of me, but the shock quickly dissipated and I felt relieved Maria had not wanted me.

And daily, I grew more and more grateful to Vincent and Mary—who had.

"Is there anything else you remember about that day, Tía?" I asked Aunt Cara as we got up to leave.

"Well . . . maybe there's one other thing," she admitted. Her eyes studied the melon ball plate as if trying to find the best words. "Your uncle and I were standing outside the house talking to your father. You know how funny your dad was, always joking around, saying sarcastic things, making everyone laugh . . ."

Mid-sentence, Aunt Cara left me hanging and asked Giselle how her dog was.

"*Tía!*" I interrupted. "What did my father say?"

Aunt Cara popped a melon ball into her mouth as she gathered her thoughts.

"It was a lot for him, having a new baby, you know? Your dad hadn't bonded with you yet . . ." Aunt Cara looked to her daughter for help, but Giselle wanted to hear what she had to say as much as I did.

"*What did he say, Tía?*" I asked again, patting the back of her hand, hoping this gentle urging and the melon ball would deliver her confession.

"I don't remember what he said *exactly*, but whatever it was your mother overheard and didn't like it. She marched out of the house yelling at your dad, 'She's my daughter! She's my daughter!!'"

Mom's reaction was as startling as hearing my biological mother say I was ugly. For years I'd harbored the notion that the mother who raised me didn't love me, or at least not the way she loved Ray, Art, or Lilly. Yet here Aunt Cara was, describing her like a tigress fighting for her cub as if it were her own and not a runt from another pack.

I understood Dad's reluctance to take on a stranger's child as his own. Daddy was forty-seven years old, caring and providing for three children and sending money back to Mexico to support younger family members. Dad and I were strangers in these early days. We had yet to share a birthday, or exchange smiles, or weave together the enduring bond of father and daughter. His mixed feelings eventually led him in front of our parish priest.

"Daddy was conflicted," Lilly shared with me not long before. "He didn't want to lie about your adoption, but even Father Rightman told him it was okay to keep that secret."

"The parish priest told him to lie?" I was incredulous, remembering Father Rightman and my mother's indignation when they thought I was being taught the sin of reincarnation. Apparently Father Rightman was on board with lying, even if it was a sin in the eyes of the church. I rolled my eyes and shrugged as I often did when I had no words to describe the quandaries of life.

At Aunt Cara's, my heart twinged upon hearing that Dad had expressed doubts about my adoption. But the encouragement, support, and love he'd given me for the rest of his life, the fact that I'd had a life at all—this was the remedy to heal any wound.

. . .

With my aunt's words still fresh in my mind, I went with Giselle to visit my father's last living sister and her sons. There, over a giant platter of guacamole, chips, and salsa, my cousins listened intently to my story. When I finished, the room was still.

My cousin Rob, sitting beside me, took my hand in his. "You will always be a part of our family," he said, eyes moistening. "We've never thought about you in any other way. You're our cousin and we love you."

While I ingested his heartfelt words, Rob's brother Mark took my other hand and met my gaze. Stone-faced and with great sincerity, he said, "Nah, you're out."

Giselle laughed so hard she inhaled her soft drink and couldn't stop coughing.

I wasn't far behind—I bent over laughing until my stomach hurt.

With this riposte, that morning's stings faded into memory.

Before I left California, I contacted my cousin Val. Her mother, Natalia—my mother's closest sister and my godmother—had passed away a few years after Mami. I figured that if anyone had any remaining pieces left to contribute to my story, it might be Val.

"My mother met your birth mother just after you were born," Val confided over the phone. "She told us she was mad at your birth mother and that she even said to her, 'How can you give up your own child like that?'"

"Wow, I can't even imagine your mother saying that," I responded.

It surprised me to hear about my godmother laying into Maria with this force. When I was a kid, Natalia was as kindhearted and gentle as a field of yellow daisies on a spring day.

"So, what did she say?" I asked.

"Nothing. My mother said she just sat there and took her anger. That's when my mother suggested to your mom that Maria might change her mind and keep you if she had the means."

"The means? Are you talking about money?" I asked, gritting my teeth.

"Uh-huh."

"Did my parents offer her money?"

"Yeah—they offered, but she said no."

I sighed. Clearly, the promise of money hadn't been enough to make Maria want me. The jab I felt hearing this once again served as a reminder that by some divine hand, I'd been spared being raised by a mother whose love would never have been mine.

"Is there anything else I should know?"

It was a question I asked everyone toward the end of all of these conversations; it usually led to the discovery that there was something more. And today was no exception.

"I don't know if you know this, but when your birth mother went into labor, she signed into the hospital using Mary Montes De Oca's name, not her own."

"What?!" I asked, trying to grasp what she was saying. "Are you telling me that I wasn't legally adopted?"

"I really don't know," Val replied. "That's all my mother told me."

After I hung up the phone, I shared Val's news with Lilly.

"I don't understand this," I said. "Am I legally adopted or not?" I rubbed my neck, feeling the beginnings of an achy throat.

"I didn't know they did that," Lilly responded, as surprised as I was by this news. "I do remember one time, not long before Mami died, she said to me, 'If Carlyn ever finds out she's adopted, just show her the birth certificate. That way, she'll see your father's name is on it.'"

"What does that prove?" I asked. "Even if his name was on the birth certificate, Dad wasn't my biological father."

"I really don't know why that was so important to her. Maybe it's the whole 'big D, little d' thing. Or maybe it was dementia talking. It just meant a lot to her that you knew you had a dad and a mom on that birth certificate named *Mary and Vincent Montes De Oca.*

I may have joked with my friends about being a terrible private detective, that I should have put two and two together and figured out I was adopted well before I did, but now I was making up for lost time; a bloodhound tracking a scent, furiously digging to unearth any unknown fragment of my origin story. I held up the document in front of my desk lamp to illuminate the background and, like a banker examining a counterfeit twenty-dollar bill; I studied every detail of my birth certificate for clues: names, dates, and signatures. But no answers lived within the document's skin. No secrets revealed themselves. Just as the identity of my birth father remained a secret, this too was a mystery.

Without the answer to this missing piece, I felt like a child of no one.

In the train car on the ride back to New Mexico, I basked in the beauty of red-striped canyons and immense cloud-filled skies until the sore throat I'd been nursing for days caught fire. My body responded in full rebellion: one moment my chest was damp with sweat, the next I was shivering. Swallowing water became difficult; eating solid food, impossible. A whisper was all my voice could manage.

The first time I saw a therapist in my early twenties, I came down with laryngitis. No other symptoms—just a complete inability to speak about the issues troubling me. And now, during the most challenging period of my life, laryngitis shut me down again.

I huddled against the train's window. The twenty-hour trip passed at a caterpillar's pace.

Once in Santa Fe, I headed straight for urgent care. The doctor examined my lungs and handed me a prescription for steroids.

The medication gave me some relief, but not enough to get well. For three weeks, I dragged myself out of bed, slipped into my sweats, and forced myself to walk to the end of the block. As soon as I got back, I climbed into bed, curled into the fetal position under the covers, and slept for hours.

One morning, a weak, high-pitched whistle that I recognized from when I was eleven years old woke me. With every inhale, my chest wheezed, straining for breath. *Maybe it will go away*, I rationalized.

The following morning, the whistle grew louder and my lungs filled with fluid.

On my third visit to urgent care, the doctor recommended a different batch of drugs. "This time they'll work," he assured me.

He was right. Slowly, gradually, finally, the wheezing dissipated. Still, my recovery was slow. For weeks I lay in bed, my voice barely above a whisper. I was a spent balloon devoid of energy and lacking motivation. Stress had taxed my immune system and had brought me to this reckoning. Rest would deliver me to the other side.

I spent half my summer lying in silence, surfing the waves of my fluctuating emotions, gazing out my bedroom window, and waited for the storm to pass.

PART SIX

"The dark thought, the shame, the malice,
meet them at the door laughing, and invite them in.
Be grateful for whoever comes, because each has been
sent as a guide from beyond."

—Rumi

CHAPTER THIRTY-SIX

Death and Rebirth

WHEN MY ENERGY RETURNED and my voice grew stronger, I picked up the phone and called a therapist.

Life experience has taught me that we can fool ourselves into assuming we are over the worst of a crisis when we are not. When I was young, I buried my emotions behind an iron curtain, unaware that doing so was creating an inferno that would later erupt as self-sabotage, insecurity, and doubt.

The healthiest way to face chaos is to dive into it. It is also the hardest. I crossed my fingers and hoped therapy would be a smooth dive and not a painful belly flop.

On the morning of my first counseling appointment, I ambled toward the therapist's office, my body a triple cocktail of excitement, anticipation, and unease. My jitters caught up with me at the front door—but then I remembered a mantra I learned in Peru while hiking the Inca trail to the ancient ruins of Machu Picchu.

The high altitude during that unforgettable hike kicked my butt. Like a fish out of water, I stopped every few feet and gasped for air, never getting enough. I thought of turning back, but a familiar voice— the same voice that spoke about *reincarnation* and refused to let me say *Okay* when my marriage was at a crossroads—whispered in my ear and offered new advice. *One step at a time*, it said, and I listened. "One step at a time, one step at a time," I repeated as I pushed my way forward.

The words guided my every step until three days later I reached the glorious ruins of Machu Picchu.

Now, I used that mantra again. "One step at a time," I said to the peephole on the therapy office door, as if it was the magical phrase for admittance, before turning the knob and stepping inside.

Elizabeth greeted me in the lobby. Her warm manner and casual southwestern attire put me at ease.

Over the next eight weeks, we tackled issues surrounding my adoption: the loss of my old identity and the building of a new one; my lingering disbelief that this happened in the first place; and feeling like I was a child of no one. I expressed to her my disappointment with my siblings for not telling me the truth after my parents died, but also my belief that although I deserved to know the information sooner, the news may have come at the perfect time.

"My parents, and in particular my mom, weren't warm and fuzzy people," I informed Elizabeth. "If they'd told me I was adopted when I was a kid, they probably would have said, 'Carlyn, we adopted you. Let's never talk about it again.'"

Elizabeth nodded and scribbled a line on her notepad.

"If they'd told me I was adopted in my twenties, that might not have been the best time; at that point I already wanted to be as far away from them as possible. In my thirties, I was struggling through a difficult marriage—not a good time either. In my forties, I was pretty stressed out, helping Ken raise the kids, rescuing dogs, and going to school at night—again, not the best time to learn you're adopted and that everybody knew about it."

The paradox of learning I was adopted so late in life but also the feeling that I should have been told earlier was a contradiction that I had trouble wrapping my head around. It was an unsolvable Rubik's cube that often left me feeling drained. Over time, I settled into a gray area, reconciling with the space between the black and the white. Learning I was adopted later in life—when anger didn't cloud my reasoning, when mistakes could be forgiven rather than held grudges against, and when love could more readily overcome the past—this balanced the scales toward *things happen for a reason.*

During my conversations with Elizabeth, we plucked away the thorny weeds that obscured my identity one by one until a new clarity grew in their stead.

"What would you like to talk about today?" Elizabeth asked as I plopped down onto her couch for our last session.

"Not sure," I said, shifting my legs and tapping my foot. This was a lie. I'd been holding back a question since our first session, fearing her expert answer. I brought the edge of my tea mug to my lips and took a sip, hoping the liquid inside it contained a tonic for valor.

"Do you remember me mentioning that my birth mother was mentally ill?" I finally asked.

"I remember," Elizabeth said, her soothing cadence assuring me that regardless of what I confessed between these four walls, her role was to support and not judge.

"Do you remember me telling you that when I was younger, my mind spent a lot of time in a really dark place?"

Elizabeth nodded, urging me to continue.

"Then as an adult I got depressed quite a bit . . . um . . . well, now I find out that my birth mother was probably bipolar or schizophrenic or . . ." I rambled, searching for the right words to ask if my biological mother's derangement would one day rear its head and her affliction would become mine. I looked into the mug as if the green tea held answers. From the glassy surface, the memory of Maria's troubled eyes looked back.

I'd like to believe that I've traveled far with my personal development. I smile now more than I frown. The shame over growing up in a junkyard and being from a different culture that once consumed me dissipated years ago. The anger and resentment I harbored toward my adoptive mother are gone. Like the Berlin Wall, the iron curtain built to keep her at bay came down with awareness, understanding, and forgiveness. But mental illness can be hereditary, traveling from parent to child, and I was Maria's daughter by blood. I feared this was her legacy.

"Your birth mother was mentally ill, Carlyn, but you are not," Elizabeth said matter-of-factly. "You are as far from that as anyone I've seen."

Elizabeth had a front-row seat into my psyche, and I trusted her. Relief surged through every cell in my body, blasting my fear to ash. Through the slits of the blinds covering the window behind her, I watched the remnants of my fear float away toward a distant world I did not intend to ever visit.

Not long after, I received an early-morning text from Martha. In the past, when I saw her name displayed across the screen, my breath stopped, as if I was bracing for an ice bath. The sessions with Elizabeth, and talking through my concerns, had changed this. Now, when my phone dinged and I read Martha's name, my mind grew curious instead of anxious.

Hi Carlyn, I hope everything is fine with you. Our mother passed this morning from a stroke . . .

I read the line several times before melting into my favorite wicker chair—the same one I'd sat in when Lilly told me I wasn't her sister by blood.

Maria's death did not sadden me. I didn't wish for a different ending to our story—or a rewrite of our beginning. My biological mother had lived alone and estranged from her family. She'd battled internal demons every day of her adult life and spent her last days living in a state hospital, surrounded by others whose aging bodies held their minds and memories under lock and key. This existence, which brought her so much emotional pain, no longer bound her. Maria was free.

I related. I'd longed for freedom when I lived on Escondido Road. When the cage opened, and I left for college, I'd felt the first sweetness of flight. Maria was soaring now.

Thank God. She's free. For the first time since this story began, I felt a connection, albeit brief, to my birth mother. From behind closed eyes, I conjured her face and imagined her stern gaze softening, smiling as she turned away from me and disappeared into the light.

I don't believe in the heaven or hell taught to us by the priests in churches. I believe that we carry our consciousness, the essence of who we are, into the next world. I mourn the people and the animals I've lost in my lifetime, but when it's my time to cross over, I suspect we'll meet again, and that Vincent and Mary, my mom and dad, will stand among them. I wonder if Maria will be among them as well, free of curses and demons, finally able to recognize the daughter she never knew.

CHAPTER THIRTY-SEVEN

Saudade

A WORD EXISTS IN PORTUGUESE that does not in English.

Saudade (soh-DAH-djee) describes a deep, sometimes painful, and always unquenchable yearning for what was and might never be again. In the wistful melancholy of separation defining *saudade*, love and longing live side by side.

I miss my mother and father. Even in the mariachi music, which once filled me with shame, when the folk singers unleash their joyful *gritos*, I look around me, searching for pieces of my parents, hearing their laughter, imagining their dance. But my *saudade* toward them is much more than that. In the middle of the night a wave of *saudade* wakes me and for minutes, sometimes an hour, it insists I submit to the drag of its undertow. I wish things had been different between my parents and me. I wish we had found greater connection while they lived. I wish I could have heard my origin story firsthand from their lips.

As if to ease my longing, my mother's youthful face appears—the enigmatic woman whom I sometimes considered a villain and at other times my North Star. Mami infused me with her strength, and encouraged me to be more, yet demanded my obedience. In protecting me from the world's censure, she also kept my identity hidden from me. My mother's intricate complexities have allowed me to look at and accept my own diverse nature, to forgive my imperfections, and to embrace my humanity—the shadow and the light.

What inspired my mother to raise a stranger's infant? What conversations did she and my birth mother have during the eight months Maria and her children lived in our home? Did Maria ever reveal who my birth father was? The answers to these questions remain a mystery. Perhaps this desire to know what cannot be known fuels the *saudade* in all children who feel the tug of unspoken words never said to their departed mothers and fathers.

I always thought that blood was thicker than water. Not knowing this phrase may have come from an earlier reference—"The blood of the covenant is thicker than the water of the womb"—a completely opposing idea which means that your bond to those you've spilled blood with is stronger than those with whom you've shared your mother's womb. I now believe this to be true.

When I heard the words *"Carlyn, you were adopted,"* a knife cut through me, severing my connection to my family and our history together. But in the disconnect, I found an alternative path forward—a path toward choice and the blood of the covenant. With this second chance, I chose the family I grew up with on Escondido Road. Not because a birth certificate demanded it, but because of a bond created by time, shared experience, and a lifetime of connection.

Officially, I may be a *child of no one,* but I am also a cousin, sister, stepmom, and daughter. I'm surrounded by a vast tribe, not bound through the water of the womb but forged by a covenant of kinship. I also have a new sister named Martha who is part of this clan. Yet my family doesn't end here.

Through their insights, inspiration, and love, I have wonderful friends of every gender and race who nourish me, encourage me, and daily restore my belief in humankind. Also, my family is not limited to my own species. The beloved dogs and extraordinary cats I've shared my life with have filled my heart and spirit since my earliest years and earned the title of *familia* in ways that no human ever could.

My adoption revelation toppled the puzzle box containing the essential pieces of my identity and scattered them across a snow-filled plateau. The task to recover these parts and make sense of them daunted me, but like all hardships, there are gifts waiting to be claimed on the shores of deliverance. Over time, as I've placed most of the puzzle pieces back together, a new image has begun to form—a more complete and genuine picture of who I am rather than the woman I was before.

My origin story changed everything about my life, and it changed nothing. I was not conceived out of love. A family of strangers taught me what love really means. In the process of yearning for my real parents to come and find me, I discovered that the perfect family I always wished for was the imperfect family I always had. I am who I always thought I was, a Junkyard Girl, *and* I am much more than that. Perhaps there's a little bit of the junkyard in all of us, a chance for discovery, revelation, and transformation in the mist of our life story. This is my truth as I see it. And the truth, indeed, sets you free.

Saving Grace

I PEERED THROUGH the chain-link fence at the white dog cringing behind a damp haystack.

The dog—Betty, the name given her by rescuers—stared back, her mistrustful eyes revealing a tale of heartbreak.

Rachel, the woman who ran the rescue, informed me that Betty was six years old. A vet would later tell me she was eight; another would say three. Whatever her age, this snow-white dog with the black-tan-gold mask and soulful eyes had lived most of her life in a barn in a ramshackle town just north of Santa Fe. Nearly one hundred dogs were being held on the rural property in deplorable conditions—suffering from neglect, abuse, and rat infestations until they were rescued. The brutal details in newspaper articles left little to the imagination.

After the dogs' former guardian landed in jail, rescuers transported them to a sanctuary set against the Sandia Mountains just south of Madrid, New Mexico. Two rows of kennels were quickly constructed, acting as temporary shelters until permanent homes could be found.

The setting sun falling over the mountains—a veil of vibrant purples and Parrish blue—made me forget the wind's sharp bite on this thirty-five-degree day.

I walked toward the kennel, constricted by the cold and the two sweaters layered under my jacket. I lifted the latch, careful not to let it clank. When I stepped inside, the dog stepped back. Then she raised her nose into the air and caught a whiff of the sweet potato treats I'd stuffed into my pockets earlier that morning. She came forward for a treat, then immediately backed away again, her fear conquering her appetite.

As she darted behind bales of hay, I glimpsed a sizable bald patch on her rump. The sanctuary folks had told me she'd been attacked by a mountain lion. The scar, according to the vet, would never heal and her exposed pink skin would always need to be protected from the intense New Mexican sun.

I leaned against the chain link and waited. Minutes later, she slunk back over to me, keeping her distance to about five feet.

Tossing treats in her direction, avoiding eye contact, and a dose of patience paid off. Feet became inches as she ventured closer.

Twenty minutes later, Betty nibbled a treat from my hand. By the end of the hour, curiosity had replaced anxiety, and in an act of fear-lessness, she licked my face. The instant our eyes met, a silent pact formed between us. We knew we belonged to one another, a recognition between two spirits. It was an agreement I pledged to never break.

"What kind of dog is she?" my friend Kai messaged me.

"No idea," I replied

"Why did you pick her?"

"Because she needs me," I said, knowing full well that I also needed her. As I said these words out loud, it dawned on me that my mother may have felt the same way when she stumbled upon Maria crying in her friend's yard. A child needed her, and she chose to help rather than walk away. My parents rescued me as I was rescuing Betty—just as I would always rescue.

"Betty, huh? You keeping that name?" another friend wondered.

"Nope, she's not a Betty," I said.

I knew this dog's name six months before I adopted her. In the middle of my own rescue story, as I swam through the waters of shock and grief, one word kept coming to mind: *grace*, the mystical favor given by divine forces to strengthen us when we are most in need. This grace was gifted to me at birth through a second chance at life and has followed me since—an invisible presence that guides me when I've lost my way. Like a tender and benevolent presence, grace stands with me on that snowy plateau helping me put my identity back together again, one puzzle piece at a time.

"Grace," I informed my friend. "Her name is Grace."

Grace. I whispered the word into my new dog's ear. It felt good to say. And I knew she liked it too when her brown eyes softened and blinked slowly, as though mesmerized by the sound.

I slipped the leash around her neck. Grace glanced up at me, and I could see that mistrust was still alive—but now, so was hope.

"Let's go, girl," I said.

Together, Grace and I went on our first walk—beyond the chain link, stepping away from the shadows and into our future.

Acknowledgments

I may have written book alone, but I was ensconced with the support and love of countless others. I'd like to thank the following people from a deep place of appreciation that I can never fully express.

As an author, I couldn't have asked for a more fantastic launch team. Thank you to the *one-hundred*. You've helped me give birth to a book I am very proud of and I'm forever grateful.

To my 63 first cousins, and especially those mentioned in this book, who reached out to make sure I knew you would always love me and that I was part of your family—*blood or not*. Thank-you Martha Barrett, Gloria Guerrero, Lori Abood, Mario Montes De Oca, Angelica Colin, Velia Rios, Jesse Rios, Robert Curiel, and Mark Curiel.

It's not easy handing your manuscript over when it's still in its infancy, but my Beta Readers shared their insights, suggestions, and honest feedback to make *Junkyard Girl* an even better book. Thank you, Lisa Bailey, Maria Jacquemetton, Charity Goodin-Sanen, and Sandina Bailo.

He read my words and answered all my questions, *over and over again*, with patience and always a good *barb* on hand. Cheers, Bob Basler!

Krista Lagos and David Aretha, and Katie Kohn, your editorial talent brought my words to another level and made me a better writer.

Eva Case-Issakov, it was a joy working with you on our publicity campaign and Gail Snyder thanks for your invaluable publicity counsel.

Christy Day at Constellation Book Services, you created a breathtaking cover that still blows me away. And Maggie McLaughlin, thanks for your patience and cyber savvy in dealing with my book's interior.

Every time an endorsement came in, I felt myself choke up. Thank you to all of my endorsers for taking the time to create such beautiful words around my book.

To my publishing sage, Martha Bullen who let me steer the boat on this project though her watchful gaze was always vigilant, making sure I got to the other side in one piece and with a published book in hand! Thank you for sharing your invaluable expertise.

Lilly, Ray, Art, and Martha, thanks for casting a light on my recall with your memories. I know you may wince from time to time reading the words written within these pages, but I appreciate you allowing me to write the truth of my story as I saw it.

To my heart—Ken, nothing brings me more joy than waking up to another day with you and Grace. Thank you for your unflinching support, unmatchable sense of humor, and being my partner on this magnificent journey of life—*para siempre.*

Mary and Vincent, mom and dad, every day I love you more.

Book Club Discussion Questions

The following questions are intended to enhance reflection and spark further discussion of *Junkyard Girl*.

1. *Junkyard Girl*—what does this title mean in the context of this story?

2. What are the book's major themes? How are those themes brought to life?

3. What does the author mean when she speaks of the *Unexplainable Knowing*?

4. Montes De Oca quotes Hafiz at the beginning of Part One – "Fear is the cheapest room in the house. I would like to see you living in better conditions." What is the significance of this quote and why do you believe the author used it?

5. If you took a DNA test and discovered you were adopted, how do you think you would feel?

6. If you discovered you were adopted, would you try to locate your biological family or not? Why do you feel this way?

7. What aspects of the author's story could you most relate to?

8. Why do you think Carlyn's parents refused to divulge that she was adopted? What were the circumstances that led them to make this decision?

9. At the beginning of Part Six, the author quotes Rumi. "The dark

thought, the shame, the malice, meet them at the door laughing, and invite them in. Be grateful for whoever comes, because each has been sent, as a guide from beyond." What do you believe the author is trying to convey by using this passage?

10. How do you define your identity?

11. Can you think of a reason that it would be better not to tell a child they are adopted?

12. How do you interpret the epigraph at the start of the book, "The blood of the covenant is thicker than the water of the womb?"Do you believe this is true or do you feel that blood is thicker than water?

13. Montes De Oca clearly has a powerful connection to animals. How did her dogs, Orange and Bandit, help her during her childhood?

14. How do your companion animals help you navigate the complexities and challenges of your life?

15. What does the author mean by *Saudade*? How does she use it to relate to her relationship with her parents after their death?

16. The author ends her book with an epilogue about her new rescue dog, Grace. Why is this part of the book so powerful?

17. What is the primary feeling you come away with after reading Junkyard Girl?

18. Are there lingering questions from the book that you're still thinking about?

19. If you could ask the author anything, what would it be?

About the Author

CARLYN MONTES DE OCA is the multi-award-winning author of *Dog as My Doctor, Cat as My Nurse*. A former film editor on movies such as *Honey, I Shrunk the Kids* and *Three Men and a Little Lady*, Carlyn holds a bachelor's degree in communications and a master's degree in Traditional Chinese Medicine.

Today, Carlyn is a popular blogger, passionate animal advocate, and the founder of The Animal-Human Health Connection where she focuses on educating others about the powerful ways human health, happiness, and longevity are improved through our connection to our animal companions.

Voted PETA's Sexiest Vegetarian Over 50, Montes De Oca has appeared on CBS, ABC, *The San Francisco Chronicle*, and other media and gave a dynamic TEDx talk—The Life-Changing Power of the Animal-Human Health Connection.

A longtime resident of Northern California, Carlyn now lives in Santa Fe, New Mexico with her husband, Ken Fischer, an award-winning sound editor, and her beloved rescue dog, Grace. Discovering she was adopted turned Carlyn's world upside down. Adopting Grace, a dog desperately in need of a second chance, set it right again.

Want More *Junkyard Girl*?
If so, please visit my photo gallery for a sneak peek
at photographs from my private album.
Junkyardgirlbook.com/photogallery

———

If You Love Animals...
Sign up for my free *Pawsitive Lifestyle Newsletter* to learn more about
the power of the animal-human bond and how it can improve your
health, happiness, and longevity.
www.AnimalHumanHealth.com

———

Did You Enjoy *Junkyard Girl*?
If so, would you kindly leave a short review on Amazon, Goodreads,
or wherever you purchased your book? Reviews make a huge
difference in helping new readers discover my books. Your generosity
in spreading the word is hugely appreciated.

———

Let's Connect!
Facebook, Instagram, Twitter, Linkedin,
You Tube @ Carlyn Montes De Oca

Made in the USA
Las Vegas, NV
16 November 2022

59672593R00174